Cryptocurrency Investing

for dummies®

A Wiley Brand

Cryptocurrency Investing

by Kiana Danial

Cryptocurrency Investing For Dummies®

Published by: **John Wiley & Sons, Inc.,** 111 River Street, Hoboken, NJ 07030-5774, www.wiley.com

Copyright © 2019 by John Wiley & Sons, Inc., Hoboken, New Jersey

Published simultaneously in Canada

For general information on our other products and services, please contact our Customer Care Department within the U.S. at 877-762-2974, outside the U.S. at 317-572-3993, or fax 317-572-4002. For technical support, please visit https://hub.wiley.com/community/support/dummies.

Wiley publishes in a variety of print and electronic formats and by print-on-demand. Some material included with standard print versions of this book may not be included in e-books or in print-on-demand. If this book refers to media such as a CD or DVD that is not included in the version you purchased, you may download this material at http://booksupport.wiley.com. For more information about Wiley products, visit www.wiley.com.

Library of Congress Control Number: 2019930733

ISBN 978-1-119-53303-0 (pbk); ISBN 978-1-119-53305-4 (ebk); ISBN 978-1-119-53307-8 (ebk)

Manufactured in the United States of America

C10008103_020619

Contents at a Glance

Table of Contents

Introduction

More than 2,000 cryptocurrencies currently exist at the time of writing. Cryptos gained a lot of mainstream hype in 2017, when Bitcoin's value increased 1,318 percent. This surge was nothing compared to the gains of some other digital assets, such as Ripple, which went up (hold your breath) a whopping 36,018 percent. These returns are more than what a stock investor could normally make in a lifetime, and they generated enough interest to create a true frenzy.

However, the bubble burst at the beginning of 2018, leaving many late investors, who bought cryptocurrencies at a very high price, at a loss. That was enough for some newbie investors to label the whole industry a scam and either give up on investing altogether or go back to traditional financial assets like stocks. Regardless, the cryptocurrency market continued evolving, became more stable, and caught the attention and support of many major financial institutions globally and in the United States. As more people get their hands on cryptocurrencies, more sellers feel comfortable accepting them as a payment method, and that's how the whole industry can flourish.

The foundation of cryptocurrencies such as Bitcoin lies in a new technology called the *blockchain*; it's the infrastructure that cryptocurrencies are built on. Blockchain is a disruptive technology that many argue is bigger than the advent of the Internet. The applications of blockchain don't end with cryptocurrencies, though, just like the applications of the Internet don't end with email.

The unique thing about cryptocurrency investing and trading is that a crypto is a cross between an asset (like stocks) and a currency (like the U.S. dollar.) Analyzing the fundamentals behind a cryptocurrency is very different from analyzing any other financial asset. The traditional ways of measuring value don't work in the crypto industry, mainly because in many cases the crypto data isn't stored in a central hub somewhere. In fact, most cryptocurrencies and their underlying blockchain are *decentralized*, which means no central authority is in charge. Instead, the power is distributed among the members of any given blockchain or crypto community.

About This Book

You may have heard of some of the famous cryptocurrencies, like Bitcoin, but the industry doesn't end there — far from it. And although the crypto market has a ton of volatility, it also has potential for you to make real money by investing wisely and developing strategies that suit your personal risk tolerance. In this book, I tap into the risks involved in cryptocurrency investing and show you the different methods you can use to get involved.

The topic of cryptocurrencies and their underlying blockchain technology can be a bit confusing. That's why I try my best to keep *Cryptocurrency Investing For Dummies* easily accessible and relatable and free of intimidating terminology. But it does contain some serious information about strategy development, risk management, and the whole industry in general.

As you dip into and out of this book, feel free to skip the sidebars (shaded boxes) and the paragraphs marked with the Technical Stuff icon. They contain interesting information but aren't essential to becoming a crypto investor.

This book contains a lot of web addresses to get you additional information about certain topics. Some of the web addresses are affiliate links, meaning that if you click them and start using a company's services through that specific web address, I may earn an affiliate payment for making the introduction. You also may note that some web addresses break across two lines of text. If you're reading this book in print and want to visit one of these web pages, simply key in the web address exactly as it's noted in the text, pretending as though the line break doesn't exist. If you're reading this work as an e-book, you've got it easy — just click the web address to be taken directly to the web page.

Foolish Assumptions

I've made some assumptions about you and your basic knowledge of investing and the cryptocurrency market:

>> You may have heard of or even own some cryptocurrencies, but you don't really know how they work.

>> Though you may have invested in other markets like the stock market before, you aren't necessarily familiar with the terminology and the technical aspects of trading and investing cryptocurrencies.

>> You know how to operate a computer and use the Internet. If you don't have high-speed access to the Internet now, be sure you have it before trying to get involved in the cryptocurrency market. You need high-speed access to be able to work with many of the valuable online tools I recommend in this book.

Icons Used in This Book

For Dummies books use little pictures, called icons, to mark certain chunks of text. Here's what they actually mean:

REMEMBER

If something is particularly important for you to take away from this book, I mark it with this icon.

TIP

Watch for these little flags to get ideas on how to improve your crypto investing skills or where to find other useful resources.

WARNING

The cryptocurrency market and investing in general have many risks. Some mistakes can cost you a ton of money, so I use this icon to point out particularly dangerous areas.

TECHNICAL STUFF

This icon designates some interesting facts and sometimes funny anecdotes that I feel you may enjoy reading but that aren't essential to your crypto investing journey.

Beyond the Book

In addition to the material you're reading right now, this product also comes with some access-anywhere goodies on the web. When you just want a quick reminder of basics like what you need before you invest and how to check crypto fundamentals, check out the free Cheat Sheet at www.dummies.com; just search for "Cryptocurrency Investing For Dummies Cheat Sheet."

Where to Go from Here

Cryptocurrency Investing For Dummies isn't your typical book, where you start from the beginning and read through the end. Depending on your interest, knowledge on the matter, and investment goals, you can start anywhere you want. For example,

» If you're already familiar with cryptocurrency basics and know how they work, where to buy them, and where to securely store them, you may want to start with Part 4 to explore different investment and trading tactics.

» Chapter 22 gives you an overview of things to consider before you start your cryptocurrency journey and cross-references to other chapters if you need further information.

» Chapter 3 is a great (and essential) place to explore methods of risk management before pulling the trigger and jumping on the crypto wagon.

» If you're looking for alternative ways to get involved in the cryptocurrency market, check out Chapter 12 for crypto mining, Chapter 11 for initial coin offerings (ICOs), and Chapter 14 for crypto futures and options.

1

Getting Started with Cryptocurrency Investing

Chapter **1**

What Is a Cryptocurrency?

S o you've picked up this book, and your first question is probably this: "What the heck is a cryptocurrency, anyway?" Simply stated, a *cryptocurrency* is a new form of digital money. You can transfer your traditional, non-cryptocurrency money like the U.S. dollar digitally, but that's not quite the same as how cryptocurrencies work. When cryptocurrencies become mainstream, you may be able to use them to pay for stuff electronically, just like you do with traditional currencies.

However, what sets cryptocurrencies apart is the technology behind them. You may say, "Who cares about the technology behind my money? I only care about how much of it there is in my wallet!" The issue is that the world's current money systems have a bunch of problems. Here are some examples:

» Payment systems such as credit cards and wire transfers are outdated.

» In most cases, a bunch of middlemen like banks and brokers take a cut in the process, making transactions expensive and slow.

» Financial inequality is growing around the globe.

» Around 3 billion unbanked or underbanked people can't access financial services. That's approximately half the population on the planet!

Cryptocurrencies aim to solve some of these problems, if not more. This chapter introduces you to crypto fundamentals.

Beginning with the Basics of Cryptocurrencies

You know how your everyday, government-based currency is reserved in banks? And that you need an ATM or a connection to a bank to get more of it or transfer it to other people? Well, with cryptocurrencies, you may be able to get rid of banks and other centralized middlemen altogether. That's because cryptocurrencies rely on a technology called *blockchain*, which is *decentralized* (meaning no single entity is in charge of it). Instead, every computer in the network confirms the transactions. Flip to Chapter 4 to find out more about the blockchain technology that enables cool things like cryptocurrencies.

In the following sections, I go over the basics of cryptocurrencies: their background, benefits, and more.

The definition of money

Before getting into the nitty-gritty of cryptocurrencies, you need to understand the definition of money itself. The philosophy behind money is a bit like the whole "which came first: the chicken or the egg?" thing. In order for money to be valuable, it must have a number of characteristics, such as the following:

>> Enough people must have it.

>> Merchants must accept it as a form of payment.

>> Society must trust that it's valuable and that it will remain valuable in the future.

Of course, in the old days, when you traded your chicken for shoes, the values of the exchanged materials were inherent to their nature. But when coins, cash, and credit cards came into play, the definition of money and, more importantly, the trust model of money changed.

Another key change in money has been its ease of transaction. The hassle of carrying a ton of gold bars from one country to another was one of the main reasons cash was invented. Then, when people got even lazier, credit cards were invented. But credit cards carry the money that your government controls. As the world becomes more interconnected and more concerned about authorities who may or may not have people's best interests in mind, cryptocurrencies may offer a valuable alternative.

Here's a fun fact: Your normal, government-backed currency, such as the U.S. dollar, must go by its fancy name, *fiat currency*, now that cryptocurrencies are around. Fiat is described as a legal tender like coins and banknotes that have value only because the government says so. Get the scoop on fiat currencies in Chapter 15.

Some cryptocurrency history

The first ever cryptocurrency was (drumroll please) Bitcoin! You probably have heard of Bitcoin more than any other thing in the crypto industry. Bitcoin was the first product of the first blockchain developed by some anonymous entity who went by the name Satoshi Nakamoto. Satoshi released the idea of Bitcoin in 2008 and described it as a "purely peer-to-peer version" of electronic money.

TECHNICAL STUFF

Bitcoin was the first established cryptocurrency, but many attempts at creating digital currencies occurred years before Bitcoin was formally introduced.

Cryptocurrencies like Bitcoin are created through a process called *mining*. Very different than mining ore, mining cryptocurrencies involves powerful computers solving complicated problems. Flip to Chapter 12 for more on mining.

Bitcoin remained the only cryptocurrency until 2011. Then Bitcoin enthusiasts started noticing flaws in it, so they decided to create alternative coins, also known as *altcoins*, to improve Bitcoin's design for things like speed, security, anonymity, and more. Among the first altcoins was Litecoin, which aimed to become the silver to Bitcoin's gold. But as of the time of writing, over 1,600 cryptocurrencies are available, and the number is expected to increase in the future. Check out Chapter 8 for just a sampling of cryptocurrencies available now.

Key crypto benefits

Still not convinced that cryptocurrencies (or any other sort of decentralized money) are a better solution than traditional government-based money? Here are a number of solutions that cryptocurrencies may be able to provide through their decentralized nature:

>> **Reducing corruption:** With great power comes great responsibility. But when you give a ton of power to only one person or entity, the chances of their abusing that power increase. The 19th-century British politician Lord Acton said it best: "Power tends to corrupt, and absolute power corrupts absolutely."

Cryptocurrencies aim to resolve the issue of absolute power by distributing power among many people or, better yet, among all the members of the network. That's the key idea behind blockchain technology (see Chapter 4) anyway.

>> **Eliminating extreme money printing:** Governments have central banks, and central banks have the ability to simply print money when they're faced with a serious economic problem. This process is also called *quantitative easing.* By printing more money, a government may be able to bail out debt or devalue its currency. However, this approach is like putting a bandage on a broken leg. Not only does it rarely solve the problem, but the negative side effects also can sometimes surpass the original issue.

For example, when a country like Iran or Venezuela prints too much money, the value of its currency drops so much that inflation skyrockets and people can't even afford to buy everyday goods and services. Their cash becomes barely as valuable as rolls of toilet paper. Most cryptocurrencies have a limited, set amount of coins available. When all those coins are in circulation, a central entity or the company behind the blockchain has no easy way to simply create more coins or add on to its supply.

>> **Giving people charge of their own money:** With traditional cash, you're basically giving away all your control to central banks and the government. If you trust your government, that's great, but keep in mind that at any point, your government is able to simply freeze your bank account and deny your access to your funds. For example, in the United States, if you don't have a legal will and own a business, the government has the right to all your assets if you pass away. Some governments can even simply abolish bank notes the way India did in 2016. With cryptocurrencies, you and only you can access your funds. (Unless someone steals them from you, that is. To find out how to secure your crypto assets, flip to Chapter 7.)

>> **Cutting out the middleman:** With traditional money, every time you make a transfer, a middleman like your bank or a digital payment service takes a cut. With cryptocurrencies, all the network members in the blockchain are that middleman; their compensation is formulated differently from that of fiat money middlemen's and therefore is minimal in comparison. Flip to Chapter 5 for more on how cryptocurrencies work.

>> **Serving the unbanked:** A vast portion of the world's citizens has no access or limited access to payment systems like banks. Cryptocurrencies aim to resolve this issue by spreading digital commerce around the globe so that anyone with a mobile phone can start making payments. And yes, more people have access to mobile phones than to banks. In fact, more people have mobile phones than have toilets, but at this point the blockchain technology may not be able to resolve the latter issue. (Flip to Chapter 2 for more on the social good that can come from cryptocurrencies and blockchain technology.)

Common crypto and blockchain myths

During the 2017 Bitcoin hype, a lot of misconceptions about the whole industry started to circulate. These myths may have played a role in the cryptocurrency crash that followed the surge. The important thing to remember is that both the blockchain technology and its byproduct, the cryptocurrency market, are still in their infancy, and things are rapidly changing. Let me get some of the most common misunderstandings out of the way:

» **Cryptocurrencies are good only for criminals.** Some cryptocurrencies boast anonymity as one of their key features. That means your identity isn't revealed when you're making transactions. Other cryptocurrencies are based on a decentralized blockchain, meaning a central government isn't the sole power behind them. These features do make such cryptocurrencies attractive for criminals; however, law-abiding citizens in corrupt countries can also benefit from them. For example, if you don't trust your local bank or country because of corruption and political instability, the best way to store your money may be through the blockchain and cryptocurrency assets.

» **You can make anonymous transactions using all cryptocurrencies.** For some reason, many people equate Bitcoin with anonymity. But Bitcoin, along with many other cryptocurrencies, doesn't incorporate anonymity at all. All transactions made using such cryptocurrencies are made on public blockchain. Some cryptocurrencies, such as Monero, do prioritize privacy, meaning no outsider can find the source, amount, or destination of transactions. However, most other cryptocurrencies, including Bitcoin, don't operate that way.

» **The only application of blockchain is Bitcoin.** This idea couldn't be further from the truth. Bitcoin and other cryptocurrencies are a tiny byproduct of the blockchain revolution. Many believe Satoshi created Bitcoin simply to provide an example of how the blockchain technology can work. As I explore in Chapter 4, almost every industry and business in the world can use the blockchain technology in its specific field.

» **All blockchain activity is private.** Many people falsely believe that the blockchain technology isn't open to the public and is accessible only to its network of common users. Although some companies create their own private blockchains to be used only among employees and business partners, the majority of the blockchains behind famous cryptocurrencies such as Bitcoin are accessible by the public. Literally anyone with a computer can access the transactions in real time. For example, you can view the real-time Bitcoin transactions at www.blockchain.com.

Risks

Just like anything else in life, cryptocurrencies come with their own baggage of risk. Whether you trade cryptos, invest in them, or simply hold on to them for the future, you must assess and understand the risks beforehand. Some of the most talked-about cryptocurrency risks include their volatility and lack of regulation. Volatility got especially out of hand in 2017, when the price of most major cryptocurrencies, including Bitcoin, skyrocketed above 1,000 percent and then came crashing down. However, as the cryptocurrency hype has calmed down, the price fluctuations have become more predictable and followed similar patterns of stocks and other financial assets.

Regulations are another major topic in the industry. The funny thing is that both lack of regulation and exposure to regulations can turn into risk events for cryptocurrency investors. I explore these and other types of risks, as well as methods of managing them, in Chapter 3.

Gearing Up to Make Transactions

Cryptocurrencies are here to make transactions easier and faster. But before you take advantage of these benefits, you must gear up with crypto gadgets, discover where you can get your hands on different cryptocurrencies, and get to know the cryptocurrency community. Some of the essentials include cryptocurrency wallets and exchanges.

Wallets

Some *cryptocurrency wallets,* which hold your purchased cryptos, are similar to digital payment services like Apple Pay and PayPal. But generally, they're different from traditional wallets and come in different formats and levels of security.

REMEMBER

You can't get involved in the cryptocurrency market without a crypto wallet. I recommend that you get the most secure type of wallet, such as hardware or paper wallets, instead of using the convenient online ones. Flip to Chapter 7 to explore how these wallets work and how you can get them.

Exchanges

After you get yourself a crypto wallet (see the preceding section), you're ready to go crypto shopping, and one of the best destinations is a cryptocurrency exchange. These online web services are where you can transfer your traditional money to buy cryptocurrencies, exchange different types of cryptocurrencies, or even store your cryptocurrencies.

WARNING

Storing your cryptocurrencies on an exchange is considered high risk because many such exchanges have been exposed to hacking attacks and scams in the past. When you're done with your transactions, your best bet is to move your new digital assets to your personal, secure wallet.

Exchanges come in different shapes and forms. Some are like traditional stock exchanges and act as a middleman — something crypto enthusiasts believe is a slap in the face of the cryptocurrency market, which is trying to remove a centralized middleman. Others are decentralized and provide a service where buyers and sellers come together and transact in a peer-to-peer manner, but they come with their own sets of problems, like the risk of locking yourself out. A third type of crypto exchange is called *hybrid*, and it merges the benefits of the other two types to create a better, more secure experience for users. Flip to Chapter 6 to review the pros and cons of all these types of exchanges and get to know other places where you can go cryptocurrency shopping.

Communities

TIP

Getting to know the crypto community can be the next step as you're finding your way in the market. The web has plenty of chat rooms and support groups to give you a sense of the market and what people are talking about. Here are some ways to get involved:

>> **Crypto-specific Telegram groups.** Many cryptocurrencies have their very own channels on the Telegram app. To join them, you first need to download the Telegram messenger app on your smartphone or computer; it's available for iOS and Android.

>> **Crypto chat rooms on Reddit or BitcoinTalk:** BitcoinTalk (https:// bitcointalk.org/) and Reddit (www.reddit.com/) have some of the oldest crypto chat rooms around. You can view some topics without signing up, but if you want to get involved, you need to log in. (Of course, Reddit isn't exclusive to cryptos, but you can search for a variety of cryptocurrency topics.)

>> **TradingView chat room:** One of the best trading platforms out there, TradingView (www.tradingview.com/) also has a social service where traders and investors of all sorts come together and share their thoughts, questions, and ideas.

>> **Invest Diva's Premium Investing Group:** If you're looking for a less crowded and more investment/trading-focused place to get support, you can join our investment group (and chat directly with me as a perk too) at https://learn.investdiva.com/join-group.

REMEMBER

On the flip side, many scammers also target these kinds of platforms to advertise and lure members into trouble. Keep your wits about you.

Making a Plan Before You Jump In

You may just want to buy some cryptocurrencies and save them for their potential growth in the future. Or you may want to become more of an active investor and buy or sell cryptocurrencies more regularly to maximize profit and revenue. Regardless, you must have a plan and a strategy. Even if your transaction is a one-time thing and you don't want to hear anything about your crypto assets for the next ten years, you still must gain the knowledge necessary to determine things like the following:

>> What to buy

>> When to buy

>> How much to buy

>> When to sell

The following sections give you a quick overview of the steps you must take before buying your first cryptocurrency.

TIP

If you're not fully ready to buy cryptocurrencies, no worries: You can try some of the alternatives to cryptos that I describe in Part 3, like initial coin offerings, mining, stocks, and more.

Select your cryptos

Over 1,600 cryptocurrencies are out there at the time of writing, and the number is growing. Some of these cryptos may vanish in five years. Others may explode over 1,000 percent and may even replace traditional cash. In Chapter 8, I go through all different types of cryptocurrencies, including the most famous ones right now, such as Ethereum, Ripple, Litecoin, Bitcoin Cash, and Stellar Lumens.

As I discuss in Chapter 9, you can select cryptocurrencies based on things like category, popularity, ideology, the management behind the blockchain, and its economic model.

Because the crypto industry is pretty new, it's still very hard to identify the best-performing cryptos for long-term investments. That's why you may benefit from diversifying among various types and categories of cryptocurrencies in order to manage your risk. By diversifying across 15 or more cryptos, you can stack up the odds of having winners in your portfolio. On the flip side, overdiversification can become problematic as well, so you need to take calculated measures. Flip to Chapter 10 for more on diversification.

Analyze, invest, and profit

When you've narrowed down the cryptocurrencies you like, you must then identify the best time to buy them. For example, in 2017 many people started to believe in the idea of Bitcoin and wanted to get involved. Unfortunately, many of those people mismanaged the timing and bought when the price had peaked. Therefore, they not only were able to buy fewer bits of Bitcoin (pun intended), but they also had to sit on their losses and wait for the next price surge.

Now, I'm not saying that by going through Part 4 of this book, you're going to become some sort of new-age Cryptodamus. However, by analyzing the price action and conducting proper risk management, you may be able to stack the odds in your favor and make a ton of profit in the future.

Chapter **2**

Why Invest in Cryptocurrencies?

Whether you're a seasoned investor who has been exposed only to investment assets other than cryptos or you're just starting to invest (in anything!) for the first time, you're probably wondering why you should consider including cryptocurrencies in your portfolio. You've probably heard about Bitcoin here and there. Heck, you may have even heard of other cryptocurrencies such as Ethereum and Litecoin. But what's the big deal about all these funny-sounding coins anyway? Is Litecoin just a very light coin that won't take much space in your physical wallet? Is a Bitcoin made of bits and pieces of other valuable coins? Why on earth should you invest in bits of coins?

You can read all about the different types of cryptocurrencies, what they're made of, and what their purpose is in Chapter 8. Here, I give you a general overview of the market as a whole. That way, you can decide whether the cryptocurrency industry is the right route for you to grow your wealth.

Cryptocurrency investing may make sense for many investors, for a growing number of reasons — from things as simple as diversification to more exciting stuff like joining the revolutionary movement toward the future of how we perceive money. In this chapter, I show you some exciting features of this new investment kid on the block.

TIP

Although you can read this book in any order, I encourage you to read Chapter 3 right after this one. That's where I explain the other side of the coin, which involves the risks surrounding cryptocurrencies.

Diversifying from Traditional Investments

Diversification is the good ol' "don't put all your eggs in one basket" thing. You can apply this advice to literally anything in life. If you're traveling, don't put all your underwear in your checked-in luggage. Put an emergency pair in your carry-on in case your luggage gets lost. If you're grocery shopping, don't buy only apples. Even though they say "an apple a day keeps the doctor away," you still need the nutrition in other kinds of vegetables and fruit.

You can go about investment diversification in so many ways. You can diversify with different financial assets, like stocks, bonds, foreign exchange (forex), and so on. You can diversify based on industry, like technology, healthcare, and entertainment. You can allocate your investment by having multiple investment time frames, both short-term and long-term (see Chapters 17 and 18 for details.) Adding cryptocurrencies to your investment portfolio is essentially one way of balancing that portfolio. Especially because the cryptocurrency industry is vastly different from traditional ones, this diversification may increase the potential of maximizing your portfolio's growth. One of the main reasons for this higher potential is that the cryptocurrency market may react differently to various global and financial events.

In the following sections, I explain more by briefly looking into some of the traditional markets and exploring their differences from the cryptocurrency market. (Find out more about diversification in Chapter 10.)

Stocks

The stock market gives you the opportunity to take a bite of the profits a company makes. By buying stocks of that company, you become a part-owner of that firm. The more stocks you buy, the bigger your slice of the cake. And of course, the higher the risk you face if the whole cake is thrown out in the garbage.

The stock market is perhaps one of the most appealing investment assets. Novice investors may pick up a stock or two just because they like the company. For most investors, the charm of stock investing is the possibility that the prices will increase over time and generate significant capital gains. Some stocks even provide you with a periodic income stream through something called *dividends*.

(I explain more about capital gains and dividend income in Chapter 3.) Regardless, for most stocks, the dividends paid within a year are nothing compared to the increase of the stock's value, especially when the economic environment is upbeat.

REMEMBER

This is precisely what stocks and cryptocurrencies have in common: When their respective markets are strong, you can generally expect to benefit from price appreciation.

Make no mistake, though, both markets have their bad days and sometimes even bad years. The stock market has a longer history that can guide investors through navigating the future. For example, even though it may not always seem like it, bad days happen less often than good ones. Figure 2-1 shows that for the 70 years between 1947 and 2017, the Dow, one of the main stock market indexes, ended the year at a lower price only 28.6 percent of the time (20 years). The other 71.4 percent (50 years), it went up.

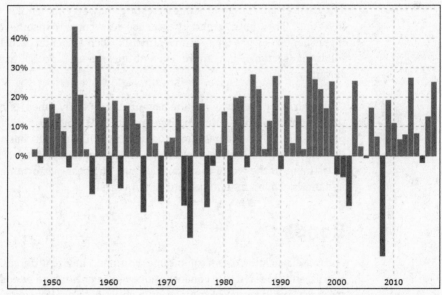

FIGURE 2-1:
Dow Jones 70-year historical chart by year.

Source: Macrotrends.net

However, stock investing naturally has some disadvantages. For example,

>> **Stocks face different types of risks.** Even the most awesome stocks have risks that you can't easily eliminate, such as the following (see Chapter 3 for details):

● Business and financial risk

● Purchasing power risk

- Market risk

- Event risk

- Government control and regulations

- Foreign competition

- The general state of the economy

>> **The stock selection process can be a pain in the neck.** You have literally thousands of stocks to choose from. Predicting how the company will perform tomorrow can also be very difficult. After all, the price today only reflects the current state of the company or what the market participants perceive it to be.

TIP

By investing in the cryptocurrency market, you may be able to balance out some of the preceding risks. The cryptocurrency selection process is also different from that of stocks, as I explain in Chapter 9.

The final disadvantage of stock investing, however, is similar to that of crypto investing. They both generally produce less current income than some other investments. Several types of investments, such as bonds (which I discuss in the following section), pay more current income and do so with much greater certainty.

TECHNICAL
STUFF

Cryptocurrency investing is quite asymmetric. Rightly timed, crypto investing can produce an enormous return on investment (ROI). For example, NXT has a 697,295 percent ROI, Ethereum has a 160,100 percent ROI, and IOTA has a 282,300 percent ROI since their initial coin offerings (ICOs; see Chapter 11). There is no other investment in the world that can top that. The best-performing stock is Netflix, and that's around 64,000 percent in ten years!

Bonds

Bonds are also known as *fixed-income securities.* They're different from cryptocurrencies and stocks in that you loan money to an entity for a period of time, and you receive a fixed amount of interest on a periodic basis. Hence its categorization as "fixed income."

Just like with cryptocurrencies and stocks (see the preceding section), you can also expect capital gains from bonds. But these capital gains work a bit differently. Because the companies issuing bonds promise to repay a fixed amount when the bonds mature, bond prices don't typically rise in correlation with the firm's profits. The bond prices rise and fall as market interest rates change.

Another similarity among bonds, cryptocurrencies, and stocks is that they're all issued by a wide range of companies. Additionally, many governmental bodies issue bonds. So if you're looking to diversify only within the bonds market, you still can choose from a range of relatively safe ones to highly speculative ones.

Compared to cryptocurrencies and stocks, bonds are generally less risky and provide higher current income. But they still are subject to a variety of risks. Some of the risks involved with bonds investing are similar to those of cryptocurrencies and stocks — namely, purchasing power risk, business and financial risk, and liquidity risk. Bonds have an additional type of risk known as the *call risk* or *prepayment risk*. Call risk is the risk that a bond will be *called*, or retired, long before its maturity date. If the bond issuer calls its bonds, you'll have to find another place for your funds.

REMEMBER

The potential for very high returns on bonds is much lower compared to cryptocurrencies and stocks, respectively. But the risk involved with bonds is also comparatively lower. You can find more about cryptocurrency risks in Chapter 3.

Forex

Here's an alternative investment that may be even riskier than cryptocurrencies. *Forex* is the geek term for the foreign exchange market. It's the first thing I ever invested in. I've written books about it (*Invest Diva's Guide to Making Money in Forex* [McGraw-Hill Education] and *Ichimoku Secrets* [CreateSpace Independent Publishing Platform]). In fact, my company's original name was Forex Diva! We then switched to Invest Diva, literally in order to emphasize the importance of diversification.

By participating in the forex market, you buy and sell currencies. Not cryptocurrencies, but fiat currencies such as the U.S. dollar, the euro, the British pound, the Australian dollar, or any other currency any government issues. A *fiat currency* is a country's legal tender that's issued by the government.

Before Bitcoin became the celebrity of financial assets in 2017, most people associated cryptocurrencies such as Bitcoin with the traditional forex market because "cryptocurrency" includes the word "currency," and crypto owners hoped to use their assets to make payments. However, as I mention earlier in this chapter, cryptocurrencies also have a lot in common with stocks.

When you participate in the forex market, you don't necessarily invest for long-term capital gains. Even the most popular currencies such as the U.S. dollar are subject to a ton of volatility throughout the year. A good U.S. economy doesn't always translate into a stronger U.S. dollar.

Heck, sometimes some countries, such as Japan, prefer to have a weaker currency because they rely heavily on exports. If their currencies are stronger than the currency of the country they're trying to sell stuff to, they get a lower rate to sell the same product abroad than domestically.

Participating in the forex market as an investor mainly consists of short-to-medium-term trading activity between different currency pairs. You can buy the euro versus the U.S. dollar (the EUR/USD pair), for example. If the euro's value appreciates relative to the U.S. dollar's, you make money. However, if the U.S. dollar's value goes higher than the euro's, you lose money.

Analyzing the forex market needs a very different approach when compared to stock and cryptocurrency analysis. When looking at the forex markets, you need to focus on the issuing country's economic state, its upcoming economic figures such as its *gross domestic product* (GDP, or the value of the goods produced inside the country), unemployment rate, inflation, interest rate, and so on, as well as its political environment.

However, just like the cryptocurrency market, you need to trade forex in pairs. In my online forex education course, the *Forex Coffee Break,* I compare these pairs to dancing couples — international couples who push each other back and forth. Traders can make money by speculating which direction the couple will move next. You can see this metaphor in Figure 2-2, where the Australian dollar (AUD, or Mr. Aussie) is dancing against the U.S. dollar (USD, or Ms. USA).

FIGURE 2-2:
Forex metaphor: Australian dollar dancing against U.S. dollar.

Source: InvestDiva.com

You can apply a similar concept to the cryptocurrency market. For example, you can pair up Bitcoin (BTC) and Ethereum (ETH) against each other. You can even pair up a cryptocurrency such as Bitcoin against a fiat currency such as the

U.S. dollar and speculate their value against each other. However, in these cases you need to analyze each currency, crypto or fiat, separately. Then you need to measure their relative value against each other and predict which currency will win the couple's battle in the future.

TIP

You can also consider cryptocurrencies as a cross between stocks and forex. Though many investors invest in cryptocurrencies for capital gain purposes, you can also trade different cryptocurrencies against each other, the way you can in the forex market. I explore cross-cryptocurrency trading in Chapter 10.

Precious metals

Time to compare one of the most recent manmade means to buy stuff (cryptocurrencies) to one of the most ancient ones! No, I'm not going back all the way to *bartering*, where people exchanged their goods and services to fulfill their needs. In the following sections, I talk about the stuff with a bling. Before the advent of paper money, precious metals such as gold and silver were long used to make coins and to buy stuff.

REMEMBER

The precious metals comparison is actually the best argument when someone tells you cryptocurrencies are worthless because they don't have any intrinsic value.

Getting a little background

Back in the days of bartering, people would exchange stuff that provided real value to their human needs: chickens, clothes, or farming services. Supposedly, people in the ancient civilization of Lydia were among the first to use coins made of gold and silver in exchange for goods and services. Imagine the first shopper who tried to convince the seller to accept a gold coin instead of three chickens that could feed a family for a week. This change was followed by leather money, paper money, credit cards, and now cryptocurrencies.

Some may argue that precious metals like gold do too have intrinsic value. They're durable. They conduct both heat and electricity and therefore have some industrial application. I know I used some gold and silver in experiments back in the day when I was studying electrical engineering in Japan. But to be honest, most people don't invest in precious metals because they're trying to conduct electricity. They primarily buy them to use as jewelry or currency. Today, market sentiment mainly determines the value of gold and silver.

Silver has more use as an industrial metal than gold does. Silver is used in batteries, electrical appliances, medical products, and other industrial items. However, despite the additional demand, silver is valued lower than gold. For example, at the time of writing, silver is priced at $16 per ounce, while gold is traded above $1,250 per ounce.

Keep in mind that England didn't establish gold as its standard of value until 1816. (*Standard of value* means tying the value of the currency to its value in gold.) In 1913, the United States finally jumped on board through its Federal Reserve system. It backed its notes by gold and aimed to ensure that notes and checks would be honored and could be redeemed for gold.

Even though precious metals don't have an arguable intrinsic value, they have long been a favorite investment tool among market participants. One of the main reasons is their historical association with wealth. Often, when investments such as bonds, real estate, and the stock market go down or the political environment is uncertain, people flock to precious metals. People prefer to own precious metals at these times because they can actually physically touch metals and keep them in their homes right next to their beds.

Comparing precious metals to cryptocurrencies

Besides the fact that you need to mine in order to get your hands on precious metals and some cryptocurrencies, one key similarity between precious metals and cryptocurrencies is that both categories have unregulated characteristics. Gold has been an unregulated currency at various times and in various places. Unregulated currencies become more valuable when investors don't trust the official currency, and cryptocurrencies just seem to be another example of this trend. (I talk about cryptocurrency mining in Chapter 12.)

Investing in precious metals comes with a number of risk factors you need to keep in mind. For example, if you're buying physical precious metals as an investment, you must consider their portability risk. Transferring precious metals can be expensive given their weight, high import taxes, and the need for a high level of security. In contrast, you don't need to make a physical transfer with cryptocurrencies, besides the hardware crypto wallets I discuss in Chapter 7. But moving cryptocurrencies is much faster and less expensive, even with a hardware wallet, than transferring precious metals.

On the other hand, cryptocurrency prices have been more volatile in the short time they've been available on the markets than all precious metals combined have. The 2017 volatility in particular was due to the hype in the market, as I explain in Chapter 3. As cryptocurrency investing becomes more mainstream and more people use it for everyday transaction, crypto prices may become more predictable.

Gaining Capital Appreciation

Capital appreciation refers to the increase in the price or value of cryptocurrencies. And it's one of the reasons many investors (and noninvestors, for that matter) look to jump on the cryptocurrency train. Initial Bitcoin owners sure waited years before they saw any sort of capital appreciation. Personally, I was one of the skeptics of the whole thing. Back in 2012, one of my investor friends in Switzerland told me to buy some Bitcoin. I arrogantly ignored him — and boy, did I regret my arrogance later! I started investing in cryptocurrencies when the price of Bitcoin had surged significantly. However, with some research, I was able to find more affordable cryptocurrencies that were expected to have similar capital appreciation.

In the following sections, I look at the history of capital appreciation for cryptocurrencies and discuss their growth potential — a big reason to consider investing in them.

REMEMBER

With great expectations of capital appreciation and huge growth potential come great expectations of capital losses. That's why I strongly recommend reading Chapter 3 before starting your trading activity in the cryptocurrency market.

Historical returns

Most of the gains in the cryptocurrency market up to 2017 were a result of market hype. In 2013, for example, many people bought Bitcoin as its price approached $1,000 for the first time. As you can see in Figure 2-3, shortly after, its price crashed to around $300, where it stayed for the following two years. The next big wave of growth came in January 2017, when Bitcoin's price broke above the $1,000 level.

FIGURE 2-3: Bitcoin price between 2013 and January 2017.

Source: tradingview.com

If you had bought one Bitcoin at $300 at the end of 2015, by January 2017 you would've had $700 worth of capital appreciation (when the price hit $1,000). But of course, the gains didn't stop there. As you can see in Figure 2-4, after the break above $1,000, Bitcoin's price managed to go all the way up to close to $20,000 by the end of 2017, when it came crashing down to a range around $6,000.

FIGURE 2-4:
Bitcoin price between 2016 and July 2018.

Source: tradingview.com

For people who had bought (or mined) Bitcoin when it was valued at around $300 and held on to it throughout the volatility, the crash to $6,000 wasn't that big of a deal. For every Bitcoin they'd bought at $300, they had around $5,700 worth of capital appreciation even if they didn't cash their Bitcoins in when the value reached above $19,000.

People who bought Bitcoin at around $1,000 and cashed it out at $19,000 at its 2017 peak would've made $18,000 for every Bitcoin they owned. Of course, those who bought Bitcoin at $19,000 had to sit on their hands and eat their losses after the crash.

Many market participants compare Bitcoin and other cryptocurrencies' appreciation to the dot-com bubble from the mid-1990s and early 2000s. According to *Fortune* magazine, since its creation in 2009 until March 2018, Bitcoin saw four bear (falling) waves, where prices dropped 45 to 50 percent, typically rebounding an average of 47 percent afterward. During the dot-com bubble, the Nasdaq composite index had five of those waves, averaging 44 percent declines followed by 40 percent rebounds. Trading volume patterns are also eerily similar.

Nasdaq has clearly rallied nicely from its low in 2002. Though history and past performance aren't indicative of future behavior, crypto enthusiasts have reasons to believe that growth potential for cryptocurrencies may be similar to the Nasdaq rebound, if not better.

Huge growth potential

Bitcoin and cryptocurrencies were the biggest investment story of 2017. Stories appeared daily on CNBC, and in the *Wall Street Journal* and *New York Times,* about people becoming millionaires practically overnight.

However, after January 2018, the price of Bitcoin fell 63 percent. The media followed suit appropriately, saying the opportunity had passed — that the cryptocurrency bull market was over and the bubble had burst.

This tune was interesting, especially because many billionaires became crypto investors at this point. For example, J.P. Morgan CEO Jamie Dimon (who had called Bitcoin a fraud and said any J.P. Morgan traders caught trading Bitcoin would be fired) became one of the most active buyers of a fund that tracks the price of Bitcoin. The price of Bitcoin fell as much as 24 percent in the few days that followed Dimon's statement, and sure enough, right in that period, J.P. Morgan and Morgan Stanley started buying for their clients at low prices.

This story isn't alone in the crypto market. For example, after slamming Bitcoin at the World Economic Forum in Davos, Switzerland, in January 2018, calling it a "bubble," hedge fund titan George Soros gave the green light to his $26 billion family office to begin buying cryptocurrencies just eight weeks later.

TECHNICAL STUFF

Interestingly, Soros attributes part of his success to his understanding of what he calls "reflexivity." In simple terms, this theory states that investors base their decisions not on reality but on their perception of reality. Soros once said, "The degree of distortion may vary from time to time. Sometimes it's quite insignificant, at other times it is quite pronounced . . . Every bubble has two components: an underlying trend that prevails in reality and a misconception relating to that trend."

The problem is that most people have no clue what's really going on in the cryptocurrency market. And most have no idea where the price is about to go next. The majority of those interested in the market are taking their cues from market noise, making it way easier for the prices to fall when the big movers downplay for their own benefit.

"Going against the crowd" is one of the key pillars in my *Invest Diva Diamond Analysis (IDDA)* that I cover in Chapter 9, as well as in the *Make Your Money Work for You PowerCourse* at `https://learn.investdiva.com/free-webinar-3-secrets-to-making-your-money-work-for-you`. When the majority of the market panics about the drops in the value of an asset, it is often the best time to stack up on it. You can say the same about the cryptocurrency market. For the cryptocurrencies with strong blockchain technology behind them, once the price bottoms out, there is nowhere for its value to go but up.

Increasing Income Potential

Although gaining capital appreciation is one of the most attractive features of cryptocurrency investing (as I explain earlier in this chapter), you can also take advantage of some cryptocurrencies that pay something similar to dividends in the stock market.

A bit about traditional dividends

By definition, a *dividend* is a sum of money public companies pay their shareholders on a regular basis. U.S. corporations pay billions of dollars' worth of dividends every year. Yet in spite of these numbers, many investors (especially young ones) don't pay much attention to dividends. They prefer capital gains because the rewards can be quicker and can way exceed any amount of dividend payment.

TECHNICAL STUFF

In the traditional stock market, companies typically pay dividends on a quarterly basis. A firm's board of directors decides how much to pay shareholders in dividends or whether to pay dividends at all. Sometimes, the directors decide to pay dividends because the stock value isn't doing so well. So they select a higher dividend rate to keep investors interested in buying the stocks.

REMEMBER

Investors with lower risk tolerance may prefer dividend payments to capital gains because dividend payments don't fluctuate as much as the value of stocks do. Furthermore, if the markets crash like they did in 2008, dividends can provide nice protection. The best way to accumulate dividends is to hold onto your assets long-term.

The basics on crypto dividends

During the crypto mania of 2017, many cryptocurrency platforms were quick to realize the importance of regular payments to keep investors happy. But these payments can be a bit different than traditional stock dividends. You can generate regular, passive income in the crypto market in several ways. Here are the two most popular ones:

>> **HODLing:** No, this term is not a typo for "holding," although it has a similar meaning. It stands for "Hold On for Dear Life." It is the closest payment to traditional dividends. Some cryptocurrencies pay out the HODLers, who simply purchase and carry the digital coins in their wallets.

>> **Proof-of-stake (PoS):** This is a lighter version of proof-of-work in cryptocurrency mining, which I explain in Chapter 7. When you "stake" a coin, it means you put it aside so it can't be used in the blockchain network. If you have a ton of stakes, you have a higher chance of getting paid at a random selection by the network. Annual returns for staking vary between 1 percent and 5 percent, depending on the coin.

Some of the most popular dividend-paying cryptos in 2018 are NEO, ARK, and exchange cryptocurrencies like Binance and KuCoin.

While receiving cash (or digital coins) just for holding onto your assets is pretty cool, sometimes it makes more sense to cash out and reinvest your holdings to get a better return.

Fueling Ideological Empowerment

Just as oil is the lubricant that allows a machine to operate, blockchain technology is the lubricant that enables the cryptocurrency market. *Blockchain* is the underlying technology for cryptocurrencies, not to mention one of those breakthrough developments that has the potential to revolutionize nearly every industry in the world completely. (I cover blockchain further in Chapter 4.)

Blockchain can offer so much more as it's aiming to resolve many economic and financial problems in the world today, from dealing with the flaws of the sharing economy to banking the unbanked and underbanked. Here are some of the kinds of social good that come through cryptocurrencies and the blockchain technology.

The economy of the future

We live in an era where the *sharing economy* is exploding. The sharing economy allows people to rent out their own property for use by others. Internet giants such as Google, Facebook, and Twitter rely on the contributions of users as a means to generate value within their own platforms. If you've ever taken an Uber or Lyft rather than a taxi or rented a room on Airbnb instead of a hotel, you're a part of the sharing economy crowd.

However, the traditional sharing economy has its issues, such as the following:

>> **Requiring high fees for using the platforms.**

>> **Hurting individual users but benefitting the underlying corporation:** In most cases, the value produced by the crowd isn't equally redistributed among all who have contributed to the value production. All the profits are captured by the large intermediaries who operate the platforms.

>> **Playing fast and loose with consumer info:** Some companies have abused their power by getting access to private data without customers knowing.

As the sharing economy expands in the future, its problems will likely become more complicated.

In order to combat these issues, several companies are developing blockchain-based sharing economy platforms. These platforms are much more affordable to use and provide much-needed transparency. They limit, and sometimes completely cut out, the need for a centralized middleman. This shift allows true peer-to-peer interactions, eliminating the 20-to-30-percent transaction fees that come with centralized platforms. Because all transactions are logged on blockchains, all users can audit the network's operations.

This approach is possible because of the decentralized nature of blockchain technology, which is ultimately a means for individuals to coordinate common activities, to interact directly with one another, and to govern themselves in a more trustworthy and decentralized manner.

WARNING

Some cryptocurrency transactions aren't entirely free. In many cases, every time there is a transaction on a blockchain, you have to pay the "network fees," which are funds payable to the blockchain network members who are mining your coins/transactions. If you take into consideration the time "wasted" waiting for a transaction to clear (for example, it takes 78 minutes for a Bitcoin transaction to reach consensus), then in reality you may not save anything in fees by going to some blockchain applications.

Blockchain remains the fuel behind the economy of the future, and cryptocurrencies are a byproduct to pave the way by distributing the global economy.

Freedom from government control of currency

The rise of Bitcoin and other cryptocurrencies as a trillion-dollar asset class in 2017 was spurred without the oversight of a central bank or monetary authority guaranteeing trust or market conduct. Unlike fiat currencies such as the

U.S. dollar and the euro, most cryptocurrencies will never be subject to money printing (officially called *quantitative easing*) by central banks. Most cryptocurrencies operate under controlled supply, which means no printing of money. In fact, networks limit the supply of tokens even in cases where the demand is high. For example, Bitcoin's supply will decrease in time and will reach its final number somewhere around the year 2140. All cryptocurrencies control the supply of the tokens by a schedule written in the code. Translation: The money supply of a cryptocurrency in every given moment in the future can roughly be calculated today.

The lack of government control over cryptocurrencies can also help with lower inflation risk. History has shown over and over again that when a particular government applies bad policies, becomes corrupt, or is faced by crisis, the country's individual currency suffers. This fluctuation in the currency value can lead to the printing of more money. Inflation is the reason why your parents paid less than a dollar for a gallon of milk while you have to pay at least three dollars. How awesome would it be if cryptocurrencies can get rid of government-controlled inflation so that your grandchildren don't have to pay more for stuff than you do?

Help for the unbanked and underbanked

One of the most noble problems cryptocurrencies can solve is banking the *unbanked.* According to Cointelegraph, "2 billion people in the world still don't have a bank account. Most of them live in low- and middle-income emerging markets, but even in high-income countries, large numbers of people are unable to use banks to meet their day-to-day financial needs. This means they don't have access to the convenience, security, and interest that banks provide."

Moreover, many people are *underbanked;* they have access to a bank account but don't have adequate access to the financial services that banks can provide. Even in the United States, for example, 33.5 million households in 2015 were unbanked or underbanked. Without access to savings and credit, these people can't participate in the cycle of economic growth.

TIP

Cryptocurrencies, with the help of blockchain technology, have the potential to help the unbanked and underbanked by letting them create their own financial alternatives efficiently and transparently. All someone needs to start using cryptocurrencies such as Bitcoin and send and receive money is a smartphone or laptop and Internet connection. (Flip to Chapter 6 for an introduction on how to buy cryptocurrencies.)

Chapter **3**

Recognizing the Risks of Cryptocurrencies

S o you're excited to jump on the crypto wagon, perhaps because you expect a gigantic *return* (profit) on your investment. That's basically the reward for investing. However, you can't consider return without also looking at risk. *Risk* is the uncertainty surrounding the actual return you generate.

In my investment education courses, I spend a lot of time speaking about risk and how everyone should approach it individually. What may represent high risk for me may not be as risky for you due to our unique lifestyles and financial circumstances.

Cryptocurrencies have shown their fair share of volatility, which has made some investors millions of dollars while wiping out some others' initial investment. In this chapter, I look at cryptocurrencies' price volatility from 2017 to 2018. I also define cryptocurrency rewards and risk, describe different types of risk, and give you pointers on managing risk.

Reviewing Cryptocurrency Returns

Different assets generate different types of returns. For example, one source of return is the change in the investment's value. Also, when you invest in the stock market or the forex (foreign exchange) market, you may generate an income in the form of dividends or interest. Investors call these two sources of return *capital gains* (or *capital losses*) and *current income*, respectively.

REMEMBER

Although most people invest in the cryptocurrency market for capital gains, some cryptocurrencies actually offer current income opportunities. You get an introduction to cryptocurrency returns in Chapter 2.

Capital gains (or losses)

The most popular reason for crypto investing is to see gains in the coins' value. Some people associate the coins with precious metals such as gold. Doing so makes sense because, just like gold, a limited amount is available for most cryptocurrencies, and one way to extract many of them is to mine. (Of course, you don't need to gear up with a pickax and headlamp when mining cryptocurrencies; head to Chapter 12 for details on cryptocurrency mining.)

With that, many investors consider cryptocurrencies to be assets even though they're technically currencies that can be used in transactions. People buy these currencies in hopes of selling them when the prices rise more. If the value of your cryptocurrency token goes higher from the time you purchase, you get capital gains when you sell the token. Congrats! If the prices go lower, you end up with capital losses.

Income

Income is a lesser-known type of return in the cryptocurrency market. Income is generated from something called *crypto dividends*.

Traditionally, dividends occur when public companies distribute a portion of their earnings to their shareholders. Traditional types of dividends include cash payments, shares of stock, or other property.

Earning dividends in the crypto market can get a bit more complicated. Different currencies have different operating systems and their own rules and regulations. However, the concept still remains the same. Crypto dividend payments are becoming increasingly popular among altcoins, which are the alternative crypto-currencies besides Bitcoin. When choosing a cryptocurrency for your portfolio, you can consider looking into crypto dividends as well as the potential of capital gains (discussed in the preceding section).

Some of the most popular ways to earn crypto dividends are

>> **Staking:** Holding a proof-of-stake coin in a special wallet

>> **Holding:** Buying and holding a crypto in any wallet

I talk more about staking and holding in Chapter 7.

At the time of writing, some dividend-paying cryptocurrencies include NEO, KuCoin, BridgeCoin, Neblio, and Komodo. Find out more about these currencies in Chapter 8. In addition, besides staking and holding, you can earn regular interest payments by participating in crypto lending. For example, you can earn up to 5 percent interest on your cryptos by allowing companies like Celsius Network to give out loans to the general public against cryptos.

Risk: Flipping the Other Side of the Coin

Investment returns are exciting, but you can't consider return without also look-ing at risk. The sad truth about any type of investment is that the greater the expected return, the greater the risk. Because cryptocurrencies are considered riskier than some other assets, they may also provide higher returns. The rela-tionship between risk and return is called the *risk-return tradeoff.*

Cryptocurrency investing isn't a get-rich-quick scheme. You shouldn't invest in cryptocurrencies by using your life savings or taking out a loan. You must consider your risk tolerance, understand the different sources of cryptocurrency risks, and then develop an investment strategy that's suitable for you — just you, not any-one else — because you're unique, and so is your financial situation.

Also keep in mind that early Bitcoin investors waited years to see any returns. If you don't have the patience required to see meaningful returns on your invest-ment, you may need to forget about investing altogether.

That being said, a healthy amount of risk appetite is essential not only when investing but also in life. Don't get so paranoid about risk that you just never leave the house for fear of getting into an accident!

Glimpsing Cryptocurrencies' Reward versus Risk

One of the main reasons cryptocurrency investing became such a hot topic in 2017 was the crazy surge in the value of major cryptocurrencies such as Bitcoin.

Although you may have heard of Bitcoin the most, it wasn't even among the ten best-performing crypto assets of 2017. Bitcoin's value grew by more than 1,000 percent, but other, lesser-known cryptocurrencies such as Ripple and NEM were among the biggest winners, with a whopping 36,018 percent and 29,842 percent growth, respectively.

Where did Bitcoin stand on the performance list? Fourteenth!

These returns made investors and noninvestors alike super excited about the cryptocurrency market. By the beginning of 2018, almost everyone you knew — your doctor, your rideshare driver, perhaps even your grandmother — was probably talking about Bitcoin, whether or not the person had any experience in any sort of investing. I know my 8-year-old nephew was asking me about it.

However, as is true of any type of investment, what goes up must come down, including the cryptocurrency market. Because the cryptocurrency prices had gone up so much, so quickly, the crash was as hard and as speedy. For example, by February 2018, Bitcoin had dropped to the three-month lows of $6,000 from highs of nearly $20,000.

The cryptocurrency then started to consolidate above the $6,000 support level, forming lowering highs as you can see in Figure 3-1. By *support level*, I'm talking about a price that the market has had difficulty going lower than in the past. In this case, the price had difficulty breaking below $6,000 back in November 2017. *Lower highs* are those mountain-like peaks on the chart. Every peak (high) is lower than the previous one, which indicated a decrease of popularity among market participants. I talk more about support (and its cousin, resistance) in Chapter 16.

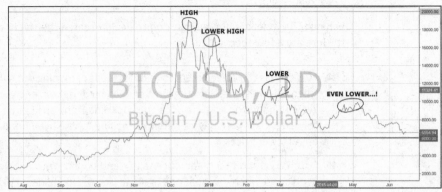

Source: tradingview.com

FIGURE 3-1:
Bitcoin's price action versus the U.S. dollar from 2017 to 2018.

Many analysts considered the great appreciation of major cryptocurrencies' value to be a bubble. This fluctuation is a heck of a roller-coaster ride in such a short period of time! The returns were great for those who invested early and took profit at the highs. But just imagine investing in the market when the prices were up and watching the value of your investment going lower and lower. That's one of the major risk factors in any type of investing.

Digging into Different Kinds of Risk

Getting educated about risk puts you right on top of your game. Knowing your risk tolerance, you can create a strategy that protects you and your wealth. The risks associated with cryptocurrencies come from many different sources. Here are the various types of crypto risks.

Crypto hype risk

Though getting hyped up in the thought of buying your dream car is a good thing, the hype surrounding cryptocurrencies isn't always as exciting. The main reason cryptos have a lot of hype is that most people don't know about what they're investing in; they just end up listening to the crowd. The crypto hype back in 2017 was one the many drivers of the fast-and-furious market surge. After people started to figure out what they'd invested in, the prices crashed. This type of behavior became so popular that crypto geeks created their very own lingo around it. Here are a few terms:

>> **FOMO:** This crypto-geek term stands for "Fear of missing out." This happens when you see a massive surge in a crypto you don't own and you hurry in to get your hands on it as the price goes up. Hint: Don't do it! What goes up must come down, so you may be better off waiting for the hype to calm down and buy at lower prices.

>> **FUD:** This is short for "Fear, uncertainty, and doubt." You can use this in a Reddit post when you hear one of those Doctor Doomsdays talking down the market. JPMorgan Chase's CEO, Jamie Dimon, spread one of the biggest FUDs in September 2017 by calling Bitcoin a fraud. In January 2018, he said he regretted saying that.

>> **ATH:** Short for "All-time high." Whenever the price of an asset reaches the highest point in its history, you can say, "It's reached an ATH."

>> **Bag holder:** You don't want this to be your nickname! Bag holders are those investors who bought out of FOMO at an ATH and missed the chance of selling. Therefore, they are left with a bag (wallet) filled with worthless coins.

>> **BTFD:** This one stands for "Buy the f@#&ing dip!" In order for you not to become a bag holder, you've got to BTFD.

REMEMBER

Before falling for the market noise, arm yourself with knowledge on the specific cryptos you're considering. You have plenty of opportunities to make lots of money in the crypto market. Be patient and acquire the right knowledge instead of betting on the current hype. An investor who trades on the hype probably doesn't even have an investment strategy — unless you call gambling a strategy! You can find different methods of strategy development in Parts 2 and 4.

Security risk

Scams. Hacking. Theft. These issues have been a common theme in the cryptocurrency market since Bitcoin's inception in 2009. And with each scandal, the cryptocurrencies' values are compromised as well, although temporarily. Your cryptocurrency can be compromised in three main ways, which I outline in the following sections. You should definitely follow safety precautions in every step of your cryptocurrency investing strategy.

Safety check #1: The cryptocurrency itself

Hundreds of cryptocurrencies are already available for investments, with thousands of new ICOs (initial coin offerings) on the way (see Chapter 11 for more on ICOs). When choosing the cryptocurrency to invest in, you must educate yourself on the blockchain's protocol and make sure no bugs (or rumors of bugs) may compromise your investment. The protocol is the common set of rules that the blockchain network has agreed upon. You may be able to find out about the nature of the cryptocurrency's protocol on its white paper on its website. The white paper is an official document that the crypto founders put together before their ICO, laying out everything there is to know about the cryptocurrency. But companies are unlikely to share their shortcomings in their white papers. That's why reading reviews on savvy websites like Reddit and my site, InvestDiva.com, can often be your best bet.

These types of bugs appear even in the major cryptocurrencies. For example, a lot of negative press surrounded EOS's release of the first version of its open source software before June 2, 2018. A Chinese security firm had found a bug in the EOS code that could theoretically have been used to create tokens out of thin air. However, EOS was able to fix the bugs. To further turn the bad press into positive, Block.one, the developer of EOS, invited people to hunt for undiscovered bugs in return for monetary rewards (a process known as a *bug bounty*).

WARNING

Reliable cryptocurrency issuers should take matters into their own hands immediately when a bug is found. But until they do, you're wise to keep your hands off their coins!

Safety check #2: The exchange

Exchanges are where you trade the cryptocurrency tokens (see Chapter 6 for an introduction). You need to make sure that your trading host is trustworthy and credible. Countless numbers of security incidents and data breaches have occurred in the crypto community because of the exchanges.

One of the famous initial hacks was that of Japan-based Mt. Gox, the largest Bitcoin exchange, in 2013. At the time, Mt. Gox was handling 70 percent of the world's Bitcoin exchanges. However, it had many issues, such as lack of a testing policy, lack of a version control software, and lack of a proper management. As all these problems piled up, in February 2014 the exchange became the victim of a massive hack, where about 850,000 Bitcoins were lost. Although 200,000 Bitcoins were eventually recovered, the remaining 650,000 have never been recovered.

Many exchanges have learned a lesson from this incident and are keeping up with the latest safety measures. However, exchange hacks still happen almost on a monthly basis.

REMEMBER

Centralized exchanges are the most vulnerable to attacks. Flip to Chapter 6 for methods to spot red flags in cryptocurrency exchanges.

I'm not trying to scare you with these stories. As time goes by, the market learns from previous mistakes and works on a better and safer future. However, you still need to take matters into your own hands as much as possible. Before choosing an exchange, take a look at its security section on its website. Check on whether it participates in any bug bounty programs to encourage safety. And, of course, ask the right people about the exchange. In Invest Diva's Premium Investing Group, we keep an eye on the latest developments in the market and keep our members informed about any shady activities. So feel free to stop by `https://learn.investdiva.com/join-group`!

Safety check #3: Your wallet

The final round of security check is all in your own hands because what kind of crypto wallet you use is entirely up to you. Though you don't physically carry your crypto coins, you can store them in a secure physical wallet. You actually store the public and private keys, which you can use for making transactions with your altcoins, in these wallets as well. You can take your wallet's security to a higher level by using a backup. I explore wallet safety methods more in Chapter 7.

Volatility risk

Volatility risk is essentially the risk in unexpected market movements. Though volatility can be a good thing, it can also catch you off guard sometimes. Just like any other market, the cryptocurrency market can suddenly move in the opposite direction from what you expected. If you aren't prepared for the market volatility, you can lose the money you invested in the market.

The volatility in the cryptocurrency market has resulted from many factors. For one, it's a brand-new technology. The inception of revolutionary technologies — such as the Internet — can create initial periods of volatility. The blockchain technology (see Chapter 4) and its underpinning cryptocurrencies take a lot of getting used to before they become mainstream.

The best way to combat the cryptocurrency volatility risk is looking at the big picture. Volatility matters a lot if you have a short-term investing horizon (see Chapter 17) because it's an indicator of how much money you may make or lose over a short period. But if you have a long-term horizon (see Chapter 18), volatility can turn into an opportunity.

You can also offset volatility risk by using automated trading algorithms on various exchanges. For example, you can set up an order like "sell 65 percent of coin 1," "100 percent of coin 2," and so on if the price drops by 3 percent. This strategy can minimize the risk of volatility and allow you to sleep well at night.

Liquidity risk

By definition, *liquidity risk* is the risk of not being able to sell (or *liquidate*) an investment quickly at a reasonable price. Liquidity is important for any tradable asset. The forex market (my first love) is considered the most liquid market in the world. But even in the forex market, the lack of liquidity may be a problem. If you trade currencies with very low volume, you may not even be able to close your trade because the prices just won't move!

Cryptocurrencies can also see episodes of illiquidity. Heck, the liquidity problem was one of the factors that led to the high volatility in Bitcoin and other altcoins described earlier in this chapter. When the liquidity is low, the risk of price manipulation also comes into play. One big player can easily move the market to his or her favor by placing a massive order.

TIP

The crypto community refers to these types of big players as *whales*. In the cryptocurrency market, whales often move small altcoins by using their huge capital.

On the bright side, as cryptocurrency investing becomes more available and acceptable, the market may become more liquid. The increase in the number of trusted crypto exchanges will provide opportunity for more people to trade. Crypto ATMs and payment cards are popping up, helping raise the awareness and acceptance of cryptocurrencies in everyday transactions.

Another key factor in cryptocurrency liquidity is the stance of countries on cryptocurrency regulations. If the authorities are able to define issues such as consumer protection and crypto taxes, more people will be comfortable using and trading cryptocurrencies, which will affect their liquidity.

REMEMBER

When choosing a cryptocurrency to trade, you must consider its liquidity by analyzing its acceptance, popularity, and the number of exchanges it's been traded on. Lesser-known cryptocurrencies may have a lot of upside potential, but they may put you in trouble because of lack of liquidity. I explore different types of cryptocurrencies and their characteristics in Part 2.

Vanishing risk

No, I'm not talking about disappearing into the ever-magical blockchain industry. Quite the contrary. Hundreds of different cryptocurrencies are currently out there. More and more cryptocurrencies are being introduced every day. In ten years' time, many of these altcoins may vanish while others flourish.

A familiar example of vanishing risk is the dot-com bubble. In the late 1990s, many people around the world dreamed up businesses that capitalized on the popularity of the Internet. Some, such as Amazon and eBay, succeeded in conquering the world. Many more crashed and burned. Following the path of history, many of the booming cryptocurrencies popping up left and right are destined to bust.

REMEMBER

To minimize the vanishing risk, you need to analyze the fundamentals of the cryptocurrencies you choose to invest in. Do their goals make sense to you? Are they solving a problem that will continue in the years to come? Who are their partners? You can't vanish the vanishing risk entirely (pun intended), but you can eliminate your exposure to a sudden bust. Check out Part 2 for more on fundamental analysis.

Regulation risk

One of the initial attractions of cryptocurrencies was their lack of regulation. In the good old days in cryptoland, crypto enthusiasts didn't have to worry about governments chasing them down. All they had was a white paper and a promise. However, as the demand for cryptocurrencies grows, global regulators are scratching their heads on how to keep up — and to not lose their shirts to the new economic reality.

REMEMBER

To date, most digital currencies aren't backed by any central government, meaning each country has different standards.

You can divide the cryptocurrency regulation risk into two components: the regulation event risk and regulation's nature itself.

>> The *regulation event risk* doesn't necessarily mean that the cryptocurrency market is doing poorly. It just means the market participants reacted to an unexpected announcement. In 2018, every seemingly small regulation announcement drove the price of many major cryptocurrencies and created a ton of volatility.

>> At the time of writing, there are no global cryptocurrency regulators, so existing regulations are all over the board. In some countries (such as Japan and the United States), for example, cryptocurrency exchanges are legal as long as they're registered with the financial authorities. Some countries, such as China, have been stricter on the cryptocurrencies but more lenient on the blockchain industry itself.

The future of cryptocurrency regulations seems to be bright at this writing, but it may impact the markets in the future. As the market grows stronger, though, these impacts may turn into isolated events.

Tax risk

When cryptocurrency investing first got popular, hardly anyone was paying taxes on the gains. A lot of underreporting was going on. However, as the market gets more regulated, the authorities may become stricter on taxation. As of 2018, the U.S. Internal Revenue Service views Bitcoin and other cryptocurrencies as property, despite the fact that they have the word *currencies* in them. Therefore, transactions using altcoins are subject to capital gains tax.

If you live in the United States or are a U.S. citizen, tax risk involves the chance that the authorities may make unfavorable changes in tax laws, such as limitation of deductions, increase in tax rates, and elimination of tax exemptions. In other countries, tax risk can get more complicated. For example, at the time of writing, the Philippines hasn't clearly established whether the Bureau of Internal Revenue will treat cryptocurrencies as equities, property, or capital gains tax.

REMEMBER

Although virtually all investments are vulnerable to increases in tax rates, cryptocurrency taxation is a fuzzy area. Most regulators can't even agree on the basic concept of what a token represents!

And of course, different countries, different rules. Personally, I have been hit hard by taxes when moving from one country to another, or when the U.S. Congress made changes to tax laws. Fortunately, though, I have been able to cover the taxes elsewhere. Had I not had enough savings in my emergency fund, I would've had to file an extension and pay a penalty, too. That's why doing your due diligence on taxing before developing your investment strategy is crucial. Flip to Chapter 21 for more details on taxes in relation to cryptocurrencies.

Exploring Risk Management Methods

The only way you can achieve your investment goals is to invest at a risk level consistent with your risk tolerance assessment. That's why I talk a lot about methods to calculate your unique risk tolerance in my Invest Diva education courses. You can measure your risk tolerance by considering objective measures like your investment goals, your time horizon for each goal, your need for liquidity, and so on. You can increase your risk tolerance by setting longer-term goals, adding to your savings by using methods other than online investing, and lowering your need for current liquidity.

These things are certainly easier said than done, especially considering you never know when you're gonna get hit financially. The following sections provide guidance on how to manage risk by building an emergency fund, being patient with your investments, and diversifying.

TIP

Check out this master class on my website where I explain how you can calculate your personal risk tolerance and give you all the analysis tools and questionnaires in order to make your money work for you: https://learn.investdiva.com/free-webinar-3-secrets-to-making-your-money-work-for-you. See the nearby sidebar for more information, too.

MEASURING YOUR OWN RISK TOLERANCE

Risk tolerance has two main components:

- Your willingness to risk
- Your ability to risk

A financial planner is likely to have you fill out a risk tolerance questionnaire that measures your willingness to risk. This questionnaire evaluates your willingness to take on risk by asking about risk issues. It can help you determine whether you are risk averse or risk tolerant. A *risk averse* investor requires significantly more return in order to consider investing in a higher-risk investment. A *risk tolerant* investor is more willing to accept risk for a small increase in return.

However, to really get an understanding about the amount you can invest in the markets, you must also find out your ability to risk based on your unique financial situation and living circumstances. To calculate your risk tolerance, you must prepare your financial statements and analyze some ratios such as

- **Your emergency fund ratio:** You can calculate this by dividing your accessible cash by your monthly necessary spending. The result must be greater than 6.

- **Your housing ratio:** Divide your housing costs by your gross pay. If you live in the United States, the result must be below 28 percent.

- **Your debt ratio:** This one calculates your total debt divided by your total assets. The benchmark varies depending on your age and financial goals.

- **Your net worth ratio:** You can calculate this by dividing your net worth (which is all your assets minus your debt) by your total assets.

Using these ratios and comparing them to benchmark numbers, you can then fill out a simple questionnaire to figure out your risk tolerance.

Build your emergency fund first

My husband and I were recently exposed to an unpredicted financial burden. After a year of financial success for both of us, we went ahead and upgraded our budget, bought a new house in an awesome neighborhood, and added some luxury expenses we normally wouldn't go after. It was good times!

Then the unexpected tax law change in the United States put us in a higher tax bracket than usual and took away some of our previously sought tax exemptions and deductions. Right after that, our daughter, Jasmine, was born, and our plans to have our parents take care of her for the first six months fell through because of sudden health issues on both sides of the family. As the saying goes, when it rains, it pours — figuratively and literally. Our area got hit by a few storms, which flooded our basement, damaged our trees, and dropped a few branches on our house. We now needed an additional budget for the damages.

I tell this story simply to point out the importance of having an emergency fund, no matter what you're investing in or what your strategy is. Thanks to our emergency fund, we were able to overcome this financially challenging time and turn our focus back on raising our little bundle of joy. Of course, now we had to rebuild the fund from scratch.

TIP

You can calculate your emergency fund by dividing the value of your total immediately accessible cash by your necessary monthly expenses. That will give you the number of months you can survive with no additional cash flow. The result *must* be greater than six months. But the more the merrier. For more on risk tolerance calculation, visit https://learn.investdiva.com/free-webinar-3-secrets-to-making-your-money-work-for-you.

REMEMBER

You must have an emergency fund before creating an investment portfolio, let alone adding cryptocurrencies to it.

Be patient

The risks involved with cryptocurrencies are slightly different from those of other, more established markets such as equities and precious metals. However, you can use similar methods for managing your portfolio risk regardless of your investments.

The most common reason many traders lose money online is the fantasy of getting rich quick. I can say with confidence (verifiably) that the vast majority of my long-term students made money, and in many cases a lot of money. The key has been patience.

"Patience is a profitable virtue" is the mantra of our investment group. The majority of our portfolio holding had been equities and forex, but the same has been true to Bitcoin holders. It took years (nine years, to be exact) for early Bitcoin enthusiasts to make any return on their holdings. And although a bit of a bubble occurred in 2017, nothing is stopping the markets from reaching and surpassing the all-time-high levels in the coming years.

The patience mantra doesn't help only long-term investors. It also goes for traders and speculators. Very often, that investment or speculative position you took may go down or sideways for what seems like forever. Sooner or later, the market will take note of the sentiment and either erase losses or create new buy opportunities.

In Figure 3-2, you can see the role patience can play in an investor's returns. Of course, you'd love for the markets to just march up to your profit target (that is, exit) price level straightaway. But more often than not, it just doesn't work that way.

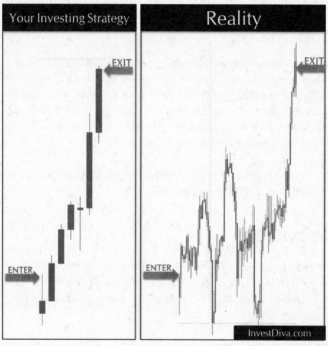

Source: InvestDiva.com

FIGURE 3-2: Demonstrating why patience is a profitable virtue.

>> The chart on the left shows a fantasy most traders have when they buy an asset. They hope the price will march up toward their profit target within their trading time frame, whether short-term or long-term, and make them money.

>> The chart on the right shows the reality. Traders and investors alike often see a lot of dips in the price before the market reaches their profit target. Some investors panic on the dips and call it quits. But in the end, those who were patient and held their position through the rough times win. This can be true to both short-term and long-term investors, so the chart's time frame doesn't really matter.

REMEMBER

Success follows a bumpy road. Your portfolio may even turn into negative territory at times. However, if you've done your due diligence of analyzing your investment, you must make time your friend in order to see long-term profit. See Chapter 18 for full details on long-term investing strategies.

A great example of this idea is the crash of 2008. Almost all markets around the world, including the U.S. stock market, dropped like a hot rock because of economic issues such as the mortgage crisis. Most people panicked and started to get out of their investments with massive losses. Had they given it some (well, a lot of) patience, they would've seen their portfolios in positive territory in around five years. By 2018, they would've more than doubled the returns on the very same investments.

Diversify outside and inside your cryptocurrency portfolio

As I note in Chapter 2, diversification is the "don't put all your eggs in one basket" rule, and this age-old investing advice remains true to the revolutionary cryptocurrency market. Besides diversifying your portfolio by adding different assets such as stocks, bonds, or exchange traded funds (ETFs), diversification within your cryptocurrency portfolio is also important. (See Chapter 10 for some diversification ideas.)

For example, Bitcoin is perhaps the celebrity of all cryptocurrencies, so everyone wants to get hold of it. But Bitcoin is also the oldest cryptocurrency, so it has some unresolvable problems. Every day, younger and better-performing cryptocurrencies make their way into the market and offer exciting opportunities. (I'm not trying to say younger is better in all facets of life. I'm talking about cryptocurrencies here, not people!)

Besides age, you can group cryptocurrencies in several different ways for diversification purposes. Here are some examples (see Chapter 8 for full details):

>> **Major cryptocurrencies by market cap:** This category includes the ones in the top ten. At the time of writing, these options include Bitcoin, Ethereum, Ripple, and Litecoin.

>> **Transactional cryptocurrencies:** This group is the original category for cryptocurrencies. Transactional cryptocurrencies are designed to be used as money and exchanged for goods and services. Bitcoin and Litecoin are examples of well-known cryptos on this list.

>> **Platform cryptocurrencies:** These cryptocurrencies are designed to get rid of middlemen, create markets, and even launch other cryptocurrencies. Ethereum is one of the biggest cryptos in this category. It provides a backbone for future applications. NEO is another prime example. Such cryptocurrencies are generally considered good long-term investments because they rise in value as more applications are created on their blockchain.

>> **Privacy cryptocurrencies:** These options are similar to transactional cryptocurrencies, but they're heavily focused toward transaction security and anonymity. Examples include Monero, Zcash, and Dash.

>> **Application-specific cryptocurrencies:** One of the trendiest types of cryptos, application-specific cryptocurrencies serve specific functions and solve some of the world's biggest problems. Some examples of such cryptos are Vechain (used for supply chain applications), IOTA (Internet of Things applications), and Cardano (cryptocurrency scalability, privacy optimizations, and so on). Some get super specific, such as Mobius, also known as Stripe for the blockchain industry, which was seeking to resolve the payment issues in the agriculture industry in 2018. Depending on the specifics of each project, a number of these cryptos may prove highly successful. You can pick the ones that are solving issues closer to your heart; just be sure to analyze their usability, application performance, and project team properly.

REMEMBER

One key problem the cryptocurrency market faces when it comes to diversification is that the whole market appears to be extremely correlated. The majority of cryptocurrencies go up when the market sentiment turns bullish (upward), and vice versa. Despite this tendency, you can diversify away risk in a crypto-only portfolio by adding more crypto assets to your portfolio. By investing in multiple crypto assets, you can spread out the amount of risk you're exposed to instead of having all the volatility of the portfolio come from one or a few assets. Flip to Chapter 10 for the full scoop on diversification in cryptocurrencies.

Chapter **4**

Looking Under the Hood: Blockchain Technology

Most people have probably heard about Bitcoin more than they have blockchain. Many who *have* heard of blockchain think it's just the technology that powers Bitcoin. Although Bitcoin became one of the most famous outcomes of blockchain technology, blockchain is capable of so much more. It's perhaps one of the most interruptive technologies in decades and may change our lives forever.

Simply put, the relationship between Bitcoin and blockchain is similar to the relationship between email and the Internet. To be able to send and receive emails, you need the Internet. Similarly, to be able to use any crypto, you need blockchain technology. In this chapter, I take a look at how blockchain technology works, why it matters, and how it can impact your life in the future. Having a better understanding of blockchain technology may help reshape your view on the cryptocurrency market. That way, you can make better investment decisions in the industry.

Breaking Down Blockchain Technology Basics

Modern technologies allow people to communicate directly. You can use them to directly send emails, text messages, pictures, and videos to others without the use of a middleman. This way, you can maintain trust with others no matter where they are in the world. Long-distance relationships aren't as hard and heart-wrenching anymore. For example, my family has maintained years and years of long-distance relationship only possible due to the advent of the Internet. I attended my sister's wedding in Los Angeles via Skype when I was in Tokyo. My Australia-based in-laws, who weren't able to travel due to a terminal illness, were able to attend our wedding in Hawaii via FaceTime.

Despite this advancement, people still have to trust a third party to complete a financial transaction. But blockchain technology is challenging this setup in a radical way. I explain the basics of blockchain technology in the following sections.

What is a blockchain, and how does it work?

Simply put, a *blockchain* is a special kind of database. According to cigionline.org, the term *blockchain* refers to the whole network of distributed ledger technologies. According to Oxford Dictionaries, a *ledger* is "a book or other collection of financial accounts of a particular type." It can be a computer file that records transactions. A ledger is actually the foundation of accounting and is as old as writing and money.

Now imagine a whole suite of incorruptible digital ledgers of economic transactions that can be programmed to record and track not only financial transactions but also virtually everything of value. The blockchain can track things like medical records, land titles, and even voting (as you find out later in this chapter). It's a shared, distributed, and immutable ledger that records the history of transactions starting with transaction number one. It establishes trust, accountability, and transparency.

REMEMBER

Blockchain stores information in batches called *blocks*. These blocks are linked together in a sequential way to form a continuous line. A chain of blocks. A block-chain. Each block is like a page of a ledger or a record book. As you can see in Figure 4-1, each block mainly has three elements:

>> **Data:** The type of data depends on what the blockchain is being used for. In Bitcoin, for example, a block's data contains the details about the transaction including sender, receiver, number of coins, and so on.

>> **Hash:** No, I'm not talking about *that* kind of hash. A *hash* in blockchain is something like a fingerprint or signature. It identifies a block and all its content, and it's always unique.

>> **Hash of previous block:** This piece is precisely what makes a blockchain! Because each block carries the information of the previous block, the chain becomes very secure.

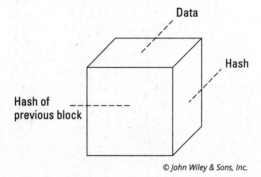

FIGURE 4-1: Three main elements of a block.

© *John Wiley & Sons, Inc.*

Here's an example of how a bunch of blocks come together in a blockchain. Say you have three blocks.

Block 1 contains this stuff:

>> Data: 10 Bitcoins from Fred to Jack

>> Hash (simplified): 12A

>> Previous hash (simplified): 000

Block 2 contains this stuff:

>> Data: 5 Bitcoins from Jack to Mary

>> Hash (simplified): 3B4

>> Previous hash: 12A

Block 3 contains this stuff:

>> Data: 4 Bitcoins from Mary to Sally

>> Hash (simplified): C74

>> Previous hash: 3B4

As you can see in Figure 4-2, each block has its own hash and a hash of the previous block. So block 3 points to block 2, and block 2 points to block 1. (*Note:* The first block is a bit special because it can't point to a previous block. This block is the *genesis block.*)

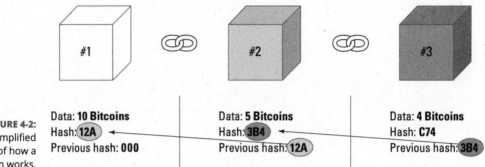

FIGURE 4-2:
Simplified version of how a blockchain works.

The hashes and the data are unique to each block, but they can still be tampered with. The following section lays out some ways blockchains secure themselves.

How does a blockchain secure itself?

Interfering with a block on the blockchain is almost impossible to do. The first way a blockchain secures itself is by hashing. Tampering with a block within a blockchain causes the hash of the block to change. That change makes the following block, which originally pointed to the first block's hash, invalid. In fact, changing a single block makes all the following blocks invalid. This setup gives the blockchain a level of security.

WARNING

However, using hashing isn't enough to prevent tampering. That's because computers these days are super fast, and they can calculate hundreds of thousands of hashes per second. Technically, a hacker can change the hash of a specific block and then calculate and change all the hashes of the following blocks in order to hide the tampering.

That's why on top of the hashes, blockchains have additional security steps including things like proof-of-work and peer-to-peer distribution. A *proof-of-work* (PoW) is a mechanism that slows down the creation of the blocks. In Bitcoin's case, for example, it takes about ten minutes to calculate the required PoW and add a new block to the chain. This timeline makes tampering with a block super difficult because if you interfere with one block, you need to interfere with all the following blocks. A blockchain like Bitcoin contains hundreds of thousands of blocks, so successfully manipulating it can take over ten years! I explore more about proof-of-work in Chapter 5.

A third way blockchains secure themselves is by being distributed. Blockchains don't use a central entity to manage the chain. Instead, they use a *peer-to-peer* (P2P) network. In public blockchains like Bitcoin, everyone is allowed to join. Each member of the network is called a *validator* or a *node*. When someone joins the network, she gets the full copy of the blockchain. This way, the node can verify that everything is still in order.

Here's what happens when someone creates a new block in the network:

1. The new block is sent to everyone in the network.

2. Each node then verifies the block and makes sure it hasn't been tampered with.

3. If everything checks out, each node adds this new block to his or her own blockchain.

All the nodes in this process create a consensus. They agree about which blocks are valid and which ones aren't. The other nodes in the network reject blocks that are tampered with.

So to successfully mess with a block on a blockchain, you'd need to tamper with all the blocks on the chain, redo the proof-of-work for each block, and take control of the peer-to-peer network!

REMEMBER

Blockchains are also constantly evolving. One of the most recent developments in the cryptocurrency ecosystem is the addition of something called a *smart contract*. A smart contract is a digital computer program stored inside a blockchain. It can directly control the transfer of cryptocurrencies or other digital assets based on certain conditions. Find out more on smart contracts in Chapter 5.

Why is blockchain revolutionary?

Here are three main reasons blockchain is different from other kinds of database and tracking systems already in use.

Blockchain may eliminate data tampering because of the way it tracks and stores data

REMEMBER

If you make a change to the information recorded in one particular block of a blockchain, you don't rewrite it. Instead the change is stored in a new block. Therefore, you can't rewrite history — no one can — because that new block shows the change as well as the date and the time of the change. This approach is actually based on a century-old method of the general financial ledger.

I can explain the difference through an example. Suppose Joe and his cousin Matt have a dispute over who owns the furniture shop they've been comanaging for years. Because the blockchain technology uses the ledger method, the ledger should have an entry showing that George first owned the shop in 1947. When George sold the shop to Mary in 1976, he made a new entry in the ledger, and so on. Every change of ownership of this shop is represented by a new entry in the ledger, right up until Matt bought it from his uncle in 2009. By going through the history in the ledger, Matt can show that he is in fact the current owner.

Now, here's how blockchain would approach this dispute differently than the age-old ledger method. The traditional ledger method uses a book, or a database file stored in a single (centralized) system. However, blockchain was designed to be *decentralized* and distributed across a large network of computers. This decentralizing of information reduces the ability for data tampering.

WARNING

Recent blockchain attacks such as the one on ZenCash show that data tampering can't be completely eliminated on the blockchain database as is. If 51 percent of miners decide to rewrite the ledger, it would be possible, and as a result, they can do whatever they want with the transaction: they can delay it, double-spend the coins, postpone it, or simply remove it from the block. Several blockchain networks are currently working on a custom solution for this. (For more information, see https://medium.com/coinmonks/is-blockchain-really-tamper-proof-88d1bc5ee338.)

Blockchain creates trust in the data

The unique way blockchain works creates trust in the data. I get more into the specifics earlier in this chapter, but here's a simplified version to show you why. Before a block can be added to the chain, a few things have to happen:

1. A cryptographic puzzle must be solved to create the new block.

2. The computer that solves the puzzle shares the solution with all the other computers in the network. This solution is the proof-of-work I discuss briefly in the earlier section "How does a blockchain secure itself?" and more about in Chapter 5.

3. Finally, all the computers involved in the network verify the proof-of-work. If 51 percent of the network testifies that the PoW was correct, the new block is added to the chain.

The combination of these complex math puzzles and verification by many computers ensures that users can trust each and every block on the chain. Heck, one of the main reasons I'm a big supporter of cryptocurrencies is that I trust in the blockchain technology so much. Because the network does the trust-building for you, you now have the opportunity to interact with your data in real time.

Centralized third parties aren't necessary

In my previous example of the dispute between Joe and Matt, each of the cousins may have hired a lawyer or a trusted *centralized* third party to go through the ledger and the documentation of the shop ownership. They trust the lawyers to keep the financial information and the documentation confidential. The third-party lawyers try to build trust between their clients and verify that Matt is indeed the rightful owner of the shop. (For the details of the example, check out "Blockchain may eliminate data tampering because of the way it tracks and stores data.")

The problem with centralized third parties and intermediaries such as lawyers and banks is that they add an extra step to resolving the dispute, resulting in spending more time and money.

If Matt's ownership information had been stored in a blockchain, he would've been able to cut out the centralized middleman, his lawyer. That's because all blocks added to the chain would've been verified to be true and couldn't be tampered with. In other words, the blockchain network and the miners are now the third party, which makes the process faster and more affordable. So Matt could simply show Joe his ownership information secured on the blockchain. He would save a ton of money and time by cutting out the centralized middleman.

This type of trusted, peer-to-peer interaction with data can revolutionize the way people access, verify, and transact with one another. And because blockchain is a type of technology and not a single network, it can be implemented in many different ways, as I explain later in this chapter.

Perusing Problems with Blockchain

The blockchain technology I describe earlier in this chapter is all sexy and revolutionary, but it sure has a bunch of problems it has to deal with before it becomes truly adapted to daily life. Here are some of the issues and barriers that blockchain has to overcome before you get too excited or too involved.

Scalability problems

Scalability is perhaps one of the most immediate problems that blockchain technology faces. Earlier in this chapter, I talk about how the blockchain secures itself, and how hackers would need a long time to be able to tamper with the system successfully. Well, this security comes at a cost for the users, too. Blockchain transactions are slow and expensive. For example, the Bitcoin network is capable of processing a maximum of seven transactions per second — for the millions of users worldwide. Additionally, to increase payment security, Bitcoin-blockchain transactions are recorded only once every ten minutes. Now imagine everyone on the planet using Bitcoins for transactions and having to wait this long for each throughput. Scary, isn't it?

Fortunately, a number of solutions are already under development for this issue. The first and most straightforward solution is to increase block size. The bigger the block size, the higher the number of transactions processed per second. For example, the current block size for Bitcoin is 1MB per block. Bumping that up to 2MB per block can double the number of transactions processed per second. As of now, this fix may be problematic in itself because of scalability issues. When you create the block, you have to send it to other people in the network. Sending a massive block to others can cause delays within the network.

TECHNICAL STUFF

Other solutions include using things like a *hard fork* (explained in Chapter 5), the *lightning network*, and *sharding*.

>> According to CoinDesk, "the lightning network effectively creates a layer on top of Bitcoin, enabling fast and cheap transactions which can net settle to the bitcoin blockchain." The concept "is based on a network that sits on top of the `Bitcoin blockchain`, and eventually settles on it. The network is comprised of user-generated channels that send payments back and forth in a secure and trust-less fashion (*trust-less* means that you don't need to trust or even know your counterparty)." Essentially, the lightning network takes the transactions away from the main blockchain and therefore reduces transaction fees and time.

>> Sharding is another proposed solution for the blockchain's scalability problem and is a concept that's widely used in databases to make them more efficient. Simply put, for cryptocurrencies sharding assigns random nodes rather than the entire network to validate a transaction on the blockchain network. The idea is that smaller sets of nodes can crunch the data faster and that the random distribution means nobody is stuck doing all the work. Sharding as a technology raises some concerns, the most basic being whether an unethical actor can manipulate a shard and whether members of a shard should be compensated.

With all the possible solutions being proposed left and right, investors can be hopeful that the blockchain's scalability problem can be solved sooner rather than later.

Environmental problems

All the blockchain security I talk about earlier in this chapter comes at yet another cost: energy and environmental cost. The way the security works today requires running complex algorithms, which in turn requires large amounts of computing power (especially with older cryptocurrencies such as Bitcoin). For example, according to Digiconomist's Bitcoin Energy Consumption Index, as of November 2017, activity related to the cryptocurrency exceeded the energy consumption of 159 countries around the world. (See `https://powercompare.co.uk/bitcoin/` for details.)

As cryptocurrency and blockchain technology evolve, more efficient hardware will be introduced that requires less energy. However, for the time being, there's an urgent need for a shift toward renewable energy instead of using fossil fuels and coal. (On the bright side, the very same blockchain technology can be used to help clean the planet, as I discuss in the later section "Energy").

Fraud problems

The blockchain industry has had a ton of hype around it, particularly regarding the cryptocurrency market (as I talk about in Chapter 3). Some companies in the financial world are trying to take advantage of the excitement surrounding blockchain. In 2018, Nasdaq delisted one company due to concerns that the company made "public statements designed to mislead investors and to take advantage of general investor interest in bitcoin and blockchain technology." And the Securities and Exchange Commission has taken action against companies that have made false and misleading statements about blockchain technology in an effort to pump up the price of the stock. This isn't a new kind of fraud; it's the same old story where a company changes its game, takes advantage of a hot trend, and makes baseless claims to attract new investors to pump, and then dump, the stock.

WARNING

Additionally, some fraudsters have attempted to capitalize on the mystery and excitement around the term *blockchain* to target investors. Scammers have posed as legitimate websites that provide services to cryptocurrency users to target unknowing users.

The list goes on. These stories only prove the importance of being educated on the subject matter before getting too hyped up and overly involved. You have the right book in your hands to get you started with that!

Political problems

The long-standing financial services industry (the establishment, if you will) has a vested interest in the failure of blockchain. Earlier in this chapter, I talk about how blockchain technology cuts out the middleman. Now consider how big this middleman industry is. All the banks, brokers, lawyers, you name it — all of them make huge profits from playing the middleman role. As of now, because the cost is distributed among millions of customers, end users usually pay very little individually. But if blockchain continues to replace these roles, it may pose a serious danger to their business.

In most countries, including the United States, banks carry huge lobbying power with governments and legislators. The established financial services industry could dramatically reduce blockchain's usefulness and restrict its availability (if not kill it altogether) should it decide doing so is to the industry's benefit. But then again, the people have power, too. And the more people know about the advantages of using blockchain technology, the harder time politicians and the financial establishment will have standing in the way of its growth.

What Can Blockchain Be Used for?

The creation of the blockchain technology has piqued a lot of people's interest. Supposedly, someone called Satoshi Nakamoto invented blockchain in 2008. Blockchain's original intent was Bitcoin. Or perhaps Satoshi used Bitcoin as a tool to introduce blockchain to the masses. Regardless, soon people realized blockchain technology can be used for different purposes, like identity verification and storing medical records. The following sections explain how a few different categories can use blockchain and, more importantly, how the cryptocurrency market uses it.

TECHNICAL STUFF

No one knows who Satoshi Nakamoto is. It can be a man, a woman, or a team of anonymous geeks. In fact, a women-on-the-block movement is out to prove that Satoshi is female!

Payments

As I cover throughout this book, money transferring was the first and most popular usage of the blockchain technology. For more than 40 years, economists have been seeking the holy grail of a digital currency that can eliminate the problem of double-spending and circumvent the issue of needing to trust an unknown third party. And then . . . bam! Satoshi's white paper was published in October 2008 and removed banks from the equation, just like that. Disregarding the scalability problem that I describe earlier in this chapter, with banks removed from transactions, most payments processed over a blockchain can be settled within a matter of seconds.

Voting

Voting fraud has been an ongoing theme in democratic, and not-so-democratic, countries. Blockchain technology can put you (and all your political debaters on Facebook) at ease. Digital voting through the blockchain can offer enough transparency that anyone would be able to see whether something were changed on the network. It combines the ease of digital voting with the security of blockchain to make your vote truly count.

Supply chain monitoring

Are you one of those people who must know where their food comes from? Is it organic, kosher, halal? Is there a food-borne illness you need to be aware of immediately? With the help of the blockchain, you can trace your food from its origin to your plate. It can help you make ethical, healthy choices about things you buy.

Blockchain can also help consumers view how products performed from a quality-control perspective as they traveled from their place of origin to the retailer. Furthermore, it can help businesses pinpoint their inefficiencies within their supply chains quickly. The blockchain removes the paper-based trails and locates items in real time.

Identity verification

This is an era where people are stuck between their digital identity and their actual physical presence. Credit agencies and social networks like Facebook and Instagram act as the main gatekeepers for online identity. Meanwhile, consumers are longing for a reliable digital identity system to maintain credit records and prove who they are to employers, banks, or car rental companies without letting private corporations make money from selling their data.

To overcome this challenge, many companies are already using blockchain technology and creating a secure digital identification system that would give users a way to control their digital identities. Some examples include Microsoft's authenticator app and Deloitte's Smart Identity System.

Legal ownership of stuff

You can get into legal trouble in so many ways. Family disputes. Lost legal paperwork. Lost assets that aren't easily traceable. Most of people's assets are currently documented on paper. And as I talk about earlier in this chapter, blockchain is hard at work to keep paper, and all the middlemen attached to it, out of the way. So if you're buying or selling land, a house, or a car, the blockchain can store titles on its network, allowing for a transparent view of this transfer and legal ownership.

Additionally, if your high-value, portable assets like bikes, jet skis, luxury handbags, and so on are stolen, you may be able to trace them back using companies who are working on providing such blockchain-based services.

Healthcare

One major problem with medical records has been paper record keeping, which the medical sector (at least in the United States) has been trying to move away from for years. Another issue has been medical identity theft. In the United States alone, the National Healthcare Anti-Fraud Association estimates the loss owing to healthcare fraud to be about $80 billion annually.

Blockchain to the rescue. All medical information related to a patient — such as past and present ailments, treatments, and family history of medical problems — will be stored on the blockchain. This approach will make every record permanent, transferable, and accessible, which will prevent the medical records from being lost or modified. Additionally, the patient, who possesses the key to access these digital records, will be in control of who gains access to that data.

Entertainment

It's not all dull around the block. The many branches of the entertainment industry can benefit from blockchain technology, if they haven't already started. The music and esports industries are a couple of examples.

The Internet democratized content creation in the early 2000s, but a new type of middleman has emerged in digital content. Platforms like YouTube (1.5 billion users), SoundCloud (175 million), Spotify (140 million), and Netflix (around 110 million) are now the middlemen controlling users and artists.

This amount of control has caused a ton of disputes around artists' compensation. Even someone as famous as Taylor Swift had to go at it with Apple Music and Spotify. As artists grow increasingly disillusioned with such platforms, blockchain technology can be an exciting new option.

The blockchain can give label companies the ability to have completely encrypted records of ownership. When applied to media consumption, the technology can solve the problems surrounding content access, distribution, compensation, managing assets, and digital rights, among others.

Another example of blockchain in the entertainment industry is esports betting. Though I don't encourage this type of gambling entertainment, esports betting is one of the biggest growth industries in the world of sports betting today. Companies such as Unikrn are among the front-runners and have rushed to incorporate blockchain technology to stand out. More specifically, Unikrn is using a cryptocurrency called UnikoinGold, which is based on the Ethereum platform, for its betting platform. And it's caught the attention of the likes of actor Ashton Kutcher and Mark Cuban (owner of the Dallas Mavericks basketball team and contributor to the popular television show *Shark Tank*). In 2015, Unikrn raised a total of $10 million from them. Pretty entertaining, wouldn't you say?

Energy

Using blockchain, people can trade energy among themselves, cutting out the energy companies (yep, the middleman.) According to RenewableEnergyWorld. com, "this shift [to peer-to-peer distribution of energy] will stimulate more renewable energy projects as a whole, ultimately forwarding our transition from carbon-emitting electricity generation. Tokenizing renewable energy allows wind, solar, and hydro producers to seamlessly connect with investors, who are willing to pay upfront for the right to consume renewable energy. As a distributed system, the middleman is removed."

Internet of Things (IoT)

The *Internet of Things* (IoT) is basically the fact that most of your stuff is connected to the Internet. For example, we control almost everything in our house, from bedside lamps to air conditioning to the microwave oven and even the baby's crib, through the Internet! While my parents were staying with us to help with our newborn, my husband would sometimes mess with them, turning off the light or TV remotely, using his phone, without their knowing. Of course, I don't think we'll get them to come back for help should we have another baby.

Besides acting as a control freak, the Internet of Things helps you send and receive data within the network of your physical devices. If you can directly integrate your physical world into computer-based systems, you may be able to reduce human exertions and improve your efficiency. According to an article in the IEEE Internet Initiative eNewsletter, "IoT capabilities are considered as 'game-changing' when combined with the concepts of big data analytics and cloud computing" (other hot topics of the tech world). Put it next to blockchain, and you may be taking the true next step into the future.

TIP

According to the article, "Blockchain technologies can help in improving the security of IoT applications in healthcare, smart cities, agriculture, energy grids, water management, public safety, supply chain management, education, and similar application areas." Basically, everything futuristic. You can find out more about these use cases by visiting https://internetinitiative.ieee.org/ newsletter/november-2017/integrating-internet-of-things-and-blockchains-use-cases.

Chapter **5**

How Cryptocurrencies Work

I n Chapter 4, I explain how blockchain technology works. Cryptocurrencies, and more specifically Bitcoin, have been one of the first use cases for blockchain technology. That's why most people may have heard about Bitcoin more than they have about the underlying blockchain technology.

In this chapter I get into more detail about how cryptocurrencies use blockchain technology, how they operate, and how they're generated, as well as some crypto geek terms you can impress your date with.

Explaining Basic Terms in the Cryptocurrency Process

Cryptocurrencies are also known as digital coins, but they're quite different from the coins in your piggy bank. For one thing, they aren't attached to a central bank, a country, or a regulatory body.

Here's an example. Say you want to buy the latest version of *Cryptocurrency Investing For Dummies* from your local bookstore. Using your normal debit card, this is what happens:

1. You give your card details to the cashier or the store's point-of-sale system.

2. The store runs the info through, essentially asking your bank whether you have enough money in your bank account to buy the book.

3. The bank checks its records to confirm whether you do.

4. If you do have enough, the bank gives a thumbs-up to the bookstore.

5. The bank then updates its records to show the movement of the money from your account to the bookstore's account.

6. The bank gets a little cut for the trouble of being the middleman.

Now if you wanted to remove the bank from this entire process, who else would you trust to keep all these records without altering them or cheating in any way? Your best friend? Your dog walker? (I hope you didn't say the crown prince of Nigeria.) In fact, you may not trust any single person. But how about trusting *everyone* in the network?

REMEMBER

As I explain in Chapter 4, blockchain technology works to remove the middleman. When applied to cryptocurrencies, blockchain eliminates a central record of transactions. Instead, you distribute many copies of your transaction ledger around the world. Each owner of each copy records your transaction of buying the book.

Here's what happens if you want to buy this book using a cryptocurrency:

1. You give your crypto details to the cashier.

2. The shop asks everyone in the network to see whether you have enough coins to buy the book.

3. All the record holders in the network check their records to see whether you do. (These record holders are called nodes; I explain their function in more detail later in this chapter.)

4. If you do have enough, each node gives the thumbs-up to the cashier.

5. The nodes all update their records to show the transfer.

6. At random, a node gets a reward for the work.

That means no organization is keeping track of where your coins are or investigating fraud. In fact, cryptocurrencies such as Bitcoin wouldn't exist without a whole network of bookkeepers (nodes) and a little thing known as *cryptography*. In the following sections, I explain that and some other important terms related to the workings of cryptocurrencies.

Cryptography

Shhh. Don't tell anyone. That's the *crypto* in *cryptography* and *cryptocurrency.* It means "secret." In the cryptocurrency world, it mainly refers to being "anonymous."

Historically, cryptography is an ancient art for sending hidden messages. (The term comes from the Greek word *krypto logos,* which means *secret writing.*) The sender *encrypts* the message by using some sort of key. The receiver then has to *decrypt* it. For example, 19th-century scholars decrypted ancient Egyptian hieroglyphics when Napoleon's soldiers found the Rosetta Stone in 1799 near Rosetta, Egypt. In the 21st-century era of information networks, the sender can digitally encrypt messages, and the receiver can use cryptographic services and algorithms to decrypt them.

What does Napoleon have to do with cryptocurrencies? Cryptocurrencies use cryptography to maintain security and anonymity. That's how digital coins, even though they're not monetized by any central authority or regulatory body, can help with security and protection from double-spending, which is the risk of your digital cash being used more than once.

TECHNICAL
STUFF

Cryptography uses three main encryption methods:

» **Hashing:** I talk about hashing briefly in Chapter 4, explaining how it's some-thing like a fingerprint or signature. A *hash function* first takes your input data (which can be of any size). The function then performs an operation on the original data and returns an output that represents the original data but has a fixed (and generally smaller) size. In cryptocurrencies such as Bitcoin, it's used to guess the combination of the lock of a block. Hashing maintains the structure of blockchain data, encodes people's account addresses, and makes block mining possible. You can find more on mining later in this chapter, and in detail in Chapter 12.

» **Symmetric encryption cryptography:** *Symmetric encryption* is the simplest method used in cryptography. It involves only one secret key for both the sender and the receiver. The main disadvantage of symmetric encryption is that all parties involved have to exchange the key used to encrypt the data before they can decrypt it.

» **Asymmetric encryption cryptography:** *Asymmetric encryption* uses two keys: a public key and a private key. You can encrypt a message by using the receiver's public key, but the receiver can decrypt it only with his or her private key.

Nodes

I mention nodes in the examples in this chapter and in Chapter 4. A *node* is an electronic device doing the bookkeeping job in the blockchain network, making the whole decentralized thing possible. The device can be a computer, a cellphone, or even a printer, as long as it's connected to the Internet and has access to the blockchain network.

Mining

As the owners of nodes (see the preceding section) willingly contribute their computing resources to store and validate transactions, they have the chance to collect the transaction fees and earn a reward in the underlying cryptocurrency for doing so. This process is known as *mining,* and the owners who do it are *miners.*

REMEMBER

Let me make something clear: Not all cryptocurrencies can be mined. Bitcoin and some other famous ones can. Some others, such as Ripple (XRP), avoid mining altogether because they want a platform that doesn't consume a huge amount of electricity in the process of mining; power usage is one of the issues with blockchain that I bring up in Chapter 4, actually. Regardless, for the most part, mining remains a huge part of many cryptocurrencies to date.

Here's how mining works: Cryptocurrency miners solve cryptographic puzzles (via software) to add transactions to the ledger (the blockchain) in the hope of getting coins as a reward. It's called mining because of the fact that this process helps extract new cryptocurrencies from the system. Anyone, including you, can join this group. Your computer needs to "guess" a random number that solves an equation that the blockchain system generates. In fact, your computer has to calculate many 64-character strings or 256-bit hashes and check with the challenge equation to see whether the answer is right. That's why it's so important that you have a powerful computer. The more powerful your computer is, the more guesses it can make in a second, increasing your chances of winning this game. If you manage to guess right, you earn Bitcoins and get to write the "next page" of Bitcoin transactions on the blockchain.

Because mining is based on a form of guessing, for each block a different miner guesses the number and is granted the right to update the blockchain. Whoever has the biggest computing power combined, controlling 51 percent of the votes, controls the chain and wins every time. Thanks to the law of statistical probability, the same miner is unlikely to succeed every time. On the other hand, this game can sometimes be unfair because the biggest computer power will be the first to solve the challenge equation and "win" more often.

Proof-of-work

If you're a miner and want to actually enter your block and transactions into the blockchain, you have to provide an answer (proof) to a specific challenge. This proof is difficult to produce (hence all the gigantic computers, time, and money needed for it), but others can very easily verify it. This process is known as *proof-of-work*, or PoW.

For example, guessing a combination to a lock is a proof to a challenge. Going through all the different possible combinations to come up with the right answer may be pretty hard, but after you get it, it's easy to validate — just enter the combination and see whether the lock opens! The first miner who solves the problem for each block on the blockchain gets a reward. The reward is basically the incentive to keep on mining and gets the miners competing to be the first one to find a solution for mathematical problems. Bitcoin and some other minable cryptocurrencies mainly use the PoW concept to make sure that the network isn't easily manipulated.

REMEMBER

But as I talk about in Chapter 4, this whole proof-of-work thing has some downsides for blockchain technology. One of the main challenges is that it wastes a lot of computing power and electricity just for the sake of producing random guesses. That's why new cryptocurrencies have jumped on an alternative wagon called proof-of-stake (PoS), covered in the next section.

Proof-of-stake

Unlike PoW, a *proof-of-stake* (PoS) system requires you to show ownership of a certain amount of money (or *stake*). That means the more crypto you own, the more mining power you have. This approach eliminates the need for the expensive mining extravaganza. And because the calculations are pretty simple to prove, you own a certain percentage of the total amount of the cryptos available.

Another difference is that the PoS system offers no block rewards, so the miners get transaction fees. That's how PoS cryptos can be several thousand times more cost-effective than PoW ones. (Don't let the PoS abbreviation give you the wrong idea.)

REMEMBER

But of course, PoS also can have its own problems. For starters, you can argue that PoS rewards coin hoarders. Under the proof-of-stake model, nodes can mine only a percentage of transactions that corresponds to their stake in a cryptocurrency. For example, a proof-of-stake miner who owns 10 percent of a cryptocurrency would be able to mine 10 percent of blocks on the network. The limitation with this consensus model is that it gives nodes on the network a reason to save their coins instead of spending them. It also produces a scenario in which the rich get richer because large coin holders are able to mine a larger percentage of blocks on the network.

Proof-of-importance

Proof-of-importance (PoI) was first introduced by a blockchain platform called NEM to support its XEM cryptocurrency. In some ways PoI is similar to PoS because participants (nodes) are marked as "eligible" if they have a certain amount of crypto "vested." Then the network gives a "score" to the eligible nodes, and they can create a block that is roughly the same proportion to that "score." But the difference is that the nodes won't get a higher score only by holding onto more cryptocurrencies. Other variables are considered in the score, too, in order to resolve the primary problem with PoS, which is hoarding. The NEM community in particular uses a method called "harvesting" to solve the PoS "hoarding" problem.

Here's how Investopedia defines harvesting: "Instead of each miner contributing its mining power in a cumulative manner to a computing node, a harvesting participant simply links his account to an existing supernode and uses that account's computing power to complete blocks on his behalf." (I talk about harvesting later in this chapter.)

Transactions: Putting it all together

REMEMBER

Here's a summary of how cryptocurrencies work (check out the preceding sections for details on some of the terminology):

1. When you want to use cryptos to purchase something, first your crypto network and your crypto wallet automatically check your previous transactions to make sure you have enough cryptocurrencies to make that transaction. For this, you need your private and public keys (explained in Chapter 7).

2. The transaction is then encrypted, broadcast to the cryptocurrency's network, and queued up to be added to the public ledger.

3. Transactions are then recorded on the public ledger through mining. The sending and receiving addresses are wallet IDs or hash values that aren't tied to the user identification so they are anonymous.

4. For PoW cryptos, the miners have to solve a math puzzle to verify the transaction. PoS cryptos attribute the mining power to the proportion of the coins held by the miners, instead of utilizing energy to solve math problems, in order to resolve the "wasted energy" problem of PoW. The PoI cryptos add a number of variables when attributing the mining power to nodes in order to resolve the "hoarding" problem that's associated with PoS.

Cruising through Other Important Crypto Concepts

Earlier in this chapter and in Chapter 4, I talk about basics of cryptocurrencies and how they're related to blockchain technology. I dig into more details about brokers, exchanges, wallets, and different types of cryptocurrencies in Part 2, but here I want to get a few more concepts out of the way, just in case someone starts talking to you about them. Other factors make cryptocurrencies so special and different from your government-backed legal tender, also known as *fiat currency*, such as the U.S. dollar.

Adaptive scaling

Adaptive scaling is one of the advantages of investing in cryptocurrencies. It means that it gets harder to mine a specific cryptocurrency over time. It allows cryptocurrencies to work well on both small and large scales. That's why cryptocurrencies take measures such as limiting the supply over time (to create scarcity) and reducing the reward for mining as more total coins are mined. Thanks to adaptive scaling, mining difficulty goes up and down depending on the popularity of the coin and the blockchain. This can give cryptocurrencies a real longevity within the market.

Decentralization

As I explain in Chapter 4, the whole idea behind blockchain technology is that it's *decentralized.* This concept means no single entity can affect the cryptocurrencies.

TECHNICAL
STUFF

Some people claim cryptocurrencies such as Ripple aren't truly decentralized because they don't follow Bitcoin's mining protocol exactly. Ripple has no miners. Instead, transactions are powered through a "centralized" blockchain to make it more reliable and faster. Ripple in particular has gone this route because it wants to work with big banks and therefore wants to combine the best elements of fiat money and blockchain cryptocurrency. Whether non-minable currencies such as Ripple can be considered true cryptocurrencies is up for discussion, but that fact doesn't mean you can't invest in them, which is the whole purpose of this book anyway!

Harvesting

Harvesting is an alternative to the traditional mining used to maintain the integrity of a blockchain network. It was designed by a blockchain platform called NEM to generate its own currency called XEM. According to finder.com, this is how harvesting works: "Every time someone carries out a transaction, the first computer to see and verify the transaction will notify nearby users of that transaction, creating a cascade of information. This process is called 'generating a block.' Whenever someone with more than 10,000 vested XEM generates a block in NEM, they receive the transaction fees on that block as payment." Also, as I explain earlier in this chapter, harvesting uses a PoI system rather than PoS and PoW.

Open source

Cryptocurrencies are typically *open source.* That means that miners, nodes, and harvesters alike can join and use the network without paying a fee.

Public ledger

As I explain in Chapter 4, a ledger is the age-old record-keeping system for recording information and data. Cryptocurrencies use a *public ledger* to record all transactional data. Everyone in the world can access public blockchains and see entire transactions happening with cryptocurrencies.

Note that not all blockchains use a public ledger. Some businesses and financial institutions use private ledgers so that the transactions aren't visible to the world. However, by doing so, they may contradict the original idea behind blockchain technology.

Smart contracts

Smart contracts are also called *self-executing contracts, blockchain contracts,* or *digital contracts.* They're just like traditional contracts except that they're completely digital. Smart contracts remove the middleman between the buyer and the seller (as I talk about in Chapter 4) so you can implement things like automatic payments and investment products without the need of a central authority like a bank.

A smart contract is actually a tiny computer program that's stored and runs on a blockchain platform. Because of that, all the transactions are completely distributed, and no centralized authority is in control of the money. Also, because it's stored on a blockchain, a smart contract is *immutable.* Being immutable means that after a smart contract is created, it can never be changed again; it can't be tampered with, which is an inherited feature from blockchain technology.

However, being immutable comes with its own disadvantages. Because you can't change anything in the smart contract, that means that if the code has any bugs, you can't fix them either. This makes smart contract security more difficult. Some companies aim to combat this problem by auditing their smart contracts, which can be very costly.

As time goes by, we can expect better coding practices and development life cycles to combat smart contract security problems. After all, smart contracts are still a pretty young practice with their whole life of trial and error ahead of them.

Stick a Fork in It: Digging into Cryptocurrency Forks

What you get from a cryptocurrency fork won't fill your tummy, but it may fill your crypto wallet with some money! Many popular cryptocurrencies were born as a result of a split (fork) in another cryptocurrency like Bitcoin. The following sections explain the basics of these cryptocurrency splits and how you may be able to profit from them.

What is a fork, and why do forks happen?

Sometimes when a group of developers disagrees with the direction a specific cryptocurrency is going, the members decide to go their own way and initiate a *fork*. Imagine an actual physical fork. It has one long handle, and then it divides into a bunch of branches. That's exactly what happens in a cryptocurrency fork.

As I explain earlier in this chapter, some cryptocurrencies are implemented within open source software. Each of these cryptocurrencies has its own protocol that everyone in the network should follow. Examples of such rule topics include the following:

>> Block size

>> Rewards that miners, harvesters, or other network participants get

>> How fees are calculated

But because cryptocurrencies are essentially software projects, their development will never be fully finished. There's always room for improvement. Crypto developers regularly push out updates to fix issues or to increase performance. Some of these improvements are small, but others fundamentally change the way the original cryptocurrency (which the developers fell in love with) works. Just as in any type of relationship, you either grow together or grow apart. When the disagreements among a group of developers or network participants intensify, they can choose to break up, create their own version of the protocol, and cause a potential heartbreak that requires years of therapy to get over. Okay, the last part doesn't really happen.

Hard forks and soft forks

Two types of forks can happen in a cryptocurrency: a hard fork and a soft fork.

Most cryptocurrencies consist of two big pieces: the protocol (set of rules) and the blockchain (which stores all the transactions that have ever happened; see Chapter 4). If a segment of the crypto community decides to create its own new rules, it starts by copying the original protocol code and then goes about making changes to it (assuming the cryptocurrency is completely open source). After the developers have implemented their desired changes, they define a point at which their fork will become active. More specifically, they choose a block number to start the forking. For example, as you can see in Figure 5-1, the community can say that the new protocol will go live when block 999 is published to the cryptocurrency blockchain.

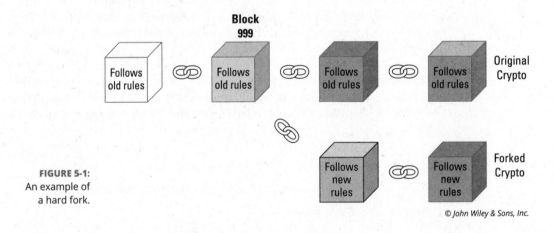

FIGURE 5-1:
An example of
a hard fork.

© John Wiley & Sons, Inc.

When the currency reaches that block number, the community splits in two. Some people decide to support the original set of rules, while others support the new fork. Each group then starts adding new blocks to the fork it supports. At this point, both blockchains are incompatible with each other, and a *hard fork* has occurred. In a hard fork, the nodes essentially go through a contentious divorce and don't ever interact with each other again. They don't even acknowledge the nodes or transactions on the old blockchain.

On the other hand, a soft fork is the type of breakup where you remain friends with your ex. If the developers decide to fork the cryptocurrency and make the changes compatible with the old one, then the situation is called a *soft fork.* You can see the subtle difference in the example shown in Figure 5-2.

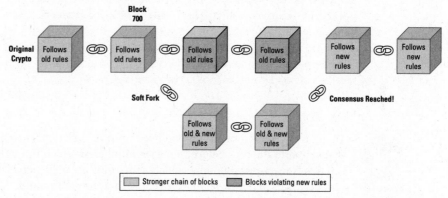

FIGURE 5-2:
An example of
a soft fork.

Say the soft fork is set to happen at block 700. The majority of the community may support the stronger chain of blocks following both the new and old rules. If the two sides reach a consensus after a while, the new rules are upgraded across the network. Any non-upgraded nodes (that is, stubborn geeks) who are still mining are essentially wasting their time. The community comes back together softly, and everyone lives happily ever after — until the next major argument, of course.

Free money on forks

Because a new fork is based on the original blockchain, all transactions that previously happened on the blockchain also happen on the fork. The developers of the new chain take a "snapshot" of the ledger at a specific block number the fork happened (like 999 in Figure 5-1) and therefore create a duplicate copy of the chain. That means if you had a certain amount of cryptocurrencies before the fork, you also get the same amount of the new coin.

A FORKING EXAMPLE: BITCOIN VERSUS BITCOIN CASH

Even the celebrity of cryptocurrencies, Bitcoin (BTC), has seen forks. One of the well-known Bitcoin forks happened on August 1, 2017. That's the birthday of Bitcoin Cash. In this case, the developers couldn't agree on what the size for a block should be. Some wanted the block size to go from 1MB to 2MB, but others wanted to increase it even more, to 32MB. Some people in the community loved the new big idea, while others thought the other group was crazy. So both groups decided to go their own ways. Bitcoin Cash adapted a brand-new symbol (BCH), too. People who already had BTC got the same amount of BCH added to their crypto wallets.

As of August 2018, BCH is valued at around $750, while BTC is worth ten times more, around $7,500. Only time will tell whether BCH ever surpasses the original protocol's value. But hey, at least the forkers got some value out of it!

REMEMBER

To get free coins from a fork, you need to have the cryptocurrency on a platform that supports the fork before the block number at which the fork occurs. You can call this free money. But how valuable the coins are all depends how well the new fork performs and how popular it gets within the community.

2

The Fundamentals of Investing in Cryptos

Pick an appropriate investing partner by finding an exchange or broker who's suitable for your level of involvement in the market.

Select a secure cryptocurrency wallet to store your digital assets based on your needs.

Find background information on a number of current cryptocurrencies.

Identify the best cryptocurrencies to invest in at any given time.

Explore diversification methods across crypto and non-crypto assets to minimize risk in your investment portfolio.

Chapter 6

Cryptocurrency Exchanges and Brokers

After you've familiarized yourself with cryptocurrencies' risks and rewards (see Chapters 2 and 3) and have decided that cryptocurrency investing is right for you, you're ready to go crypto shopping! As you may guess, most of crypto shopping, investing, and trading occurs online; after all, we're talking about digital assets. There are ways to pay cash to purchase digital currencies, but such transactions are uncommon. I mean, sure, if you have a friend who became a crypto millionaire and is looking to sell some crypto assets, you can simply give that person your cash in exchange for the cryptocurrencies.

The most popular way to buy cryptocurrencies, though, is to go directly through an online cryptocurrency exchange. However, depending on your cryptocurrency investing goals, you may need to consider alternative methods. For example, if you're an active crypto trader, you may find a traditional cryptocurrency exchange or a broker easier to use. But if you want just to buy some cryptos and park them in your wallet, a trusted online/local exchange can do the job. In this chapter, I tell you all about different types of exchanges, brokers, and other cryptocurrency providers and show you how to choose the right one(s) for your cryptocurrency goals.

Choosing a method to get your hands on these hot digital assets can be a lengthy process. However, with the changing regulatory stance, increasing adoption and acceptance, and overall market confidence in cryptocurrencies, the hard work may very well pay off. Regardless of the method you use to purchase cryptocurrencies, you must have a cryptocurrency wallet ready to store your digital assets. You find out all you need to know about cryptocurrency wallets in Chapter 7.

Distinguishing Crypto Exchanges

A *cryptocurrency exchange* is also called a *digital currency exchange,* or DCE for short. It's a web service that can help people exchange their cash into cryptocurrencies and vice versa. Most exchanges are more focused on providing services to help you exchange a cryptocurrency such as Bitcoin into other digital currencies like Ethereum, Litecoin, and so on.

Most exchanges operate online. However, a number of brick-and-mortar businesses do exist; they provide customers services to exchange traditional payment methods and cryptocurrencies. Those options are similar to the currency exchange booths at international airports where you exchange your country's money into the currency of the country you're visiting.

The most distinguished forms of cryptocurrency exchanges are the following:

>> **Centralized cryptocurrency exchange (CEX):** CEXs are similar to traditional stock exchanges.

>> **Decentralized cryptocurrency exchange (DEX):** DEXs aim to stay true to the pure philosophy behind the cryptocurrency industry.

>> **Hybrid cryptocurrency exchange:** Hybrid exchanges are known to be the next-generation crypto trading marketplace. They combine the best of CEXs and DEXs.

In the following sections, I give you the lowdown on CEXs, DEXs, and hybrid exchanges. Finally, I give you guidance on choosing an exchange.

Centralized exchanges

Centralized exchanges are like traditional stock exchanges. The buyers and sellers come together, and the exchange plays the role of a middleman. These exchanges typically charge a commission to facilitate the transactions made between the buyers and the sellers. In the cryptoworld, *centralize* means "to trust somebody else to handle your money."

Here's how a centralized exchange typically works:

1. You give your money to the exchange.

2. The exchange holds it for you (like a bank or a trusted middleman).

3. You watch the prices of the available cryptocurrencies on the exchange.

4. Depending on the exchange, you can trade your *fiat* currency (a traditional currency, like the U.S. dollar) for a cryptocurrency (like Bitcoin). With most exchanges, however, you find better luck exchanging two cryptocurrencies for one another. I talk more about cryptocurrency pairings in Chapter 10.

5. You place your order.

6. The exchange finds a seller to match your buy order. If you're selling, the exchange finds you a buyer.

7. Tada! You just crypto shopped on an exchange.

Most centralized crypto exchanges have crypto/crypto pairings. But not all of them provide fiat/crypto pairings.

>> A *crypto/crypto pairing* involves exchanging one cryptocurrency (like Bitcoin) for another cryptocurrency (like Ethereum).

>> A *fiat/crypto* pairing involves exchanging a traditional currency (like the U.S. dollar) for a cryptocurrency (like Bitcoin).

I dig into the exchanges that offer these pairings in the following sections.

One of the main issues with centralized cryptocurrency exchanges is their vulnerability to hacks. In some past hacking scandals, however, the exchange has paid the customers back out-of-pocket. That's why choosing a centralized exchange wisely, knowing it has the financial ability to combat hackers and pay you in case it gets hacked, is important. Of course, with the popularity of cryptocurrencies, more centralized cryptocurrency exchanges are bound to pop up in the market. Some will succeed, and some may fail. Therefore, you need to pick your crypto shop wisely. I talk about methods for picking the best exchange later in this chapter.

Centralized exchanges offering fiat/crypto pairings

If you're new to crypto investing, starting at an exchange that offers fiat/crypto pairings may make the most sense. That's precisely the reason why exchanges that provided this service became some of the most popular ones in 2017 and 2018.

At the time of writing, some of the most popular centralized exchanges that offer fiat/crypto pairings include the following:

>> **Coinbase:** This exchange, the most popular in the world, supports Bitcoin (BTC), Bitcoin Cash (BCH), Litecoin (LTC), and Ethereum (ETH). On the fiat currency side, you can use the U.S. dollar (USD), the euro (EUR), and the British pound (GBP), depending on where you're located. Here's my referral link for you, so that we both get some free Bitcoin as a gift: www.coinbase. com/join/59d39a7610351d00d40189f0.

>> **Bittrex:** Based in Seattle, this fast-growing exchange supports the U.S. dollar (USD), Bitcoin (BTC), Ethereum (ETH), Tether (USDT), and a variety of other pairings. You can check them out here: https://bittrex.com/.

>> **Kraken:** Kraken has a variety of crypto/fiat pairings with more than just the U.S. dollar (USD) and the euro (EUR); you can view the list on the exchange's website. Personally, I had problems with Kraken's services and customer support in 2018. Check them out here: https://www.kraken.com/.

>> **Gemini:** Gemini is based in New York with high regulation standards in the United States. It supports Bitcoin (BTC), Ethereum (ETH), Zcash (ZEC), and the U.S. dollar (USD). Check them out here: https://gemini.com/.

>> **Robinhood:** A popular financial services and trading app originally offering stocks and ETF (exchange traded fund) services, Robinhood now provides fiat pairings to Bitcoin (BTC) and Ethereum (ETH). It also supports real-time market data for more cryptos such as Dash (DASH), Ripple (XRP), Stellar (XLM), and more. It's one of my personal favorites due to ease of use. Here's my referral link so that we both get some free stocks in our portfolio: http://share. robinhood.com/kianad1.

>> **Bitfinex:** Bitfinex is for active cryptocurrency traders and requires a minimum of $10,000 equity to start functioning. It offers a variety of fiat currencies such as the U.S. dollar (USD), the Japanese yen (JPY), the euro (EUR), and the British pound (GBP) traded against a growing list of cryptocurrencies. One thing to keep in mind about Bitfinex is that it charges an "inactivity fee" if you hold your balances in your account and don't actively participate in the markets. Find out more about Bitfinex here: www.bitfinex.com/.

However, as I explain later in this chapter, you need to consider other characteristics of an exchange beyond its fiat/crypto pairings before choosing one.

Centralized exchanges offering crypto/crypto pairings

Some centralized crypto exchanges provide only crypto/crypto pairings. Some of the most popular ones at the time of writing include these:

- » **Binance:** Binance is one of the fastest growing exchanges in 2018 and offers a mobile app. I personally use it for my crypto investments. Here's my link for you: www.binance.com/?ref=18381915.

- » **Huobi:** This exchange supports Tether (USDT), Bitcoin (BTC), Ethereum (ETH), and Huobi Token (HT) against a variety of other cryptos. As of 2018, Huobi isn't available for U.S. users due to government policies. Check them out here: www.huobi.com/.

- » **KuCoin:** This fast-growing exchange supports a variety of cryptos found on its website: www.kucoin.com/#/. It also offers a mobile app.

Decentralized exchanges

A decentralized cryptocurrency exchange (DEX) is an exchange that doesn't rely on a middleman to hold your funds. It's a marketplace where buyers and sellers come together and process the transactions directly between one another. In other words, DEXs facilitate peer-to-peer trades.

TECHNICAL STUFF

On a decentralized exchange, you can buy and sell your crypto assets directly from other market participants. You'd be able to make the deals through things like smart contracts and atomic swaps. *Smart contracts,* as explained on Investopedia, are "self-executing contracts where the terms of the agreement between buyer and seller are directly written into lines of code." They're the underlying technology for *atomic swaps,* which enable exchange of one cryptocurrency for another without using centralized exchanges. With the DEX, smart contracts, and atomic swaps, instead of giving your cryptocurrencies to the CEX, you'll give them to an escrow that's centralized by the network running the exchange. Escrow still exists because transactions take as long as five days to clear. As a buyer, you'll have your cash taken out from your account immediately, although the funds aren't moved to the seller's account until the crypto transaction clears.

You may think that a decentralized exchange makes more sense to buy and sell cryptocurrencies on because the whole market is often billed as decentralized. Heck, cryptocurrencies became popular because they allow you to become your own bank and be in charge of your own assets. That's why many DEX fans argue that if you utilize centralized exchanges, you're essentially jeopardizing the whole point behind using cryptocurrencies.

The following sections give you more information on some of the issues facing DEXs, plus a rundown of some noteworthy DEX options.

Potential problems

Though DEXs may replace centralized exchanges completely in the future, at this point decentralized exchanges have their own problems.

WARNING

Decentralized cryptocurrency exchanges are harder to hack. On the flip side, you're more vulnerable to locking yourself out of your money. That means if you forget your log-in info, you may get your account locked because the system thinks you're a hacker! Other problems with DEXs include low volumes and low liquidity. *Liquidity* is how fast you can buy or sell cryptocurrencies on the marketplace. Because DEXs are less popular than centralized exchanges (at least for now), you may face more difficulty finding someone to match your buy/sell orders on a DEX. This issue is a vicious cycle because as long as DEXs are less popular, their liquidity remains low. As long as the liquidity is low, DEXs may remain less popular. That's why, at least for now, centralized exchanges are more popular than DEXs.

Additionally, most DEXs don't offer services to deposit or withdraw fiat currencies such as the U.S. dollar. They can also be expensive and slow. Everything from canceling orders to transferring crypto requires paying a fee and waiting for block confirmations — at least a few minutes, sometimes hours.

Popular decentralized exchanges

Regardless of possible DEX issues, here are some of the most popular decentralized cryptocurrency exchanges as of 2018:

>> **IDEX:** A decentralized exchange for trading Ethereum (ETH) tokens, this exchange is among the most user-friendly DEXs and can easily connect to your crypto wallet, something I cover in Chapter 7. Here's the website: https://idex.market.

>> **Waves DEX:** This exchange allows you to trade Bitcoin (BTC), Ethereum (ETH), Litecoin (LTC), Monero (XMR), and a variety of other cryptos, including the exchange's own crypto token, Waves (WAVES). You can also trade fiat currencies such as the U.S. dollar and the euro. As of July 2018, Waves DEX has seen $5 million daily volume. You can check it out here: https://wavesplatform.com/product/dex.

>> **Stellar DEX:** Based on StellarTerm.com, this exchange is Stellar platform's DEX system. It supports Bitcoin (BTC), Ethereum (ETH), Ripple (XRP), and Litecoin (LTC), as well as some fiat currencies such as the U.S. dollar, Japanese yen, Hong Kong dollar, and Chinese yuan. To start trading on this DEX, you have to deposit 20 Stellar Lumens (XLM). I talk more about these cryptocurrencies in Chapter 8. Find out more about Stellar's distributed exchange here: www.stellar.org/developers/guides/concepts/exchange.html.

>> **Bisq DEX:** Bisq DEX is based on pure peer-to-peer infrastructure. You can exchange fiat currencies such as dollars, euros, or yen for Bitcoin and trade a wide range of alternative cryptocurrencies for Bitcoin. Check it out here: https://bisq.network/.

Such DEXs are the purest form of decentralized exchanges. They're entirely *on-chain,* which means all orders interact with each other directly through the blockchain (see Chapter 4 for more about this technology). However, as I talk about in the preceding section, these kinds of exchanges have their own sets of problems. Many of those problems don't exist in the centralized cryptocurrency exchanges that I describe earlier.

Hybrid exchanges

The hybrid approach to cryptocurrency exchanges aims to merge benefits from both centralized and decentralized exchanges to give consumers the best of both worlds. More specifically, hybrids seek to provide the functionality and liquidity of a CEX with the privacy and security of a DEX. Many believe such exchanges are the real future of the cryptocurrency trading experience.

TECHNICAL
STUFF

Hybrid exchanges look to provide cryptocurrency trading services with the speed, ease, and liquidity institutional users are used to in traditional exchanges. A hybrid exchange connects its centralized elements to a network of decentralized elements. This approach allows users to access the trading platform as they do in a CEX and then engage in a peer-to-peer trading activity as they do in a DEX. The hybrid then provides confirmation and record transactions on the blockchain.

Hybrids are also called *semi-decentralized exchanges* because they incorporate both on-chain and off-chain components. An *off-chain* transaction moves your cryptocurrency value outside of the blockchain.

The first ever hybrid exchange was Qurrex (https://qurrex.com), which launched in 2018. The Qurrex team got together in 2016, consisting of experts who had years of experience working in the forex (foreign exchange) markets, developers of trade terminals, and founders of successfully operating stock and futures exchanges. They all saw the significant potential in applying the best practices of the traditional exchanges to create a new generation of cryptocurrency exchange, providing a harmonious merge of centralized and decentralized elements.

Another hybrid cryptocurrency exchange that's gaining attention is NEXT. exchange (https://next.exchange/). If you own its native token, NEXT, you can trade between fiat and crypto pairs such as Bitcoin (BTC) versus the euro (EUR), or Ethereum (ETH) versus the U.S. dollar (USD).

How to choose an exchange

In the preceding sections, you may notice the Internet has no lack of cryptocurrency exchanges. And more variations of exchanges are bound to make their way into the market. Which type of exchange is best for you: CEX, DEX, or hybrid? Even then, which one of the many exchanges in each category should you choose?

I can't give you a solid answer for these questions, but I can offer ways to cycle through some of the most important characteristics in an exchange to help you make the best decision. The following sections note a few things to consider when choosing a cryptocurrency exchange.

TIP

First-time traders are better off doing their research on the cryptocurrencies first and then choosing an exchange. But once you become more experienced, you can simply choose cryptos to trade based on the current market conditions.

TIP

Personally, I'm a big fan of diversification in anything. Because many of these exchanges offer different sets of pros and cons, you may be wise to diversify your cryptocurrency activities across a number of exchanges, just like what many people do when they go grocery shopping. You may go to one store for its better-quality meat but get all your pasta from another.

Security

REMEMBER

Security is one of the biggest issues in the cryptocurrency industry. Exchanges are at constant risk of hacks, frauds, and pump-and-dump schemes. A pump-and-dump scheme is when someone encourages investors to buy a crypto asset in order to artificially inflate its value (the "pumping" part) and then sells his own assets at a high price (or "dumps"). That is why one of the most important things to do before choosing your crypto shop(s) is to do your research. Word-of-mouth and online reviews on sites like Reddit or news organizations like Forbes are some of the ways to help you choose a legitimate and secure platform. Some of other safety features you must check on the exchange include the following:

>> **Two-factor authentication (2FA):** *Two-factor authentication* is a method of confirming your claimed identity by using a combination of two different factors: something the exchange knows (like your password) and something it has (like a six-digit number it sends to your mobile phone or your email address for the second step of the verification).

>> **Cold storage for the majority of funds:** This term means the exchange stores your funds offline so risk of online hacking is lower. I explain more about this feature in Chapter 7.

>> **Proof of reserve:** This element requires the exchange to be audited to verify that the total amount of funds held by the exchange matches the amount required to cover an anonymized set of customer balances.

Supported currencies (crypto and otherwise)

When you decide which of the thousands of available cryptocurrencies are right for you, you must make sure your exchange carries them. You can read more about various crypto options in Chapter 8.

Additionally, if you're looking to purchase cryptocurrencies for the very first time, you probably need an exchange that allows you to deposit your country's fiat currency.

As I cover earlier in this chapter, some exchanges use solely cryptocurrency for purchases, and some allow you to use fiat currencies such as the U.S. dollar, the euro, or your country's currency.

Liquidity

Without sufficient liquidity, the prices and the speeds of your transactions may be compromised. After you decide which cryptocurrencies you want to purchase, make sure your exchange offers sufficient liquidity and trading volume for fast and easy transactions. Liquidity also ensures you're able to buy and sell without the cryptocurrency's price being significantly affected by big market movers. The more buyers and sellers there are, the more liquidity that exists.

TIP

The best way to measure an exchange's liquidity is to look up its most recent trading volume. Coinmarketcap.com and bitcoincharts.com are two of the many cryptocurrency information websites that rank exchanges based on their volume and liquidity.

Fees

Exchanges charge their customers in a number of different ways. It would be great if they didn't, but exchanges aren't charities. Charging customers fees is precisely how they make money to stay in business. The most common method is taking a small percentage of the amount you trade. Most exchanges charge a percentage lower than 1 percent; to stay competitive, some exchanges go as low as around 0.2 percent. Often, a sliding scale decreases the fee percentage as the user's monthly trading volume rises.

Paying less is always attractive, but prioritize security and liquidity over the fees. Your investment will defeat its purpose if you pay next to nothing on transaction fees and then lose all your funds in a hacker's attack.

Ease of use

This one is especially important for newbies. You want your exchange to provide you with an easy-to-use, intuitive, and fast user interface. This factor also depends on what kind of device you want to use for your cryptocurrency investing activities. If you're always on the go, you may want to choose an exchange with great mobile app services.

A good user experience helps you take more informed and more efficient actions on the exchange. Another benefit of exchanges with great interface and mobile support is that they're more likely to grow more quickly and therefore provide more trading volume and liquidity in their markets.

Location

Depending on where you live, you may find a specific exchange that works better for you in your country than another, more popular one on an international level does. Some of the things to keep in mind are issues like which fiat currency exchanges accept and what fees they charge locals compared to international customers.

Additionally, the location of the exchange dictates the laws it has to comply with. At the time of writing, many countries don't have any specific regulations on cryptocurrencies. However, if and when they start to regulate, any restrictions may significantly affect your ability to participate in the market through the exchanges in those countries.

Method of payment

Look into the methods of payment the exchange accepts. Some exchanges require deposits by bank transfer, some use PayPal, and some accept credit and debit cards. Typically, the easier it is for you to pay, the more fees you're going to have to pay. For example, few services allow you to pay with a credit or debit card, and the ones that do will make you pay for the convenience. (Head to the earlier section "Fees" for more on fee issues; the later "PayPal" section has info on that option.) One example of such services is xCoins (https://xcoins.io/?r=62hcz9), which accepts credit cards and PayPal to exchange Bitcoins. They call it "lending," but their concept is similar to buying and selling.

Customer support

Poor customer support was precisely the reason I decided not to go with one of the major exchanges when I first started crypto investing. I always feel more comfortable knowing the place I'm trusting with my funds has a responsive customer support service. You can check this factor either by directly contacting the customer support department and asking any questions that you haven't been able to find on the exchange's FAQ page or by perusing online cryptocurrency forums like BitcoinTalk (https://bitcointalk.org/). You may find complaints about the exchanges in these forums. However, keep in mind that fast-growing exchanges often combat these complaints by improving their customer services, which is always a good thing.

TIP

Another point you may be able to find on forums is whether an exchange has spurred complaints about locking people out of their accounts. If it has, you may want to consider other options.

Trading options

Trading options are especially important for active and advanced traders. For example, depending on your risk tolerance and financial goals, you may want to have access to certain order types or margin trading. On these occasions, make sure you understand the risks involved with such trading activities (check out Part 4) before getting yourself in trouble.

Transaction limits

Most exchanges have a daily withdrawal/deposit limit. Unless you're an institutional trader who wants to make millions of transactions per day, these restrictions may not be an issue. But these limits are still something you may need to keep in mind depending on your investing style and goals. You can typically find out about the exchanges' transaction limits on their websites without having to create an account.

Considering Brokers

If you're looking to purchase cryptocurrencies online and invest in them as an asset, then cryptocurrency exchanges are the way to go. You can read about these earlier in the chapter. However, if you're thinking of simply speculating the price action of cryptocurrencies, then you may want to consider brokers.

As cryptocurrencies became more popular, some traditional forex currency brokers started extending their services to cryptos. But keep in mind that the concept of a "broker" doesn't really exist in pure cryptocurrency investing. You can't purchase cryptocurrencies such as Bitcoin through traditional forex brokers. Even though the brokers may carry them, all they're really providing is streaming a tradable price on their platform. That way, you may be able to take advantage of the market volatility and make/lose money based on your speculated trading orders.

In the following sections, I explain how traditional forex brokers work. Then I get into the pros and cons of utilizing them in your crypto trading activities.

How brokers work

Traditional forex brokers are market intermediaries who help traders execute trades on their platforms. They're the middlemen between an individual retail trader and networks of big banks. The forex brokers typically get a price from one or multiple banks for a specific currency. They then offer you the best price they've received from their banks. You can then trade your favorite currencies based on the prices that are streaming on your broker's platform.

TECHNICAL STUFF

Such brokers operate on something called the *over-the-counter (OTC)* markets. This means that the currencies are traded via a dealer network as opposed to on a centralized exchange. The brokers unload their trading risk to third-party or internal backend warehouses called *liquidity providers*. When it comes to cryptocurrency services on their platforms, these liquidity providers are often cryptocurrency exchanges that I talk about earlier in this chapter.

WARNING

Forex brokers mainly make money through transparent — and sometimes hidden — commission fees. Some brokers even make money when their customers lose money. That's one reason the forex industry as a whole started getting a bad reputation; some such brokers started getting caught by government regulators. I explain all about forex brokers and the scams involved with the industry in my book *Invest Diva's Guide to Making Money in Forex*: https://learn.investdiva.com/ebook-new-edition-invest-divas-guide-to-making-money-in-forex-31.

The pros and cons of using a broker

REMEMBER

Forex brokers who provide cryptocurrency services have started hardcore marketing to advertise speculative crypto trading. Here are some of the advantages and disadvantages of trading through a broker as opposed to using a cryptocurrency exchange:

>> **Pro: You get improved liquidity.** Because the brokers get their quotes from multiple exchanges, they're able to provide increased liquidity to customers. That means you have a higher chance of getting your buy/sell orders fulfilled in a timely manner. You also may be able to get a price closer to your initial buy/sell order because the broker has multiple channels to find a buyer and seller to fulfill your order.

>> **Pro: You can start trading immediately.** If you go through an exchange, you sometimes need to wait for days before your account is confirmed. With most brokers, the account confirmation can be quicker.

>> **Con: You can't invest in cryptos as an asset.** By trading through a broker, you're simply speculating on price volatility of the market. You aren't actually purchasing, or investing in the cryptocurrency market. This distinction means you don't own your cryptos even if you buy them on the brokerage account.

>> **Con: You don't have access to wallets.** For the same reason as in the preceding point, no real portfolio or wallet is available for you. This fact also means you can't realize your transfers or cryptocurrency acquisitions.

In addition to the preceding pros and cons, some conditions can be both advantages and disadvantages of trading cryptocurrencies on a broker. Of course, if you go to the brokers' websites, they've featured these characteristics as advantages. However, you must understand the risks beneath the surface. Here are a couple of the most common ones.

Pro or con: You can take advantage of a down market

This tricky advantage is one that many brokers advertise. Because you aren't actually purchasing the currencies (fiat or crypto), you can bet on the markets to go down. If the prices do go down as you predicted, you can make money. This process is called *short-selling*. Short-selling is actually also available on exchanges and traditional stock markets as well. However, it involves a lot of risk because you need to borrow money from your broker, exchange, or whoever is providing your trading services.

Pro or con: You can trade on leverage

Trading on leverage means borrowing money from your broker to trade. With some brokers, you can open an account with $100 and then use 50-times leverage (or even more), which means you control a $5,000 account with your mere $100! But unless you're Nostradamus or have a crystal ball, using leverage can be problematic because leverage enlarges the risks of gains and losses by the same magnitude.

Here's how leverage can make or break your account: Say you have a $1,000 account. You place a trade order without using any leverage, and you end up making $50. If you had used a 10-time leverage, you would've made $500 instead. That's awesome!

But (and that's a very big but) on the flip side, if the markets go against your speculation when you're trading on that leverage, you lose $500 rather than $50, wiping half of your account. Newbie traders often wipe out their accounts completely within the first few days. Sometimes, depending on the broker's policy, investors' losses can even exceed their initial deposits, which means they actually owe the broker money!

REMEMBER

Using leverage can be an advantage if you know what you're doing and you have high enough risk tolerance to be prepared for a worst-case scenario, which means losing parts or all of your initial investment through the broker.

How to choose a broker

REMEMBER

The steps in choosing a broker can be very similar to those of choosing an exchange (covered earlier in this chapter). Some additional rules you need to keep in mind when choosing a broker include the following:

>> **Make sure it's regulated.** Each country has strict international regulatory authorities that audit brokers on a regular basis to ensure their security. Your best bet is often to make sure the broker is regulated by two or more regulatory bodies in your country. You can find regulation information on brokers' websites.

>> **Consider ease of deposit and withdrawals.** Good brokers will allow you to deposit funds and withdraw your earnings without a hassle. Brokers really have no reason to make it hard for you to withdraw your profits because the only reason they hold your funds is to facilitate trading. (This point is part of my Invest Diva's *Forex Coffee Break Education Course*.)

>> **Beware of promotions.** Some brokers have discovered that people love discount sales! So they use such promotions to attract customers. Nothing is wrong with promotions, but you must be careful because sometimes brokers use these promotions to push new traders into making risky investments or using unreliable products and signals. That's why you need to do your due diligence and know your broker before you take advantage of a promotion.

TIP

One of the major brokers in this field is eToro (http://partners.etoro.com/ A75956_TClick.aspx). Otherwise, here's a place you can check out to help you with your broker hunt: Forest Park FX (https://forestparkfx.com/?id=UU1Uck hZSVN3OW1WNnNuNHIxaH1qUT09). They help you find a broker suitable for you in your location.

Looking at Other Methods for Buying Cryptos

I cover some of the most popular methods to purchase or invest in cryptocurrencies earlier in this chapter. However, these options aren't the only ones. Check out the following sections for a few other handy ways to buy cryptos. (I cover where to store your cryptocurrencies after you purchase them in Chapter 7.)

Funds

Many people seek exposure to the cryptocurrency market but don't want to invest in a specific cryptocurrency such as Bitcoin or Ripple. They may be looking for an equivalent of a *mutual fund* or an *exchange traded fund* (ETF), which tracks a basket of different assets such as stocks and indexes. (See Chapter 13 for more information.)

The upside of a fund is that it's somewhat diversified. That's because you get to invest in a number of popular cryptos in one fund, without the hassle of selecting just a few. The downside of most funds is their costs and restrictions.

TIP

At the time of writing, no cryptocurrency ETFs or mutual funds are available for investors. The closest thing to a crypto fund is the Coinbase GDAX. By providing diversified exposure to a broad range of assets, Coinbase's index funds enable investors to track the performance of an entire asset class instead of having to select individual assets. Coinbase is still working on launching more internationally accessible funds to cover a broader range of digital assets. You can find out more about Coinbase and GDAX here: www.coinbase.com/join/59d39a7610351d00d40189f0.

Credit card

Financial services like Coinmama allow you to buy cryptocurrencies like Bitcoin (BTC), Ethereum (ETH), Litecoin (LTC), Bitcoin Cash (BCH), Cardano (ADA), Qtum (QTUM), and Ethereum Classic (ETC) using a credit card. But they are not available in all countries yet at the time of writing. You can check them out here: http://go.coinmama.com/visit/?bta=53881&nci=5360.

PayPal

Earlier in this chapter, I touch on various methods of payment cryptocurrency exchanges may offer, including transferring money from your bank account and using your credit card/debit card. PayPal is another form of online payment system that supports money transfers and serves as an electronic alternative to traditional money.

PayPal started out working on Bitcoin integration earlier than many other financial services, back in 2014. However, it then slowed its services down. At the time of writing, you still can't simply send and receive Bitcoins or other forms of crypto currencies directly via your PayPal account. However, a few exchanges do accept PayPal money transfers, which means you can use PayPal to indirectly buy crypto currencies. To do so, you need to choose the third party or a middleman like an exchange or a broker who accepts PayPal payments. I talk about exchanges and brokers earlier in this chapter.

Back in the day, you were even able to transfer money to the Coinbase exchange (introduced earlier in this chapter) using PayPal. However, at the time of writing, one of the only viable exchanges that accepts PayPal as a form of money transfer is an exchange called VirWox. One major problem with VirWox is its high fees. If you're looking to trade cryptos through a broker, eToro (`http://partners. etoro.com/A75956_TClick.aspx`) is one famous one that accepts PayPal.

TIP This type of information is constantly subject to change due to cryptocurrencies' volatile current state. The best way to stay on top of cryptocurrency news is on websites such as `www.newsbtc.com/` and `www.coindesk.com/`.

Cash

TIP The process for paying cash to buy cryptocurrencies such as Bitcoin is to find someone who owns cryptocurrencies and is willing to sell them in exchange for cash:

>> One place you can find buyers and sellers of cryptocurrencies for cash is `https://localbitcoins.com/?ch=w7ct`. On this website, you can sign up for free, enter the amount you're looking to buy or sell, and choose your preferred payment method — in this case, cash — to find a counterpart.

>> Other sites connect buyers and sellers in a way where the seller provides bank details that let the buyer make a cash deposit at the bank. You must keep the receipt to provide proof, and the seller can send you the Bitcoins. Some options in this vein include `https://www.bitquick.co/` (part of Athena Bitcoin based in Chicago) and `https://paxful.com/` (based in Delaware).

Note: If you do an Internet search on how to buy cryptocurrencies with cash, you may get directed to a mobile app called Square Cash, which is indeed an app that helps you buy and sell Bitcoin from friends! However, this isn't the type of cash payment I'm talking about in this section.

Cryptocurrency ATMs

Cryptocurrency ATMs are becoming more popular. Many individuals are even trying to start their own such machines to make passive income. Bitcoin (and other cryptocurrency) ATMs work like any other ATM. The first step in the process is to find one near you, something you can do via a quick online search or at https://coinatmradar.com/.

There are several different brands of ATMs with differing methods of verifying your ID and *cryptocurrency address* (a code in your cryptocurrency wallet). Naturally, you need to do some research in finding a secure and trustworthy ATM with a good online reputation. One simple research method is entering the ATM name on Google or Bing, and checking whether it has any negative press.

The process of buying cryptocurrencies at an ATM may vary from machine to machine. However, here are the general steps most ATMs require:

1. **Verify your identity (using an ID card, for example).**

2. **Select the cryptocurrency you want to purchase.**

3. **Provide a cryptocurrency address for deposit.**

   Chapter 7 has more on this address.

4. **Select the amount of cryptocurrency you want to purchase.**

5. **Insert cash into the cryptocurrency ATM.**

6. **Confirm the operation.**

REMEMBER

Some cryptocurrency ATMs even provide services to sell digital coins as well as buy. Keep in mind that these types of cryptocurrency machines aren't ATMs in the traditional sense, where they help you connect with your bank account. Instead, they're machines that are connected to the Internet and direct you to a cryptocurrency exchange in order to provide you with your cryptocurrency.

Chapter **7**

Using Cryptocurrency Wallets

A traditional wallet is where you keep your valuable personal items such as cash, credit cards, and identification cards. But now that you're using the most advanced, futuristic form of money (cryptos, baby!), you're gonna need a brand-new type of wallet to go with it: a cryptocurrency wallet.

With a cryptocurrency wallet, you can not only store the value of your digital money but also send and receive currencies. Additionally, you can monitor your balance the way you'd do with your banking account. In this chapter, I walk you step-by-step through understanding and choosing your very first cryptocurrency wallet.

Defining Cryptocurrency Wallets

A *cryptocurrency wallet* is a software program that helps you manage your digital money. Though you may be the type of person who doesn't like to carry around traditional wallets and would rather put your cash and credit cards right in your back pocket, you must have a digital cryptocurrency wallet if you want to use any type of cryptocurrency. There's no way around it. Cryptocurrencies aren't stored in a bank reserve like other types of traditional assets such as gold and cash. Without crypto wallets, the whole idea of cryptocurrencies dies! Cryptocurrency wallets are the air that keeps the system alive.

TECHNICAL
STUFF

While in theory Bitcoin is decentralized and nobody controls anything, it's in fact run by a network that's controlled and maintained by someone (whoever is hiding behind the name Satoshi Nakamoto). In other words, Bitcoin is distributed and miners are somewhat anonymous, but the actual blockchain is stored in its entirety by the network. It's so large in size that miners have maybe 30 days' worth of transactions and blocks stored on their devices; the full blockchain is actually stored somewhat centralized by the network.

A few important terms

REMEMBER

Before you get started, take a look at some geek terms that you may encounter as you explore the world of crypto wallets:

>> **Hot wallet:** A wallet connected to the Internet.

>> **Cold wallet:** A wallet that isn't connected to the Internet.

>> **Wallet address:** A number that functions something like a traditional bank account number.

>> **Public key:** A code that allows you to receive cryptocurrencies into your account or wallet. It's mathematically linked to your wallet address, but it isn't identical.

>> **Private key:** A code that's coupled with the public key to ensure your security. It's something like your own private password you use to enter your bank account in the real world.

The following section explains how some of these items work together so you can complete crypto transactions.

How a wallet works

Crypto wallets don't actually store the cryptocurrency itself; rather, they store the cryptocurrency's private and public keys. These keys are something like the PIN code you use to access your bank account.

No two wallet addresses are ever the same. They're something like fingerprints. This distinction means that there is a very low chance that somebody else can get your funds by mistake. Also, you have no limit to the number of wallet addresses you can create.

There have been cases where a wallet ID was intercepted and changed and funds went to the wrong wallet. For example, some malware recently replaced wallet IDs in the clipboard of a computer so when the user cut and pasted the IDs of the intended recipient, the wrong ones were actually pasted — that of the perpetrator.

To give you an example of what a cryptocurrency address looks like, here is the wallet address believed to belong to the creator of Bitcoin, Satoshi Nakamoto!

1A1zP1eP5QGefi2DMPTfTL5SLmv7DivfNa

As you can see, it uses a combination of numbers and letters, both uppercase and lowercase. Don't worry; as long as you have a safe and secure wallet, you don't have to memorize your crypto wallet address. Personally, I keep my wallet address and other keys in a locked document on a secure computer. You can also consider printing your keys and storing them somewhere safe that you won't forget about.

A private key does the job of a unique individual password to your individual crypto wallet address. A public key then adds an extra layer of security and ensures that your wallet can't be hacked. Here is a quick example of what the keys look like:

Private key:
03bf350d2821375158a608b51e3e898e507fe47f2d2e8c774de4a9a7edecf74eda

Public key: 99b1ebcfc11a13df5161aba8160460fe1601d541

These addresses look completely different to the eye, but the software technology knows that they two keys are specifically linked to each other. That proves that you're the owner of the coins and allows you to transfer funds whenever you want.

When someone sends you any type of cryptocurrency, he or she is essentially signing off ownership of those cryptos to your wallet's address. To be able to spend those cryptos and unlock the funds, the private key stored in your wallet must match the public address the currency is assigned to. If the public and private keys match, the balance in your wallet increases, and the sender's balance decreases accordingly. No exchange of real coins actually occurs. The transaction is signified merely by a transaction record on the blockchain (see Chapter 4) and a change in balance in your cryptocurrency wallet.

Looking at Different Types of Wallets

First, let me clear up the difference between a traditional digital wallet and a cryptocurrency wallet. You may already be using digital wallets, also known as e-wallets, through your mobile phone. Personally, I use wallet apps for my train tickets, parking tickets, and Apple Pay (a mobile payment and digital wallet service by Apple Inc. that allows users to make payments in person, in iOS apps).

Cryptocurrency wallets are a whole different animal; furthermore, they come in several different species catering to different needs. The following sections cover the five most popular types of cryptocurrency wallets, in order of their security level (from least secure to most).

In Figure 7-1, you can see a summary of most common crypto wallets and their examples that I shared with Invest Diva students in 2018. *Note:* According to Bitcoin Wiki, a "seed phrase, seed recovery phrase, or backup seed phrase is a list of words which `store` all the information needed to recover a Bitcoin wallet. Wallet software will typically generate a seed phrase and instruct the user to write it down on paper. If the user's computer breaks or their hard drive becomes corrupted, they can download the same wallet software again and use the paper backup to get their bitcoins back." A POS stands for proof-of-stake, a mining concept I explain in Chapter 5.

SUMMARY OF CRYPTOCURRENCY WALLETS

	SOFTWARE	ONLINE	HARDWARE	PAPER
PROS	User-controlled Security For POS coins, allows minting	High convenience, Accessible from any browser without needing to download the Blockchain	Protects user's private keys, which are stored on the device Can be recovered with PIN and seed	Extremely secure. Can't be hacked using digital means Great for long term storage
CONS	Must download entire Blockchain for each type of coin/token	Susceptible to key logging hacks Can't stake POS coins Unknown level of security	Doesn't support all coins/tokens Can't stake POS coins	Inconvenient to use for transactions
EXAMPLES	Electrum Armory	Blockchain MyEtherWallet	Ledger Trezor	

FIGURE 7-1: Popular cryptocurrency wallet types.

REMEMBER Specific wallet brands I mention here aren't the only options available, and you shouldn't take their inclusion as a recommendation. You must do your own research to find the best options available in your area and for your needs and chosen cryptocurrencies. I discuss choosing a crypto wallet in more detail later in this chapter.

Online wallet

Online wallets may be less secure, but they do have a bunch of advantages for small amounts of cryptocurrencies. An *online* (or *web*) *wallet* allows you access to your cryptos via the Internet. Therefore, as long as you're connected to the Internet (the cloud), you can reach and store your coins and make crypto payments. The online wallet provider stores your wallet's private key on its server. The provider may send you the crypto code but store your keys and give you the ability to access your keys. Different services offer various features, with some of them linking to multiple devices such as your mobile phone, tablet, and computer.

Advantages of online wallets include the following:

>> They enable fast transactions.

>> They may be able to manage multiple cryptocurrencies.

>> They're convenient for use on the go and for active trading.

Disadvantages include these:

>> They risk your online security because of potential vulnerability to hacks and scams.

>> They risk your personal security because of potential exposure to computer viruses.

>> You aren't storing your cryptos; a third party is.

Mobile wallet

Mobile wallets are available on your cellphone through an app. You can use mobile wallets when shopping in physical stores as cryptocurrencies become more acceptable. *Note:* Other types of wallets, such as online wallets (see the preceding section), offer mobile versions as well. But some wallets are specifically and only used for mobile phones.

Mobile wallets (which fall into the category of software wallets) have their advantages:

>> They can be safer than online wallets.

>> They're convenient for use on the go.

>> They offer additional features such as QR code scanning.

Some disadvantages of mobile wallets include the following:

>> You risk losing your crypto assets if your phone is lost or damaged.

>> They run the risk of getting mobile viruses and malware.

Desktop wallet

You can download a *desktop wallet* and install it on your computer. Some argue that desktop wallets are safer if your computer isn't, or even better, has never been connected to the Internet. If a desktop computer has never been connected to the Internet, it essentially becomes a cold wallet. On the other hand, a computer that has never been connected to the Internet may expose you to malware that may automatically move from the wallet drive that you connect to the computer and infect the desktop since it's never been patched with software updates that require an Internet connection. Talking about a catch-22!

TIP

To set up your wallet on a computer that has never been connected to the Internet, you must first download the latest version of the wallet on a computer that *is* connected to the Internet. You then move the file to a USB drive or something similar in order to move it to your offline computer.

Some advantages of desktop wallets (which fall into the category of software wallets) include these:

>> They're a convenient choice if you trade cryptos from your computer.

>> You aren't storing your private keys on a third-party server.

>> If your computer has never been connected to the Internet, a desktop wallet can be safer than an online wallet.

But desktop wallets do come with some disadvantages:

>> Using your crypto assets on the go is more difficult.

>> If you connected the wallet to the Internet, it turns into a less secure hot wallet.

>> If you don't back up your computer and it dies, you lose your cryptos.

Hardware wallet

A *hardware wallet* can arguably be one of the safest types of crypto wallets out there. These wallets store your private keys on a device like a USB drive. You're still able to make online transactions, but the wallets are offline most of the time, so you can consider them cold wallets.

TIP

For security purposes, a hardware wallet is an absolute must (and a bare minimum) for large crypto amounts. Keeping a ton of your assets on other, less secure types of wallets increases your risk of unrecoverable hacking attacks. Even safer than hardware wallets are paper wallets, which I talk about in the next section.

Here are some advantages of hardware wallets:

>> They're one of the safest crypto wallet options.

>> They're great for storing large amounts of cryptocurrencies that you don't want to use on a day-to-day basis.

Some disadvantages of hardware wallets include the following:

>> They're the most expensive type of wallet.

>> They aren't as user-friendly as other wallets, especially for beginners.

Paper wallet

A *paper wallet* is a super cold crypto wallet. To use it, you print out your private and public keys. You can send funds by transferring the money to the wallet's public address, and you can withdraw or send your currencies by entering your private keys or by scanning the QR code on the paper wallet.

Some of the advantages of paper wallets include these:

>> They're ultra hacker-proof.

>> You don't store them on a computer, mobile phone, or third-party server.

Paper wallets do have some disadvantages, though:

>> They aren't user-friendly for non-geeks.

>> They're harder to use for day-to-day transactions than other wallet types are.

>> They can catch fire.

TIP

Some paper wallet generators include `Bitaddress.org`, `WalletGenerator.net`, `Bitcoinpaperwallet.org`, and `Mycelium` (`https://mycelium.com/mycelium-entropy.html`). Mycelium offers an original and even more secure way to generate paper wallets, with a USB device that you plug directly into your printer. The device generates a paper wallet that automatically gets printed out without ever having touched your computer.

Choosing a Crypto Wallet

Depending on your cryptocurrency needs and goals, you may need more than one type of cryptocurrency wallet. Personally, I use cold wallets to store my larger crypto reserves and hot wallets for active trading. Regardless, you can choose your cryptocurrency wallet(s) based on different characteristics, some of which I discuss in the following sections.

REMEMBER

Make sure you've gathered everything you need to know about a given wallet before committing to getting one.

Based on security

REMEMBER

Even if you're an active crypto trader, I recommend that you have a super secure cold wallet where you store your larger amounts of crypto assets. As I note earlier in this chapter, online wallets aren't the most secure option, however convenient they may be. You can always transfer your assets to an online wallet if you need immediate access to your cryptocurrencies for an investment/shopping opportunity.

Another point to keep in mind is that the most secure hardware wallets are normally the most expensive ones. So you should calculate whether spending that much money for a particular wallet makes sense for the amount of crypto you're going to store in it.

Some questions you must ask before choosing the most secure wallet include the following:

>> What sort of authentication does the wallet use?

>> Is the website secure?

>> What do online reviews say?

TIP

CoinCentral.com, 99Bitcoins.com, and CryptoCompare.com are among the websites that provide an annual crypto wallet review. I normally check with two or more websites before making a decision.

TIP

At the time of writing, Ledger Nano S hardware wallet (priced at $99) is one of the most popular and highly rated secure wallets out there. Here's my personalized link to get you the best deal: www.ledger.com/products/ledger-nano-s?r=2acaa6bf4b8d&tracker=MY_TRACKER. You can find out about other Ledger products here: www.ledger.com. Trezor Bitcoin hardware wallet (created by SatoshiLabs) is another example. One catch about these is that if the USB drive dies, all your cryptos go with it. That's why you should always have a backup and keep your security codes elsewhere so that you can recover your assets.

Based on your crypto ownership

Not all crypto wallets can handle your different types of cryptocurrency assets. In fact, some wallets are purpose-built for just one cryptocurrency; many cryptocurrencies have their own official wallets, which can handle only that one crypto. For example, Bitcoin-specific wallets include Bitcoin Core Wallet (https://bitcoin.org/en/choose-your-wallet), Mycelium (https://wallet.mycelium.com/), and Electrum (https://electrum.org/#home). For Ethereum, you have options such as Ethereum Wallet (www.ethereum.org/) and MyEtherWallet (which is a paper wallet; see www.myetherwallet.com/). If you're not planning to diversify among other types of cryptocurrencies, a singular official cryptocurrency wallet may be right for you. Most of the time, you can find the official wallet of a cryptocurrency on the company's website.

Multicurrency wallets are an option for people who want to hold more than one cryptocurrency. The majority of online wallets provided on the exchanges (introduced in Chapter 6) give you the opportunity to store and transact among multiple cryptos. However, if you're using these wallets to store your crypto assets, know that your wallet security may be compromised.

I do *not* recommend leaving your coins on an online exchange wallet.

Coinomi (www.coinomi.com/) is a popular multicoin mobile wallet. It supports more than 200 different digital tokens and a number of blockchains. It's a great multiasset cryptocurrency wallet, but at this writing, it's available for mobile devices only. Exodus (https://www.exodus.io/) is another multicoin wallet, available only on desktop. Your private keys remain secure on your device and never leave it. Exodus can even encrypt the private keys for you.

Based on transaction fees

If you're planning to do a lot of crypto shopping and use digital coins on the go, you may need to be mindful of the transaction fees you're paying along the way. This point is especially true for active traders. If you're a day trader and you're paying more on transaction fees than what you're making in the market, doesn't that defeat the purpose of trading?

Based on anonymity

Anonymity is an extra layer of security you can take into consideration when choosing a crypto wallet. If you use an anonymous wallet, you can separate your personal information from your funds, therefore making it harder for anyone to track down your cryptos and potentially steal them. This factor is something that can be very personal. Some wallets offer full anonymity, while others don't. If anonymity is something that's really important to you, choose among more-private wallets. Note that prioritizing anonymity may affect transaction fees and the price of the wallet.

To find the latest, most popular anonymous wallets, you can simply search the term "anonymous cryptocurrency wallets" on your favorite search engine. Anonymous wallets come in the forms of mobile, hardware, software, and so on. With that, you can have one or more anonymous wallets based on your needs. Some of the popular anonymous wallets at the time of writing include these:

>> **BitLox:** This hardware Bitcoin wallet ensures both security and anonymity. It's capable of holding over 100 wallets with the ability to create millions of addresses for each wallet. Check it out here: http://www.bitlox.com?ref=196.

>> **Electrum:** This desktop Bitcoin wallet appears to be one of the most trusted software wallets by the cryptocurrency community. Check it out here: https://electrum.org/#home.

>> **Samourai:** This wallet is a mobile Bitcoin wallet. According to the Samourai website, the aim is to "to keep your transactions private, your identity masked, and your funds secure." You can check out the company here: `https://samouraiwallet.com/index.html`.

Keeping Your Wallet Secure

After you've selected the cryptocurrency wallet(s) aligned with your goals, you want to actively keep your investment safe. No matter how secure a wallet is, you still need to take personal steps to enhance that security, just like you'd do with your traditional personal wallet. Because you may be storing a higher value in your cryptocurrency wallets, keeping them safe becomes that much more important. This effort is basically the price you pay for wanting to manage your own money without having to rely on third parties, governments, and big banks. Here are some tips on keeping your wallet safe.

Back up your wallet

A famous *Sex and the City* episode has main character Carrie Bradshaw losing her journalism portfolio because she didn't back up her computer. Don't let that happen to your crypto portfolio. Back up your cryptocurrency wallets like you back up your photos, work files, and computer data.

REMEMBER

A backup of your wallet can protect you against computer failures and many human mistakes. It can also allow you to recover your wallet if your mobile phone or computer is stolen. Of course, you need to keep your backup wallet in a safe place, away from your original wallet. And make sure you back up regularly to ensure that all recent crypto addresses are included in your original wallet.

Additionally, you should also consider keeping a backup of PIN codes, usernames, and passwords if your wallet provides these features. This measure is just in case it has been long enough for you to forget these things. Personally, I keep a hidden file with these items on a secure local cloud for our personal use that is almost impossible to hack.

Have multiple wallets

It's diversification time, baby! If you're having a hard time choosing among the many secure wallets, don't worry. Keeping your assets across multiple wallets is actually a great practice anyway. That way, if any of your wallets are somehow compromised, you don't go bankrupt of cryptocurrencies.

TIP

A good combination is using two or more hardware wallets for larger crypto amounts, with the rest of your smaller amounts spread across mobile, desktop, or online wallets, depending on your everyday use of cryptocurrencies. Of course, all these need to have their own specific backups (as I explain in the preceding section).

Add more security levels

You can add to the security level of your wallets in a number of ways. Here are some suggestions:

>> **Use two-factor authentication (2FA).** If your wallet allows it, *two-factor authentication* is a great way to take the security of your wallet to the next level. It's simply a double authentication of who you are, though it can be done in different ways. Personally, I use the Google Authenticator app, which provides a six-digit code that changes every minute and is unique to you.

>> **Encrypt your wallet.** Encrypting your wallet or your smartphone allows you to set a password for anyone trying to withdraw any funds. This act helps protect against thieves, though it can't protect against keylogging hardware or software (which tracks your keystrokes). You should also consider encrypting your backups. *Note:* Some methods to encrypt may need a bit more technical familiarity. The best way to encrypt your wallet is to contact your wallet provider for more information.

>> **Use a strong password.** A strong password must contain letters, numbers, and punctuation marks and must be at least 16 characters long. Avoid passwords that contain only letters, only numbers, or only symbols. Recognizable English words are also a no-go because they're easy to break.

TIP

You can make a very long, strong password by memorizing a pattern on your keyboard instead of selecting a word. For example, start from the left side of the keyboard and type, top to bottom, the keys along the lines of this pattern (using the shift key after the last lowercase letter): 1qaz2wsx!QAZ@WSX. It's an extremely strong password, and you don't have to memorize it! Of course, if you try to log in to your software from a mobile phone, things can get complicated.

Update your software

REMEMBER

If you're using mobile or desktop wallets, make sure you're using the latest version of the wallet's software. Reputable companies constantly send stability and security fixes. By updating your software regularly, you can make sure that you're using the newest safety features that can prevent problems from minor to severe.

(Updating your wallet's software isn't the same as backing it up, which I discuss in the earlier section "Back up your wallet.")

Remember where you hide it!

This suggestion may sound a bit silly, but you have no idea how many times I've tried to hide something valuable, just to lose it forever! If you're one of those people who hides things so well that even you can't remember where they are, make sure you choose a location you won't forget. If you lose your cryptocurrency wallets, you may very well lose your shirt as well in the long run.

Chapter **8**

Different Types of Cryptocurrencies

By now, you probably have heard of the cryptocurrency that started it all: Bitcoin. But Bitcoin is hardly the only famous or even investment-worthy cryptocurrency out there anymore. Heck, some people even think that Bitcoin may be the worst cryptocurrency to own or to invest in. So many other digital coins are available that have made massive improvements to the Bitcoin model to avoid its disadvantages.

In this chapter, I go over some of the most famous cryptos as of 2018. But because the cryptocurrency market is ever-changing, I explain how you can navigate your way through all the up-and-coming cryptos for years to come.

Celebrating Celebrity Cryptocurrencies by Market Cap

One of the fastest ways to navigate through popular cryptocurrencies is to check out their ranking based on their *market capitalization,* or *market cap.* Traditionally, market cap is the value of a company that's traded on the stock market. You can calculate it by multiplying the total number of shares by the present share price.

In the cryptoworld, market capitalization shows the value of all units of a specific cryptocurrency that are for sale right now. To calculate a cryptocurrency's market cap, simply multiply the cryptocurrency's current price by its *circulating supply*. Circulating supply is the best approximate number of coins that are circulating in the market and in the general public's hands.

Market cap = Price × Circulating supply

REMEMBER

Knowing about a crypto's market cap and its ranking versus other coins is important because that info can quickly show you how popular the coin is and how much money you may be able to make from it. You can find out about all cryptocurrencies' market caps by visiting websites such as http://coinmarketcap.com, www.cryptocompare.com/, https://coincodex.com/, and www.coingecko.com/.

WARNING

Market cap can't tell you everything about a cryptocurrency's investment potential. Lots of other factors, such as forks, regulation, rumor, and so on, can affect a cryptocurrency's value. I talk more about analyzing a cryptocurrency's performance in Chapter 9.

TIP

A higher market cap isn't necessarily a good thing. Investors who can take higher risks may prefer cryptocurrencies with a lower market cap because those may offer more room for the market cap to increase. However, if you want to play it safe and avoid volatility or vanishing risk (as I explain in Chapter 3), you may prefer going with cryptocurrencies with a higher market cap.

With a knowledge of what role a coin's market cap plays in the industry, you can start to evaluate cryptocurrencies based on that metric. I discuss Bitcoin and other major cryptocurrencies in the following sections.

Bitcoin

Ranking number one on the list, Bitcoin was developed in 2008. As of October 2018, Bitcoin's market cap is around $115 billion.

A bit of Bitcoin background

TECHNICAL
STUFF

An entity called Satoshi Nakamoto invented Bitcoin. Satoshi claimed to be a man living in Japan, born on April 5, 1975. I was actually living in Japan, completing my studies in electrical engineering in Tokyo, when Bitcoin hit the scene. I can tell you that Bitcoin wasn't really a big thing in Japan at that time. That's why most speculation about the true identity of Satoshi points to a number of cryptography and computer science experts of non-Japanese descent living in the United States and various European countries.

But Satoshi's anonymity isn't really a big deal, because Bitcoin (and other crypto-currencies, for that matter) are supposed to be open source and decentralized, as I explain in Chapter 5. In fact, according to Bitcoin.org, no single person or entity "owns the Bitcoin network much like no one owns the technology behind email." Bitcoin users around the world control Bitcoin, with the developer improving the software and the forkers making some radical changes. However, the main idea behind Bitcoin and Bitcoin's protocol can't be changed.

Almost ten years after Satoshi published Bitcoin's white paper, Bitcoin's market cap went up to as much as $320 billion by the end of 2017. If you had invested $100 to buy one Bitcoin in 2011 (something my investor friends told me to do that I ignored), you would've had $20,000 worth of Bitcoin by the end of 2017. Of course, many initial investors bought more than one Bitcoin at the time, which is exactly how all those Bitcoin millionaires were made. If you had bought 100 Bit-coins in 2011, by the end of 2017 they would have been worth $2 million.

But by the time everyone started talking about Bitcoin, it went crashing down to around $120 billion and stayed there for most of 2018. It maintained its number one ranking among all other cryptocurrencies, though. The main reason behind this position may be that most people have heard a lot (relatively speaking) about Bitcoin but not so much about other cryptocurrencies. So even though they have several hundred other altcoins to choose from, even some that may be better long-term alternatives to Bitcoin, most newbies who want to get involved in the market start out with Bitcoin.

Another reason for Bitcoin's huge market cap is its accessibility. I can pretty safely say that all cryptocurrency exchanges (see Chapter 6) carry Bitcoin. But not all exchanges list all altcoins, at least for now.

Bitcoin characteristics

Here are some main features of Bitcoin:

- » Bitcoin's trading symbol is BTC.
- » Bitcoin is minable.
- » Coin creation occurs through proof-of-work (PoW; see Chapter 5).
- » Transaction time is between 30 minutes and 24 hours.
- » Transactions aren't fully anonymous.
- » Bitcoin is decentralized.
- » Mining Bitcoin requires a lot of (wasted) energy.

Because Bitcoin has been the superstar of all cryptocurrencies, it tends to pull the entire market along. Generally speaking, the whole market sentiment follows the volatility of Bitcoin in longer-term time frames (with many past exceptions). You can use this piece of information in technical analysis for investing, as I cover in Chapter 16. You can find out more about Bitcoin on its website, `https://bitcoin.org/`.

Ethereum

Ranked number two based on coin market cap as of 2018, Ethereum is another major cryptocurrency. As of October 2018, its market cap is around $23 billion.

Brief Ethereum background

Compared to Bitcoin, Ethereum is a pretty young currency; Russian American Vitalik Buterin proposed it in 2013. It's almost five years younger than Bitcoin, which in the cryptoworld is still a big deal.

Buterin was born in 1994. That's the year the Cranberries sang their hit song "Zombie" and two years before the Backstreet Boys and Spice Girls became famous. If this math makes you feel old, imagine how Bitcoin's Satoshi must feel.

Ethereum uses the old Bitcoin's wisdom and philosophy, but it has a different purpose and capability. According to its website, `www.ethereum.org`, "Ethereum is a decentralized platform that runs smart contracts." As I explain in Chapter 5, *smart contracts* allow people to create agreements without a middleman. Ethereum creates these smart contracts by employing the same blockchain technology as Bitcoin. Just as Bitcoin's blockchain and network validate Bitcoin ownership, Ethereum's blockchain validates smart contracts, which the encoded rules execute.

Ethereum versus Bitcoin

The main difference between Ethereum and Bitcoin is that Ethereum wants to be the place users go to execute their decentralized applications. In fact, its goal is to be a sort of massive, decentralized computer that executes smart contracts. That's why many other cryptocurrencies can run on the Ethereum platform. The Ethereum blockchain forms a decentralized network where these programs can be executed.

Bitcoin is different in this sense. Its platform gets the miners to compete and solve the complicated blockchain math problems I talk about in Chapter 4. The first one who solves the problem is the winner and gets rewarded. But miners can use Ethereum's platform as a co-working space to create their own products. They get compensated for providing the infrastructure so that inventors can cook their own new types of products.

TIP

In fact, even major technology players like Intel and Microsoft and financial behemoths like J.P. Morgan and Credit Suisse are using the Ethereum platform to create new stuff of their own. Along with other giant founding members, various blockchain start-ups, research groups, and Fortune 500 companies have created a group called the Enterprise Ethereum Alliance (EEA). By October 2018, the alliance had more than 500 members, including Accenture, AMD, Credit Suisse, Dash, Pfizer, Samsung, and Toyota, to name a few. You can find out more about the EEA at `https://entethalliance.org/`.

Ethereum characteristics

Here are some main attributes of Ethereum:

>> Ethereum's token symbol for investors is ETH.

>> Ethereum is minable.

>> Coin creation occurs through proof-of-work (PoW).

>> Transaction time can be as little as 14 seconds, although it can go higher based on confirmation requirements.

>> Transactions aren't fully anonymous.

>> Ethereum is more decentralized than Bitcoin.

>> As of 2018, mining Ethereum requires less wasted energy than Bitcoin mining does.

TIP

You can find out about different cryptocurrencies' mining profitability at any given time by visiting `www.cryptocompare.com/mining/calculator/eth?Hashing Power=20&HashingUnit=MH%2Fs&PowerConsumption=140&CostPerkWh=0.12& MiningPoolFee=1`.

Ripple

For most of 2018, Ripple was the third largest cryptocurrency by market cap at around $19 billion. However, at the end of 2017 and beginning of January 2018, it temporarily surpassed Ethereum's ranking for ten days.

Some Ripple background

The idea of Ripple actually goes all the way back to 2004. That's way before Satoshi and Bitcoin. In 2004, Ryan Fugger founded a company called RipplePay. According to `https://blog.bitmex.com/the-ripple-story/`, the idea behind the protocol was a "peer-to-peer trust network of financial relations that would replace banks." (If that sounds familiar, that's probably because it's also how blockchain works, as I discuss in Chapter 4).

By 2011, Ripple's target demographic started paying attention to Bitcoin, which was just becoming popular and was doing a better job as a peer-to-peer payment network than Ripple. Ripple's architecture started to shift when an early Bitcoin pioneer, Jed McCaleb, joined the Ripple network in May 2011. Others joined the Ripple bandwagon as time went by.

Finally, Ripple's XRP, a cryptocurrency that also acts as a digital payment network for financial institutions, was released in 2012, according to their website, `https://ripple.com/xrp/`. Like many other cryptocurrencies, XRP is based on a public chain of cryptographic signatures. That being said, Ripple is very different from traditional cryptos like Bitcoin and even Ethereum.

REMEMBER

As I explain later, some people don't consider Ripple a true cryptocurrency. Also, Ripple as a company and Ripple the cryptocurrency are two different things, although they're connected. Ripple the coin, which trades as XRP, is the cryptocurrency used with some of the company's payment systems. Ripple the company does business as Ripple Labs, Inc., and provides global payment solutions for big banks and such using blockchain technology.

Ripple versus Bitcoin

Here are some of the key differences between these two cryptocurrencies:

>> **Ownership and decentralization:** As I talk about earlier in this chapter, Bitcoin is owned by no particular person or entity, and Bitcoin the cryptocurrency is pretty much the same as Bitcoin the open-source platform. That's why Bitcoin is highly decentralized and open source, owned by a community that agrees on changes. This setup can make upgrades tough and is why Bitcoin has had a ton of forks (hard and soft; see Chapter 5) in its history.

By contrast, Ripple is a private company called Ripple Labs, with offices all over the world. Ripple's digital asset (cryptocurrency) is called XRP and is also owned by Ripple Labs. The company constantly looks to please everyone (especially its partners) and come up with consensus, which can allow for faster upgrades. It has an amendment system with which the developers seek consensus before making changes to the network. In most cases, if an amendment receives 80 percent support for two weeks, it comes into effect, and all future ledgers must support it. Basically, Ripple is a democracy that tries to avoid hard forks and nasty splits!

TIP

You can find out more about Ripple and its most recent updates at `https://ripple.com/`.

>> **Transaction speed and fees:** This area is where Ripple really starts to shine. Bitcoin's transaction speed can sometimes go up to an hour depending on fees. And the fees can reach $40 depending on demand.

Ripple's transactions, on the other hand, can settle in as little as four seconds. Fee-wise, even when the demand was super high at the end of 2017, Ripple's transaction fees averaged $0.007 — a fraction of that of Bitcoin.

You can compare different cryptocurrencies' historical transaction fees at `https://bitinfocharts.com/comparison/transactionfees-btc-xrp.html`.

TIP

>> **Number of transactions per second:** At any given second, you can make around ten Bitcoin transactions. Enter Ripple, and raise the number to 1,500. Although some Bitcoin forks aim to resolve this issue, at the time of writing Ripple appears to be ahead of the game.

>> **Coin amount limits:** Bitcoin and other minable cryptocurrencies have finite numbers of coins, which come into the market only through mining. But XRP is limited to the 100 billion coins in circulation now, largely to appeal to Ripple's (the company's) biggest clients, which are large financial institutions.

Ripple characteristics

The following list gives you a summary of Ripple's main features:

>> Ripple's token symbol for investors is XRP.

>> Ripple's XRP isn't minable. No miners whatsoever.

>> Coin creation and algorithm processing happens through consensus, *not* PoW.

>> Transaction time can be as little as four seconds.

>> Transactions can be made anonymous.

>> Ripple isn't fully decentralized.

>> Energy cost per transaction is minor.

REMEMBER

Because these unique features are so different from Bitcoin's, some people believe Ripple's XRP isn't truly a cryptocurrency. Ripple is actually a strange hybrid of a *fiat currency* (the traditional form of currency backed by a local government, such as the U.S. dollar) and a traditional cryptocurrency. This deviation is because Ripple primarily seeks to serve financial institutions like American Express instead of focusing on the spread of Ripple's XRP among everyday users, at least as of October 2018. This may very well change in the future.

Litecoin

Litecoin has been hovering around the top ten largest cryptocurrencies by market cap since its inception in 2011. Its ranking has gone up as high as number two and dropped as low as number seven, so its market cap has been one of the more volatile ones among celebrity cryptos. As of October 2018, its market cap is around $3 billion, making it the seventh largest cryptocurrency after Bitcoin, Ethereum, Ripple, Bitcoin Cash, EOS, and Stellar.

A little Litecoin background

Litecoin is a result of a Bitcoin hard fork that happened in 2011. (Chapter 5 has details on cryptocurrency forks.) It wanted to become the lighter and faster version of Bitcoin. Litecoin was released by Charlie Lee, a Google employee and an MIT graduate. It reached $1 billion market capitalization by November 2013. Check out the Litecoin project here: `https://litecoin.org/`.

TECHNICAL
STUFF

If you had invested in Bitcoin end of 2016, it would've grown 2,204 percent by the end of 2017. But if you had invested in Litecoin then, it would've grown over 9,892 percent. Not too shabby.

Litecoin versus Bitcoin

Litecoin's technology isn't *that* different from that of Bitcoin. Lee didn't even want it to compete with Bitcoin; he wanted it to complement Bitcoin, like silver complemented gold in the old days. As the gold of cryptos, Bitcoin is great for buying expensive stuff like houses and cars. That's because Bitcoin may be presumed as more secure than Litecoin, although many crypto enthusiasts insist neither are truly secure. Litecoin, on the other hand, can be used for buying cheap things and day-to-day stuff where security isn't that much of a concern and transaction speed is more important. Here are some of other differences between the two:

>> **Mining difficulty:** The real difference between Litecoin and Bitcoin may be mining difficulty. Mining Bitcoin is becoming more difficult and expensive as time goes by. To really make money mining Bitcoin, you need a very powerful computer. You can mine Litecoin, on the other hand, using normal computers.

TECHNICAL
STUFF

Bitcoin mining uses something called the SHA-256 algorithm. Litecoin uses a new algorithm known as Scrypt. SHA-256 is generally considered to be a more complex algorithm than Scrypt, while at the same time allowing a greater degree of parallel processing. Scrypt is faster. I explain more about these ideas in Chapter 12.

>> **Total number of coins:** Bitcoin has a finite number of 21 million coins. Litecoin can accommodate four times that amount, up to 84 million coins.

>> **Transaction speed and fees:** On Bitcoin's network, transaction confirmation time averages around ten minutes and can sometimes take up to an hour. For Litecoin, the speed is roughly 2.5 minutes, according to data from BitInfoCharts.com. Litecoin's transaction fee is also considerably lower than Bitcoin's, averaging less than $0.08. Its highest point until October 2018 was around $1.40 ,when the crypto demand was super high in December 2017.

Litecoin characteristics

Litecoin's main traits include the following:

>> Litecoin's token symbol for investors is LTC.

>> Litecoin is minable.

>> Coin creation and algorithm processing occurs through the proof-of-work (PoW) process.

>> Transaction time is around 2.5 minutes.

>> Transactions can be made anonymous.

>> Litecoin is decentralized.

>> Litecoin's energy cost per transaction is lower than Bitcoin's.

TIP

Although team Bitcoin and team Litecoin argue their respective cryptocurrencies are the best, at the time of writing neither is a clear winner. The best way to go about your investment strategy may be to diversify your assets not only between these options but also well among the other categories of cryptocurrencies I cover in this chapter. Find out more about diversification in Chapter 10.

Other top ten major cryptos

In the preceding sections, I introduce some of the most well-known cryptocurrencies that also have some of the largest market capitalization on average. But being famous doesn't mean they're necessarily better. In fact, many analysts and investors believe some of these celebrity cryptocurrencies may vanish within ten years (as I explain in Chapter 3). Also, having a bigger market cap doesn't necessarily mean having a brighter future. Their current popularity may just be the proverbial 15 minutes of fame, and they may therefore have lower growth opportunity compared to those that are less known.

REMEMBER

Chances are that if anything should happen to a core cryptocurrency, a hard fork may come along that saves it. As I explain in Chapter 5, if you've already invested in a cryptocurrency when it forks, you get the same amount of new coins anyway. That's why I've recommended to my Premium Investing Group members in 2017–2018 to start their cryptocurrency portfolio by first diversifying among the top ten largest ones by market cap and then get into other, different categories. You can stay up-to-date with my most recent cryptocurrency investing strategies here: https://learn.investdiva.com/join-group.

The remaining cryptocurrencies in the top ten keep bouncing on and off the list, but Table 8-1 shows some (in alphabetical order) that were on the list more consistently during 2017 and 2018 and that I personally invested in, in 2018.

TABLE 8-1   **Some Top Ten Cryptos As of 2018**

Crypto	Symbol	Description
Bitcoin Cash (www.bitcoincash.org/)	BCH	A Bitcoin fork that provides cheaper transactions and a more open development process
Cardano (www.cardano.org/en/home)	ADA	Established by a co-founder of Ethereum; smart contracts platform; the "Ethereum of Japan"
Dash (www.dash.org/)	DASH	Digital cash; private transactions via masternodes (computer wallets that host the full copy of the coin's ledger); quick confirmation times and low fees
EOS (https://eos.io/)	EOS	A smart contract platform similar to Ethereum but with performance and scalability benefits
IOTA (www.iota.org/)	MIOTA	No blockchain; instead uses something called Tangle; no mining; no transaction fees
Stellar (Lumens) (www.stellar.org/)	XLM	Similar to Ripple; an open platform for building financial products that connect people everywhere

Top 100 major cryptos

You can dive into the top 100 major cryptocurrencies and still not find *the one* you want to have a long-term relationship with. At this point, selecting cryptocurrencies that match your portfolio really becomes like online dating. You've got to make some decisions based on first impressions and then go on dates (start making small investments and do more research) to discover whether a currency is worthy of a bigger chunk of your crypto portfolio. Table 8-2 lists some options, in alphabetical order, that I've been following on my daily broadcast for NewsBTC.

TABLE 8-2   **Some Top 100 Cryptos as of 2018**

Crypto	Symbol ·	Description
Golem (https://golem.network/)	GNT	Worldwide supercomputer network; aims to become the Airbnb for computing, machine learning, and AI
Monero (https://getmonero.org/)	XMR	Famous for anonymous, untraceable, and private transactions
NEM (https://nem.io/)	XEM	The world's first "smart asset" blockchain; built with businesses in mind
NEO (https://neo.org/)	NEO	"Ethereum of China"; aims to become a smart economy platform
OmiseGo (https://omisego.network/)	OMG	Smart contract platform using proof-of-scale (see Chapter 5) based on Ethereum platform that wants to "unbank the banked"
Populous (https://populous.com/)	PPT	Provides small and medium-sized enterprises an invoice discounting platform on the Ethereum blockchain
SiaCoin (https://sia.tech/)	SC	Decentralized cloud storage platform that uses a blockchain to facilitate payments
TRON (https://tron.network/)	TRX	Decentralized entertainment and content-sharing platform that uses blockchain
VeChain (https://www.vechain.org)	VET	Blockchain-based platform that gives retailers and consumers the ability to determine the quality and authenticity of products they buy
Verge (https://vergecurrency.com/)	XVG	Just like Bitcoin but with faster transactions, aiming to bring block-chain transactions into everyday life through its open-source software

Cryptocurrencies by Category

As an alternative to selecting cryptocurrencies by market cap, the best way to truly diversify your portfolio, for both value and growth purposes, may be to go about selecting cryptocurrencies by category. After you've flipped through the categories and selected the finalists that best fit your risk tolerance (see Chapter 3), you can then move on to the advanced techniques I discuss in Chapters 9 and 10 and in Part 4.

Here are some of the most popular cryptocurrency categories and the leading cryptos in each space. I cover these based on their popularity and total market cap as of 2018. The following sections describe just a few examples of many categories in the exciting cryptocurrency world; you may recognize some of the currencies from their coverage earlier in this chapter. Other people may categorize these cryptos differently. Some popular cryptocurrency categories include the following:

>> Gaming/gambling

>> Supply chain

>> Transportation

>> Medical

>> Internet of Things (IoT)

REMEMBER

Keep in mind that some categories are hotter as of this writing, but others may have become more popular by the time you get this book in your hands. Also know that some cryptos are hybrids of multiple categories and are hard to fit in only one box. You can find different crypto categories on websites such as www.upfolio. com/collections#Go and www.investitin.com/altcoin-list/.

Payment cryptos

Payment cryptos are by far the biggest category in terms of total market cap. In this group, you find cryptocurrencies that mainly aim to be used as a store of value, transaction, and payments, just like fiat currencies like the U.S. dollar. Examples of cryptocurrencies that fall into this category include these:

>> Bitcoin (BTC)

>> Litecoin (LTC)

>> Bitcoin Cash (BCH)

>> OmiseGo (OMG)

>> Dash (DASH)

>> Ripple (XRP)

>> Tether (USDT; https://tether.to/)

TIP

With Bitcoin as the pioneer, no wonder this category started out so popular. But as I say multiple times throughout this book, blockchain technology can be applied to so much more than just payment systems, so be on the lookout for the next big thing within other hot categories!

Privacy cryptos

Privacy cryptos are heavily focused toward transaction security and anonymity, a lot more than those in the payment category are. In fact, the idea that Bitcoin and other cryptocurrencies in the payment category are fully anonymous and untraceable is a common misconception. Many blockchains only disguise users' identities while leaving behind a public record of all transactions that have occurred on the blockchain. The data in the ledger often includes how many tokens a user has received or sent in historical transactions, as well as the balance of any cryptocurrency in the user's wallet.

Privacy cryptos can be a bit controversial because authorities see them as an illicit tool that for criminals to engage in illegal activities, such as money laundering. Nonetheless, some of them have gained popularity. Here are some examples:

>> **Monero (XMR):** Monero is the most famous privacy crypto as of 2018.

>> **Zcash (ZEC):** Zcash is similar to Monero but has a different protocol (set of rules). Check it out here: https://z.cash/.

>> **CloakCoin (CLOAK):** A lesser-known privacy crypto, CloakCoin has a number of added layers of security. See www.cloakcoin.com/en.

>> **Dash (DASH):** Also mentioned in the payment category, Dash is a bit of hybrid. In addition to Bitcoin's core features, Dash also includes the option for instant and private transactions.

Platform cryptos

Platform cryptos are also referred to as *decentralized application protocol cryptos, smart contract cryptos,* or a hybrid of all three. In this category, you can find cryptocurrencies that are built on a centralized blockchain platform; developers use them to build decentralized applications. In other words, such cryptocurrencies act as platforms where people build upon blockchain applications (and thus other cryptocurrencies).

TIP

In fact, some analysts suggest you may want to forget about payment cryptocurrencies and invest in crypto platforms instead. They're generally considered good long-term investments because they rise in value as more applications are created on their blockchain. As blockchain technology becomes more mainstream, the number of applications and their usage will increase, along with the price of such coins. The most famous example in this category is Ethereum (ETH). Others include the following:

>> **NEO (NEO):** A smart contracts ecosystem similar to Ethereum, NEO wants to be a platform for a new smart economy. NEO is China's largest cryptocurrency.

>> **Lisk (LSK):** Lisk is a smart contracts platform similar to Ethereum but based on JavaScript. See https://lisk.io/.

>> **EOS (EOS):** Another smart contracts platform similar to Ethereum, EOS has performance and scalability benefits.

>> **Icon (ICX):** Icon wants to "Hyperconnect the World" by building one of the largest decentralized global networks. See https://m.icon.foundation/?lang=en.

>> **Qtum (QTUM):** Qtum is a Singapore-based Ethereum and Bitcoin hybrid. See https://qtum.org/.

>> **VeChain (VEN):** VeChain is a blockchain-based platform that gives retailers and consumers the ability to determine the quality and authenticity of products they buy.

>> **Ark (ARK):** Ark wants to provide an all-in-one blockchain solution for developers and start-ups. See https://ark.io/.

>> **Substratum (SUB):** Substratum wants to create a new generation of Internet. See https://substratum.net/.

These are just a few of hundreds of cryptocurrencies that are emerging in this category.

Exchange-specific cryptos

Exchange-specific cryptos are the cryptos that mainly the cryptocurrency exchanges introduce and use. You can think of these cryptos as incentives that bring people to the exchanges' platforms. To select the best exchange-specific cryptocurrency, you can consider taking the steps I introduce in Chapter 6 to choosing the best cryptocurrency exchange. Here are a few examples of these currencies:

>> **Binance Coin (BNB):** Issued by Binance exchange, Binance Coin runs on the Ethereum platform and has a strict maximum limit of 200 million BNB tokens. See www.binance.com/.

>> **KuCoin Shares (KCS):** KuCoin Shares is just like Binance Coin but for the KuCoin exchange. See www.kucoin.com/.

» **Bibox Token (BIX):** Bibox Token is one of the smaller exchanges that has successfully launched its own token. See www.bibox.com/.

» **COSS Coin (COSS):** COSS Coin is a much smaller exchange than KuCoin, but it's looking to introduce new features as of 2018. See https://coss.io/.

Finance/fintech cryptos

Here I group pure financial cryptos with financial technology (fintech) cryptocurrencies. These cryptos facilitate the creation of a financial system for the blockchain and for people around the world:

» **Ripple (XRP):** Ripple is a blockchain payment system for banks, payment providers, digital asset exchanges, and other companies. It's designed to move large amounts of money quickly and reliably.

» **Stellar Lumens (XLM):** Stellar Lumens aims to develop the world's new financial system. It's building an open system where people of all income levels can access financial services.

» **Populous (PPT):** Populous is a global invoice trading platform to help businesses. Smart contracts automatically perform funding and release payment without a third party.

» **OmiseGo (OMG):** OmiseGo is designed to enable financial services for people without bank accounts. It works worldwide and with both traditional money (fiat currency) and cryptocurrencies.

» **Quoine (QASH):** Quoine wants to solve the liquidity problem in the cryptocurrency market through its LIQUID platform. See https://quoine.com/.

» **Bancor (BNT):** Bancor lets you convert between two cryptocurrencies of your choice without another party. See www.bancor.network/.

» **Crypto.com (formerly Monaco, MCO):** This cryptocurrency-funded Visa debit card allows you to spend your coins on everyday purchases. See https://crypto.com/.

Legal and property cryptos

More cryptocurrencies are emerging in the two categories of legal and property cryptos. But because they're related, I've grouped them together here for now. Here are a couple of examples:

» **Polymath (POLY):** Polymath helps provide legal advice for token investors and smart contract developers. See https://polymath.network/.

>> **Propy (PRO):** Propy solves problems of purchasing properties across borders when using fiat currencies or cryptocurrencies. It's the first company to ever sell a property on the blockchain and using Bitcoin. See https://propy.com/.

Other up-and-coming property cryptocurrencies include REAL and REX, but at the time of writing they're way down on the cryptocurrency market cap ranking list.

Chapter **9**

Identifying Top Performing Cryptocurrencies

I n Chapter 8 I open a huge window to all the different categories of cryptocurrencies because this whole industry isn't just about Bitcoin or a few other famous cryptos you may have already heard of. Having so many options to choose from is exciting! But just like dating in the digital age, having too many options can be tricky. You're always keeping an eye open for the next best thing.

The good news is that you can have multiple "right" cryptocurrencies for you. But swiping through so many cryptocurrencies can become challenging, especially if you don't know exactly what you're looking for.

In this chapter, I guide you through finding your best crypto match(es) by introducing you to my golden strategy development method, the Invest Diva Diamond Analysis (IDDA).

Introducing the Invest Diva Diamond Analysis

Most individual traders learn one or two methods for analyzing the markets before pulling the trigger and actually executing an investment strategy. For example, most newbie investors rely on things like technical analysis and their favorite economic news anchors on TV. Unfortunately, depending on only one type of analysis can be incredibly dangerous.

Enter the Invest Diva Diamond Analysis (IDDA). The IDDA suggests analyzing the markets from five different points, as you can see in Figure 9-1:

1. Fundamental analysis

2. Sentimental (market sentiment) analysis

3. Technical analysis

4. Capital analysis (personal risk management)

5. Overall analysis

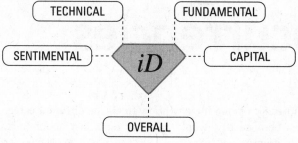

© John Wiley & Sons, Inc.

FIGURE 9-1: Five points of the Invest Diva Diamond Analysis (IDDA).

Flip to Chapter 3 to read about risk management (part of the capital analysis point); for overall analysis and the latest strategies in the market, please visit `https://learn.investdiva.com/services`. In the rest of this chapter, I discuss fundamentals and market sentiment analysis and introduce technical analysis to help you pick the right cryptocurrencies for your portfolio. Here's a brief overview of these concepts:

» **Fundamental analysis:** As a fundamental analyst, you look at data from facts to rumors to decide whether that coin is worth buying.

» **Sentimental analysis:** *Market sentiment* gauges the emotions and attitudes of traders in the market about a specific security. Using sentimental analysis, even non-animal-lovers in the investing world compare market expectations to bulls and bears.

If traders expect upward price movement of a specific security, the sentiment is said to be *bullish.* On the contrary, if the market sentiment is *bearish,* most traders expect downward price movement.

» **Technical analysis:** As a technical analyst, you look at how a cryptocurrency's price has been performing, and then you make an investment decision that is right for you. More specifically, you analyze the price action of your favorite cryptocurrency to see the best time to jump into a relationship and a good time to call it quits. You can see the history of the crypto price actions on something called *charts* that are available on your cryptocurrency exchange. (Head to Chapter 16 to discover all the dirty secrets about technical analysis methods.)

I first introduced the Invest Diva Diamond Analysis (IDDA) investment strategy development method in my book *Invest Diva's Guide to Making Money in Forex* (McGraw-Hill Education), and it then became the key strategy for all my clients and students, from investing.com and Nasdaq to my own educational products for universities in New York and on my website (`https://learn.investdiva.com/free-webinar-3-secrets-to-making-your-money-work-for-you`).

Using Fundamental Analysis to Pick Cryptocurrencies

Fundamental analysis is the art of using all the gossip, stories, and facts about a cryptocurrency, its financial situation, and upcoming risk events that may move the market. Going back to the earlier dating metaphor, finding the right crypto category is like picking your type in a significant other. Except in this case, you should most certainly think with your brain. And maybe a little bit with your gut feeling. But nothing more than that (if you catch my drift). Here are some methods you can use to cherry-pick the best cryptos for you.

Go with what you know

Going with what you know is a golden yet simple method also used in the stock market. If you've already been exposed to certain types of cryptocurrencies or, better yet, used them in real life and have liked their performance, consider adding them to your portfolio. In the stock market, for example, many newbie investors make several profitable investments by simply observing their own buying habits. If they prefer to buy from healthier fast-food services like Chipotle (CMG on the New York Stock Exchange, or NYSE) rather than McDonald's (NYSE: MCD), they may consider adding CMG to their portfolio.

Similarly, say you notice that your favorite online store has already added a cryptocurrency payment option to its checkout page and you place an order with it smoothly. That success may be an indication that the trading volume for that cryptocurrency will increase in the future, and the crypto may become a valuable asset for your portfolio.

Choose the right categories

In Chapter 8, I talk a huge deal about crypto categories and where you can find them. Certain categories perform better at certain times in the overall market, not just the crypto market. So, for example, if you notice that the financial technology (fintech) sector is heading higher in equities and that everyone is talking about artificial intelligence (AI), you may want to consider browsing through the AI category and finding cryptocurrencies that are involved with it.

Another way to pick the best categories for medium-term investments is to choose from categories that are already outperforming the overall market. I'm not talking about a category that did well just today but rather something that either has been doing well for a few months or even years or is showing signs of picking up. You can pick the hottest category as your top pick and then add on the second and third ones for diversification purposes. I talk more about diversification in Chapter 10.

For more-up-to-date information on hottest cryptocurrency categories, consider joining the Premium Investment group at `https://learn.investdiva.com/join-group`.

REMEMBER

The cryptocurrency categories may not always follow the rest of the market. Because cryptocurrency is a very new industry to begin with, you may find opportunities in it that you may not necessarily find in the more traditional equities market. Heck, the crypto industry may turn into the safety net if the stock market crashes.

TIP

Exchange traded funds (ETFs) normally consist of a basket of a number of assets in the same category. They're super popular in the equities market because they make the choosing process much easier. They're also cheaper to purchase than their big, fancy hedge-fund equivalents, mutual funds. At the time of writing, cryptocurrency ETFs aren't really a thing yet. After cryptocurrency ETFs become popular, you can view and compare their charts to identify best-performing crypto categories. You can find out more about ETFs in Chapter 13 and at https://www.investdiva.com/investing-guide/category/etf-trading/.

Check out cryptos' websites

Whether you have a number of cryptocurrencies in mind based on your own experience or you've picked a category and now want to choose the best crypto within that sector, you must now start a more detailed analysis on your finalists.

If you've ever watched *The Bachelor* or *The Bachelorette* on TV (guilty as charged — I'm addicted), you're probably already familiar with the process. You start out with around 30 potential matches for your portfolio. By the time you're down to the three or four finalists, you're ready to see what their worlds are all about. In the cryptocurrency world, the company's website is the equivalent of the TV hometown dates. Here are a few ideas to consider when you're picking your crypto sweethearts that don't involve visiting their high schools and getting a grilling from their families.

Flip through their white papers

A *white paper* is something like a business proposal for new cryptocurrencies. It includes everything potential investors need to know about the crypto, such as technology, purpose, financial details, and so on. More-established cryptocurrencies may already have a page that breaks down all this critical information into easy-to-understand video clips and cool infographics on tabs titled "About" or "How It Works." For others, you may just need to find the white paper on the website and try to digest the information by reading. The good news is that white papers are often written in a language that people who aren't experts in the field can understand.

Identify their teams

No one really knows who created Bitcoin, but the rest of the cryptocurrencies out there normally have a team behind them who guide the company and its blockchain technology (see Chapter 4). The team behind the crypto is important even if its platform is completely open source, which means anyone can access and modify it.

REMEMBER

When you invest in anything, whether it's stocks, a new start-up, or a hot date, understanding the background and how it came to life can play a major role. Here are some things to look for in the management:

- >> Bios
- >> Resumes
- >> Experience in the field

In addition to the core management, I also like to check the backgrounds of the members of the board of advisors if the company has it. You normally can find such information on the company's website, under tabs labeled things like "About Us" or "Our Team."

TIP

When you invest in a cryptocurrency, you're essentially investing in a start-up company and an entrepreneur. Sometimes these entrepreneurs are young with no qualifying resume, just like Facebook's Mark Zuckerberg or Ethereum founder Vitalik Buterin. That's when the creator's personality can become a factor in your decision making. As Mark Cuban (*Shark Tank* investor and Dallas Mavericks owner) told CNBC, "When you invest in an entrepreneur, you get the personality. And if that's not appropriate or you don't think it's right, buy another stock" (or in this case, crypto).

Browse their partnerships

If you're not willing to take a lot of risk, seeing who in the industry has put their trust in the hands of the cryptocurrency you're considering buying is very important. More established cryptocurrencies have been able to team up with traditional giants like IBM and Microsoft and banks like Goldman Sachs. These companies have expert analytic teams perform due diligence before jumping on board with new investments and partnerships. Having reputable partners can be a sign that the company is solid and on the right track to get ahead of the competition.

Another good thing about having partners in the traditional world is that the cryptocurrency may have a higher chance of getting accepted by the masses. If a cryptocurrency has established partnerships with other companies, they are normally listed under a tab named "Our Partners" or "About Us."

Familiarize yourself with their technology

Many cryptocurrencies are tokens from blockchain companies with multiple products. Well-developed websites walk you through their technology and their products in a not-so-intimidating way. The more you get to know the products and the technology behind the cryptocurrency, the easier you can make your decision about the finalists on your cryptocurrency list. Chapter 5 can be your go-to "cryptionary" along the way.

Check out their contribution to society

What problems are your shortlist cryptocurrencies trying to solve? Does it matter to you? Are they just here to get rich quick, or do they have a long-term plan for the betterment of society? Finding an answer to these questions can also help you narrow down your list of finalists. Companies like Ripple describe their social contributions under a subtab called "Ripple for Good." Other companies often use a similar format or simply put their core social contributions first thing on their home page.

Analyze their road maps

Many companies behind cryptocurrencies have sections on their websites dedicated to their road maps: where they come from, what they've achieved, and what they're planning to accomplish in the future. If available, road maps are a great way to discover a ton of fundamental information about the crypto in a few minutes.

Get involved

Here's your lucky seven! Just like dating, the more you get involved, the more you get to know about the dirty secrets. The majority of cryptocurrency platforms love to increase their followings and encourage people to get involved right there on their websites. Depending on the cryptocurrency, getting involved can mean anything from mining (see Chapter 12) to joining its social forums or even starting a new cryptocurrency project on its blockchain platform (like Ethereum)! Of course, getting involved also means investing more of your time, so you need to find a balance there.

Choosing Cryptos with Sentimental Analysis

After you've done the essential background check on your prospective cryptocurrencies, you can move on to the second point of IDDA, sentimental analysis. *Sentimental analysis* is the study of the love-hate relationship with cryptocurrencies and traders.

Key sentimental elements

Without getting too sentimental, here are some essential elements to check before setting your heart on your favorite cryptocurrencies.

The crypto community

The company behind the cryptocurrency can play a role in the direction the crypto goes, but the network that participates in the currency's blockchain technology (see Chapter 4) is an important key to its success. Many cryptocurrencies directly depend on the participation of their communities, like miners and developers. Most of the crypto communities have their own forums on places such as the following:

>> Reddit (www.reddit.com/)

>> Bitcointalk (https://bitcointalk.org/)

>> Steemit (https://steemit.com/)

These forums are great not only because they give you a sense of what type of people are involved in the cryptocurrency but also because you can find out more about the cryptocurrency itself.

TIP

More and more cryptocurrencies use their Telegram channel as a way to communicate with their userbase. To join, you must download the Telegram app on your mobile phone (see https://telegram.org/ for more information).

Exchanges that carry the crypto

REMEMBER

As I discuss in Chapter 6, cryptocurrency exchanges are a big part of the whole ecosystem. You want to make sure your cryptocurrency exchange carries your cryptos of choice, but choosing cryptos that are listed on many different exchanges is also a good idea. Exchanges choose the cryptocurrencies they carry carefully. Finding your finalists on many different exchanges may be a sign that many exchanges have found that crypto to be valuable enough to carry. Therefore, the demand for it may be higher, and you may be able to do more with your investment. You can discover which exchanges carry your crypto of choice on websites such as coinmarketcap.com.

For example, say you want to know which exchanges carry Ripple's XRP. After selecting Ripple's XRP on coinmarketcap.com, go the tab labeled "Markets," as shown in Figure 9-2; you may need to scroll down the webpage a bit to find it. There you can view the full list of exchanges that carry XRP.

Volume

TIP

Volume means how much cryptocurrency got traded in a specific time frame. It's important because it tells you how easily you can buy or sell that cryptocurrency. The higher the volume, the more easily you can trade it off. You can check and compare cryptocurrency volume on websites such as www.cryptocompare.com and coinmarketcap.com, where they show the number of coins that have been traded in the last 24 hours. You can also examine which exchanges had what volume. Generally, the biggest and most popular coins are traded the most. But if you're trying to choose a cryptocurrency within a specific category (and not simply going for the celebrity cryptos), trading volume can be a very important indicator in making your decision.

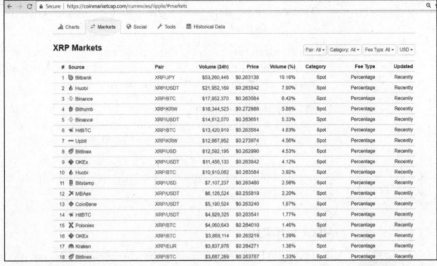

FIGURE 9-2:
Locating exchanges that carry XRP on coinmarketcap. com.

Coin market capitalization

One of the fastest ways to navigate through cryptocurrencies is to check out their ranking based on their *market capitalization,* or *market cap.* A bigger market cap shows a higher value of all units of a specific cryptocurrency that are for sale right now. This metric can again come handy when you're trying to select "the one" within a specific category of cryptos. For more on market capitalization analysis, flip to Chapter 8.

Circulating supply

Circulating supply (CS) is the number of coins or tokens that people have mined or that companies have generated. The key is that the circulating supply number shows you how many of these coins are currently in the market and that the general public has access to.

You can look at the importance of the CS in a couple of different ways:

>> Some crypto investors believe less is more in terms of the CS. That's if you look at it as an oversupply issue. Any market generally moves based on a principle called *supply and demand.* For example, when stores have a lot of

apples and not enough people to buy them, they drop their apple prices because they want to get rid of their stock before it goes bad. The same theory can apply to cryptocurrencies. Although most coins don't have an expiration date (unless the company goes bankrupt, that is), a smaller CS may be more attractive if you're looking to invest short-term to medium-term. Fewer coins available and a higher demand may signal that the prices may go higher in the future.

» On the other hand, a lower CS number may indicate a lack of popularity. Fewer people have put in the effort to mine the coin, which may impact the long-term forecast of the cryptocurrency.

» In some cases, the CS may not even matter. For example, Ripple's XRP has a circulation supply of almost 40 billion, while Dash has a CS of only 8 million. Meanwhile, they both gained around 3,000 percent in 2017!

You can find out about cryptocurrencies' circulating supply on websites such as coinmarketcap.com.

Total supply

TECHNICAL STUFF

When you add the newly mined cryptocurrencies to the circulating supply (see the preceding section), you get the *total supply* number. In other words, total supply is the total number of coins currently in existence, not just those circulating. For several reasons, some coins are reserved or locked and aren't sold in the public market. Total supply doesn't really impact a coin's price and isn't more important than the circulating supply. I just threw it out here in case you come across it on a website and wonder what it is.

Stuff to check in the news

The news has the power to make someone or something so incredibly popular. Take reality stars, that whole Yanny/Laurel thing, or the floss dance that became popular thanks to the Instagram sensation @thebackpackkid.

The same thing goes for cryptocurrencies. The media was behind the whole cryptocurrency hype and bullish market sentiment of 2017. Just like you may do a quick cyber check about your potential date before agreeing to meet, you may want to consider looking into the following about your finalist coins.

Recent coverage

TIP

Has your finalist been in the news a lot lately? Is it a hot topic? If the answer is yes, find out whether the news coverage is organic or paid. Of course, crypto companies are aware of the impact of the media, so they pay a ton of money to popular search engines to bring them right up on top of the search results ranking system. Some trustworthy crypto news providers include NewsBTC (www.newsbtc.com), Nasdaq (https://www.nasdaq.com/topic/cryptocurrency), CoinDesk (www.coindesk.com), and of course, www.investdiva.com/investing-guide/category/cryptocurrencies/.

Another way you can approach this task is to simply go to the "News" tab on your search engine. When you search a topic on Google, for example, you're automatically directed to the "All" tab, which includes everything, from advertisements to news and general information. Find the "News" tab, and you'll get the relevant news coverage that's less likely to be paid ads.

Upcoming events

TIP

You can look for upcoming events in the early stages of finding your crypto soul mate or right at the very end:

>> For the first method, you can check out websites such as https://coinmarketcal.com/ and www.newsbtc.com/crypto-calendar/ and see which cryptos have a busy lineup of announcements and events that may impact the crypto in a positive way. Then take the other approaches I talk about earlier in this chapter to see whether that crypto is right for your portfolio.

>> For the second method, compile the list of your finalists, and then you can either check the cryptocurrency's website to see whether it has a blog where it shares its upcoming events or check out the third-party crypto calendars for additional information.

Of course, you can also combine both approaches.

Negative press

Public Relations 101 says any press is good press. The reason for that is that people tend to enjoy reading about negative stuff more. Then they get passionate about it and are more likely to remember the entity associated with the bad press in the future — but not necessarily in a bad way anymore. That certainly is the mentality of some celebrities, who believe any coverage of them, good or bad, will bring them positive outcomes in the long run.

And it certainly can be true in cryptocurrency investing as well. During the period when the negative press is a hot topic, the prices are likely to plummet. However, contrary to what you may think, that exact period may be a good time to purchase because everyone is likely dumping the asset. Catch them when they're down, and go to the top with them. A perfect romantic fairy tale, eh?

WARNING

Buying during negative press works only if all the other IDDA analysis points indicate the cryptocurrency is worthwhile long-term. If the negative press consists of something ultra-damaging that the crypto is unlikely to recover from, then go ahead and pass.

Trying Technical Analysis to Select Cryptos

When you've got your heart set on a few cryptocurrencies to add to your portfolio, you're ready to decide the best time to buy them. The golden rule to any type of investment comes down to four important words:

"Buy low, sell high."

REMEMBER

But how can you decide when the price is at its lowest point to buy? That's where technical analysis, the third point of IDDA, comes in. *Technical analysis* is the art of using history to predict the future. Read on here for a brief introduction to price action and the best price analysis methods. Part 4 is where I dive deeper into technical analysis.

>> **Technical analysis basics:** So many fabulous tools and gadgets can help you understand the historical movements and patterns of a cryptocurrency's price. By discovering how each pattern and indicator works, you can have a higher accuracy in predicting future price actions. Flip to Chapter 16 to explore some of the most important chart patterns and indicators that can help you develop your winning investment strategy for your favorite cryptocurrency.

>> **Recent price action:** Although the current price of one coin isn't a very good indicator of a cryptocurrency's overall value, analyzing the price action becomes *very* important when you're trying to figure out when to buy and sell. You can check the most recent price action of your selected cryptocurrency on websites such as coinmarketcap.com to see how much the price has dropped or surged in the past day, week, or even months. Analyzing recent price action is more important for short-term traders who are looking to get in and out of the market more rapidly, say within a day or a week. Chapter 17 has more on short-term trading strategies.

>> **Big picture:** If you're a long-term investor like I am, you may find looking at the big picture more useful in your technical analysis. Many cryptocurrencies are too young to have a well-developed price history, but you still can use similar techniques by comparing older cryptocurrencies in the same category and applying big-picture analysis to the new ones. In Chapter 18, I discuss technical analysis methods for long-term investors.

Chapter **10**

Diversification in Cryptocurrencies

talk a lot about diversification throughout this book, specifically in Chapters 3, 8, and 9, and in my education products and seminar. In this chapter I get to the bottom of what diversification means for your crypto portfolio, why it's important, and how you can manage your portfolio's risk by properly diversifying your assets.

Breaking Down Some Basics on Diversification

Small investors regularly hear about the topic of diversification for their personal stock portfolio. One of the first things a financial expert tells you when you want to get started with investing is "don't forget to diversify!" You don't want to put all your eggs in one basket, regardless of whether that basket is stocks or cryptos. The following sections dig into what that really means, especially for cryptocurrency investing.

What is traditional diversification?

When you're building your personal stock portfolio, *diversification* often means having more than one or two stocks. The most conventional diversification method in a personal stock portfolio is to have around 15 to 20 stocks that are spread across different industries.

REMEMBER

When you diversify among industries, assets, or investment instruments that aren't correlated, you're less likely to see major drops in your portfolio when one of the categories is doing poorly. Diversification doesn't guarantee you have no risk of losses, though. It just reduces that risk if done correctly.

TIP

Websites such as `https://pro.benzinga.com/?afmc=2f` can help you be in the know about the most recent developments across different industries so that you can make better diversification decisions.

How does diversification reduce risk?

You encounter two types of risk in a stock portfolio: unsystematic and systematic. *Unsystematic risk* is the type of risk that you can mitigate by combining multiple industries into one portfolio. Unsystematic risk includes the following:

» **Business risk:** This risk is associated with a company's earnings and its ability to meet its financial obligations. This risk is also tied to the company's industry, as sometimes all the businesses within a category are exposed to a similar degree of uncertainty.

» **Country risk:** This is the risk of political and economic instability in the country where the company does business.

» **Default risk:** This is the risk that a company isn't able to repay its debt and therefore is subject to default.

» **Executive risk:** This risk is associated with the moral character of the executives who run the company. If they get into legal or ethical trouble, the company's stock may suffer both short term and long term.

» **Financial risk:** This risk is associated with the amount of leverage (a measure of the amount of debt) a company uses in its financial structure. The more debt the company has, the more leverage it's using, and therefore the higher the risk.

>> **Government/regulation risk:** This is the risk that a country may pass a new law or regulation that negatively impacts the industry that a company is in.

Systematic risk you can't get rid of simply by diversifying across various industries. That risk category includes

>> **Market risk:** The risk that the market moves against your position due to various reasons, such as political reasons, social reasons, or general change in market sentiment

>> **Exchange rate risk:** The risk that the exchange rate goes higher or its movements negatively impact your investments

>> **Interest rate risk:** The chance that changes in interest rates adversely affect the asset's value

>> **Political instability risk:** The risk that political uncertainties or changes negatively impact the market

>> **Reinvestment risk:** The chance that you won't be able to reinvest your funds at a favorable rate of return

>> **Event risk:** The chance of something unpredictable (like bankruptcy and hacker attacks) happening to the company/exchange/broker/wallet that holds your asset, therefore contributing to negative market fluctuation

Traditional diversification in a stock portfolio helps reduce unsystematic risk. This is when things get interesting. You can't diversify away systematic risk within your stock portfolio, but how about diversifying across other markets? This approach is actually how I got into investing in the first place during the crash of 2008. (You can read about the details in the nearby sidebar "My foray into forex.")

REMEMBER

As we get closer to the next inevitable stock market crash, I think adding unconventional investment instruments such as cryptocurrencies to your portfolio is more important than ever. Here's why: At the time of writing, the cryptocurrency market couldn't be more different from the traditional markets. It's new. It's unregulated, and therefore traditional systematic risks such as political instability or interest rate risks don't really apply to it. In fact, investors may well see cryptocurrencies as a safety net for when things go south in other markets during a major economic crisis.

Using Cryptocurrencies in Long-Term Diversification

When it comes to adding cryptocurrencies to your portfolio, keep the following two types of long-term diversification in mind:

>> Diversifying with non-cryptocurrencies

>> Diversifying among cryptocurrencies

Here's a bit more about these two types of crypto diversification. (I talk more about diversification from traditional markets such as stocks, bonds, and forex in Chapter 2.)

TIP

For more information on many of the topics in this section, check out these Invest Diva resources:

>> The *Forex Coffee Break* education course at `https://education.investdiva.com/forex-coffee-break-with-invest-diva-education-course`

>> My book *Invest Diva's Guide to Making Money in Forex* (McGraw-Hill Education)

>> Other service listings at `https://learn.investdiva.com/services`

Diversifying with non-cryptocurrencies

You have so many financial instruments to choose from when you consider diversifying your portfolio across the board. Stocks, forex, precious metals, and bonds are just a few examples. As I explain in Chapter 2, each of these assets has its unique traits. Some assets' inherited risks can offset the risks of the other ones through long-term market ups and downs. The following sections provide guidance on how to use cryptos and non-cryptos together in the long term.

REMEMBER

No single golden diversification rule works for all investors. Diversification percentages and the overall mix greatly depend on the individual investor and his or her unique risk tolerance, as I talk about in the sidebar in Chapter 3 and on my website (`https://learn.investdiva.com/free-webinar-3-secrets-to-making-your-money-work-for-you`).

TIP

The more risk you're willing to take, the higher the chances of a bigger return on investment, and vice versa. If you're just starting out and have a lower risk tolerance, you may consider allocating a bigger portion of your portfolio to bonds and then systematically adding stocks, precious metals, and cryptocurrencies. For tips on calculating your unique risk tolerance, check out the sidebar in Chapter 3.

Some background on trading fiat currencies

Fiat currencies are the traditional money that different countries' authorities declare legal. For example, the U.S. dollar is the official currency of the United States. The euro is the official currency of the European Union and its territories. The Japanese yen is backed by Japan. You get the idea.

The *foreign exchange market,* or *forex,* is a huge market where traders trade these fiat currencies against one another. Having a bit of a background in forex can help you better understand the cryptocurrency market and how you can trade the different types of currencies against one another. I compare this market to a big international party where all the couples are made up of partners from different regions. So if one is the Japanese yen (JPY), her partner may be the euro (EUR). I call them Ms. Japan and Mr. Euro. If one is the U.S. dollar (Ms. USA), her partner can be British, Portuguese, or Japanese.

In the forex market, these international pairs get together and start "dancing." But oftentimes, the paired-up partners aren't compatible, and their moves aren't correlated. For example, every time Ms. USA makes a good move, her partner screws up. Every time her partner picks up the rhythm, she's stuck in her previous move. These incompatibilities gain some attention, and a bunch of people who are watching the dancers start betting on which of the partners is going to screw up next. Those folks are the forex traders. You can watch this forex metaphor in action in my video here: `https://www.youtube.com/watch?v=abQuHfjaGug&list=PLt3BW8jrlMZvmObHLMjpVySPmex987wyC&index=1`

REMEMBER

The point is that when trading currencies — fiat or crypto — you can only trade them in pairs. For example, you can trade the U.S. dollar (USD) versus the Japanese yen (JPY); this is the USD/JPY pair. You can trade the Australian dollar (AUD) versus the Canadian dollar (CAD); that's the AUD/CAD pair.

Quote currency versus base currency

When trading currency pairs, the *base currency* is listed first, and the *quote currency* is listed second. Which currency in a given pair is the base currency and which is the quote currency is normally fixed across the trading markets. For example, when talking about trading the U.S. dollar versus the Japanese yen, the currency of the United States always comes first, followed by the currency of Japan (USD/JPY). In the EUR/USD pair, the euro always comes first, followed by the U.S. dollar.

REMEMBER

These set patterns have nothing to do with whether a certain currency's country is more important or whether one currency in a pair is more popular than the other. It's just how the trading crowd set things up. The system doesn't change, which means everyone is on the same page and navigating through the pairs is easier.

As the base and quote come together, the currency pair shows how much of the quote currency is needed to purchase one unit of the base currency. For example, when USD/JPY is trading at 100, that means 1 U.S. dollar is valued at 100 Japanese yen. In other words, you need 100 Japanese yen (the quote currency) to buy 1 U.S. dollar (the base currency).

The same concept applies to cryptocurrency pairs. Many cryptocurrency exchanges offer a select number of quote currencies, mainly popular ones such as a fiat like the USD and cryptos such as Bitcoin, Ethereum, and their own exchange cryptos. Then they offer trading opportunities versus all the hundreds of other cryptocurrencies they may carry versus these quote currencies. I talk more about this topic the later section "Cross-crypto trading."

Trading cryptos versus fiat currencies

Similar to the forex market, you can trade cryptocurrencies versus other currencies. The most common approach at the time of writing is trading them versus a fiat currency, typically the one backed by the country you live in. For example, in the United States, most people trade Bitcoin versus the USD. They don't really think of it of trading these currencies in pairs because it feels a lot like buying a stock. But the fact is that when you buy Bitcoin using the U.S. dollar in hopes of capital gain, you're essentially betting that the value of Bitcoin will move higher against the U.S. dollar in the future. That's why if the U.S. dollar decreases in value (not only against Bitcoin but also against other currencies) at the same time that Bitcoin increases in value, you're likely to make more return on your investment.

This is where diversification can help you reduce your trading risk. As I explain in the later section "Diversifying among cryptocurrencies," most cryptos are correlated to Bitcoin in shorter time frames. That's why you can diversify your portfolio with the fiat currencies you trade them against. For example, if you think that at the time you're trading, the U.S. dollar and the Japanese yen aren't correlated, you can open up two Bitcoin trades: one versus the U.S. dollar and one versus the Japanese yen. Of course, in order to do so, you should make sure your exchange or broker carries these different fiat currencies and offers such trading opportunities.

WARNING

Speculating the markets and short-term trading carry a lot of risk. It may not be suitable for all investors, and you may end up losing all your investment. Before deciding to trade such assets, you should carefully consider your investment objectives, level of experience, risk tolerance, and risk appetite. Also, you should *not* invest money that you can't afford to lose. (If you're still curious, I delve more into short-term trades later in this chapter and in Chapter 17.)

Diversifying among cryptocurrencies

The majority of cryptocurrency exchanges offer a wider selection of cross-crypto pairs than they do fiat/crypto pairs. In fact, some exchanges don't even accept any type of fiat currencies altogether. That's why many traders have no choice but to trade one cryptocurrency against another. Bitcoin (BTC) versus Ethereum (ETH) gives you the BTC/ETH pair, for example.

As you can imagine, the thousands of different cryptocurrencies available to trade mean the mixes and matches can be endless. Many cryptocurrency exchanges have categorized these mixes by creating different "rooms" where you can trade the majority of the cryptos they carry versus a number of more popular cryptos. For example, as you can see in Figure 10-1, the Binance exchange has created four rooms or categories for the main cross-cryptos: Bitcoin (BTC), Ethereum (ETH),

Binance Coin (BNB), and Tether (USDT). By clicking on each of these categories, you can trade other cryptos versus the selected quote currency that I talk about earlier in this chapter.

Pair ▲	Price	Change
★ ADA/BTC	0.00001490	-5.10%
★ ADX/BTC	0.00002809	-1.89%
★ AE/BTC	0.0001597	-6.99%
★ AGI/BTC	0.00000659	-9.23%
★ AION/BTC	0.0000731	-9.98%
★ AMB/BTC	0.00001947	-8.07%
★ APPC/BTC	0.00001257	-6.26%
★ ARDR/BTC	0.00001675	-4.07%
★ ARK/BTC	0.0001045	-2.06%
★ ARN/BTC	0.00004063	-5.31%
★ AST/BTC	0.00001255	-3.83%
★ BAT/BTC	0.00003133	-7.09%
★ BCC/BTC	0.082501	-6.40%
★ BCD/BTC	0.001515	-4.96%

★ Favorites | BTC | ETH | BNB | USDT
🔍 Search ... | ◉ Change | ○ Volume

FIGURE 10-1: Binance exchange cryptocurrency pairing options.

Source: Binance.com

TIP

When trading currency pairs, fiat or crypto, the best bet is always to pair a strong base currency versus a weak quote currency and vice versa. This way, you maximize the chances of that pair moving strongly in the direction you're aiming for.

As I talk about earlier in this chapter, the reason you diversify your portfolio is to reduce its exposure to risk by including assets that aren't fully correlated. The big problem about diversifying within your cryptocurrency portfolio is that, at least at the time of writing, most cryptocurrencies are heavily correlated to Bitcoin. Most of the days where Bitcoin was having a bad day in 2017 and 2018, the majority of other cryptocurrencies were, too. Figure 10-2, for example, shows a snapshot of the top 12 cryptocurrencies on August 18, 2018. All are in red. In fact, 94 out of the top 100 cryptocurrencies by market cap were plummeting that day. (*Market cap* shows the value of all units of a crypto that are for sale right now; head to Chapter 8 for more on this topic.) In the crypto market, this type of short-term market correlation has become the norm.

August 19, the very next day, Bitcoin turned green, and so did the majority of the cryptos in the top 100, as you can see in Figure 10-3. In this snapshot of the top 17 cryptocurrencies, all tokens besides Tether (USDT) surged about the same amount Bitcoin did, around 1.72 percent.

Cryptocurrencies ▾	Exchanges ▾	Watchlist					USD ▾ Next 100 → View All
#	Name	Market Cap	Price	Volume (24h)	Circulating Supply	Change (24h)	Price Graph (7d)
1	Bitcoin	$110,649,855,082	$6,426.55	$4,110,066,955	17,217,625 BTC	-1.73%	•••
2	Ethereum	$30,275,253,926	$298.55	$1,815,655,842	101,409,291 ETH	-3.57%	•••
3	XRP	$13,067,008,532	$0.331882	$500,290,020	39,372,399,467 XRP *	-6.18%	•••
4	Bitcoin Cash	$9,727,259,913	$562.26	$438,690,267	17,300,163 BCH	-1.91%	•••
5	EOS	$4,681,414,609	$5.17	$864,785,525	906,245,118 EOS *	-4.09%	•••
6	Stellar	$4,271,146,076	$0.227530	$79,898,204	18,771,755,700 XLM *	-2.51%	•••
7	Litecoin	$3,313,730,889	$57.23	$253,969,516	57,903,334 LTC	-4.81%	•••
8	Tether	$2,719,405,730	$0.998995	$3,350,590,344	2,722,140,336 USDT *	-0.10%	•••
9	Cardano	$2,631,037,998	$0.101478	$107,934,610	25,927,070,538 ADA *	-5.37%	•••
10	Monero	$1,596,232,879	$97.75	$33,423,127	16,329,214 XMR	-0.48%	•••
11	TRON	$1,439,869,868	$0.021900	$146,381,621	65,748,111,645 TRX *	-3.83%	•••
12	Ethereum Classic	$1,393,191,044	$13.41	$298,225,866	103,884,149 ETC	-6.22%	•••

FIGURE 10-2: Correlation between the top 12 cryptocurrencies and Bitcoin as BTC drops.

Source: CoinMarketCap.com

Cryptocurrencies ▾	Exchanges ▾	Watchlist						USD ▾ ← Back to Top 100
#	Name	Symbol	Market Cap	Price	Circulating Supply	Volume (24h)	% 1h	% 24h	% 7d
1	Bitcoin	BTC	$112,236,198,598	$6,517.98	17,219,487	$3,313,453,845	1.71%	1.72%	2.86%	•••
2	Ethereum	ETH	$30,846,261,019	$302.14	101,429,296	$1,454,877,279	1.35%	2.93%	-6.14%	•••
3	XRP	XRP	$13,731,051,598	$0.348748	39,372,399,467 *	$332,539,987	2.20%	7.12%	15.86%	•••
4	Bitcoin Cash	BCH	$9,845,137,274	$569.02	17,301,888	$371,039,772	1.61%	2.55%	-0.85%	•••
5	EOS	EOS	$4,829,548,557	$5.33	906,245,118 *	$826,193,474	2.51%	5.35%	5.44%	•••
6	Stellar	XLM	$4,333,386,117	$0.230846	18,771,755,850 *	$61,335,714	3.63%	2.41%	3.77%	•••
7	Litecoin	LTC	$3,372,794,706	$58.23	57,917,023	$205,830,556	1.90%	2.84%	-2.25%	•••
8	Tether	USDT	$2,715,888,857	$0.997703	2,722,140,336 *	$2,617,530,199	-0.32%	-0.54%	-0.41%	•••
9	Cardano	ADA	$2,675,764,489	$0.103204	25,927,070,538 *	$53,269,411	2.25%	2.95%	-8.70%	•••
10	Monero	XMR	$1,604,253,760	$98.23	16,331,966	$17,505,936	1.52%	1.36%	4.94%	•••
11	IOTA	MIOTA	$1,539,626,433	$0.553916	2,779,530,283 *	$47,593,558	2.58%	13.79%	2.39%	•••
12	TRON	TRX	$1,465,481,396	$0.022289	65,748,111,645 *	$98,160,769	2.05%	4.41%	-1.85%	•••
13	Ethereum Classic	ETC	$1,403,395,647	$13.51	103,907,893	$195,425,979	1.28%	2.42%	1.44%	•••
14	Dash	DASH	$1,289,364,836	$155.97	8,266,740	$245,592,938	0.20%	3.75%	-7.19%	•••
15	NEO	NEO	$1,271,796,082	$19.57	65,000,000 *	$72,961,966	1.94%	6.25%	4.94%	•••
16	NEM	XEM	$974,044,126	$0.108227	8,999,999,999 *	$10,775,110	1.77%	2.41%	-0.05%	•••
17	Binance Coin	BNB	$968,626,021	$10.14	95,512,523 *	$20,230,185	1.72%	2.91%	-13.33%	•••

FIGURE 10-3: Correlation between the top 17 cryptocurrencies and Bitcoin as BTC surges.

Source: CoinMarketCap.com

On the other hand, if you look at the bigger picture, say the seven-day price change, you notice that the market correlation to Bitcoin is more mixed, as shown in Figure 10-4. For example, while Bitcoin gained 1.25 percent in the seven days before August 18, Ripple's XRP gained 8.51 percent, and Dash lost 9.79 percent.

Cryptocurrencies ▾	Exchanges ▾	Watchlist						USD ▾	← Back to Top 100	
#	Name	Symbol	Market Cap	Price	Circulating Supply	Volume (24h)	% 1h	% 24h	% 7d	
1	ⓑ Bitcoin	BTC	$110,736,482,332	$6,431.58	17,217,625	$4,111,810,813	0.58%	-1.69%	1.25%	•••
2	♦ Ethereum	ETH	$30,312,762,760	$298.92	101,409,291	$1,818,755,064	2.74%	-3.45%	-7.42%	•••
3	✕ XRP	XRP	$13,058,424,828	$0.331664	39,372,399,467 *	$499,677,279	1.92%	-6.41%	8.51%	•••
4	Ⓑ Bitcoin Cash	BCH	$9,739,156,000	$562.95	17,300,163	$438,840,268	2.07%	-1.79%	-1.33%	•••
5	ⓔ EOS	EOS	$4,668,751,666	$5.15	906,245,118 *	$863,755,878	2.42%	-4.48%	0.53%	•••
6	⚡ Stellar	XLM	$4,268,885,433	$0.227410	18,771,755,700 *	$79,814,068	1.26%	-2.68%	3.35%	•••
7	Ⓛ Litecoin	LTC	$3,313,806,803	$57.23	57,903,334	$253,654,509	1.40%	-4.90%	-2.59%	•••
8	ⓣ Tether	USDT	$2,724,937,528	$1.00	2,722,140,336 *	$3,355,187,045	-0.15%	0.12%	-0.20%	•••
9	ⓐ Cardano	ADA	$2,630,299,721	$0.101450	25,927,070,538 *	$107,974,564	0.86%	-5.51%	-10.62%	•••
10	ⓜ Monero	XMR	$1,596,412,015	$97.76	16,329,214	$33,408,728	1.43%	-0.52%	3.43%	•••
11	ⓣ TRON	TRX	$1,438,597,367	$0.021880	65,748,111,645 *	$146,225,110	3.17%	-3.91%	-5.39%	•••
12	Ⓔ Ethereum Classic	ETC	$1,391,586,196	$13.40	103,884,149	$297,763,972	2.54%	-6.39%	0.20%	•••
13	ⓘ IOTA	MIOTA	$1,381,908,847	$0.497174	2,779,530,283 *	$47,610,739	2.99%	-8.27%	-7.14%	•••
14	ⓓ Dash	DASH	$1,249,230,719	$151.15	8,264,930	$164,713,102	1.36%	-6.96%	-9.79%	•••
15	ⓝ NEO	NEO	$1,245,268,169	$19.16	65,000,000 *	$89,028,728	5.62%	-4.25%	1.32%	•••
16	ⓝ NEM	XEM	$959,252,944	$0.106584	8,999,999,999 *	$17,941,269	1.55%	-6.91%	-1.33%	•••
17	◈ Binance Coin	BNB	$951,601,420	$9.96	95,512,523 *	$30,765,186	1.14%	-5.42%	-15.00%	•••

FIGURE 10-4: The top 17 cryptocurrencies are less correlated in the seven-day time frame.

Source: CoinMarketCap.com

REMEMBER

This correlation is one key reason short-term trading cryptocurrencies is riskier than many other financial instruments. Considering long-term investments when adding cryptocurrencies to your portfolio may be best. That way, you can reduce your investment risk by diversifying within different crypto categories.

On the bright side, as the cryptocurrency market continues to develop, the diversification methods can also improve, and the whole market may become less correlated to Bitcoin.

Tackling Diversification in Short-Term Trades

If you've calculated your risk tolerance based on the information in Chapter 3 and the results are pretty aggressive, you may want to consider trading cryptocurrencies in shorter time frames. Here are some suggestions to keep in mind. To read more about developing short-term strategies, flip to Chapter 17.

WARNING

>> **Beware of commissions.** Cryptocurrency trading exchanges generally require lower commission and transaction fees than brokers who offer forex or stocks. But you shouldn't completely ignore the commission cost to your wallet. When day trading, you may end up paying more in commission than what you're actually making by trading if you trade way too often, getting in and out of trades way too fast without calculating your returns! Also, as I talk about in Chapter 6, cheaper isn't always the best option when choosing an exchange. You always get what you pay for.

TIP

>> **Keep expanding your portfolio.** Some people invest a lump sum in their investment portfolios and then either wipe it out in dangerous day-trading actions or get stuck in a strategy that's working but isn't maximizing their returns. A healthy portfolio requires nourishment. Consider leaving a monthly investment fund aside out of your paycheck in order to expand your portfolio and make your money work for you.

>> **Observe the rule of three.** You have a ton of options when trading currencies. You can mix and match crypto/crypto and fiat/crypto pairs like there's no tomorrow if your account size lets you. However, the key in having a healthy diversified portfolio is to avoid double-dipping the same quote currency in your trades. Try to limit your open short-term positions against each quote currency to three. For example, trade one crypto versus Bitcoin, another versus Ethereum, and a third versus your exchange's cryptocurrency. This approach also helps you keep your portfolio at a reasonable size so it's not too big to monitor.

3
Alternatives to Cryptos

Understand how new cryptocurrencies are funded and how you can profit from getting involved in initial coin offerings (ICOs).

Dig into cryptocurrency mining and find out whether it's a better alternative for you than straight up buying and investing is.

Discover how to get indirect exposure to the cryptocurrency and blockchain industries by investing in traditional assets like stocks and exchange traded funds (ETFs).

Find out the basics of cryptocurrency futures and options.

See how cryptocurrencies are related to government-based currencies and the foreign exchange (forex) market.

Chapter **11**

Getting Ahead of the Crowd: Investing in ICOs

CO is short for initial coin offering. In an age where ICOs aren't subject to many regulations, some would call them the easiest path to scams. And though a ton (and I mean a *ton!*) of ICO scams are out there, if you do your homework, you may be able to catch a few diamonds in the rough as well. In this chapter, I explain ICO basics and show how you can get involved.

Understanding the Basics of Initial Coin Offerings

Initial coin offerings are something like fundraising for a new start-up, except that your new idea revolves around a new cryptocurrency rather than a business idea or product. You're trying to raise "money" in the form of other, already established cryptocurrencies such as Bitcoin and Ethereum. In other words, an ICO is crowdfunding, using other cryptocurrencies, for a new cryptocurrency that's (hopefully) connected to an awesome product. The following sections provide the basics on ICOs.

How an ICO works and how to start one

REMEMBER

Simply put, an ICO works exactly how start-up fundraising works. You come up with a cool idea for a cryptocurrency. The cryptocurrency may be used for an existing product, or perhaps you have an idea for a product that can work well with a brand-new crypto.

As an example, say a fashion website in New York City showcases display windows in real time. (Okay, this is actually my friend Jon Harari's website, WindowsWear — check out www.windowswear.com. I've been trying to pitch him the ICO idea, but he doesn't really understand how it can work for his business.) But for the sake of argument, say that Jon decides he wants to change his business strategy, make his website available to the masses, and let people shop on his app using WindowsWear's very own digital currency. Call this brand-new crypto WEAR Coin. But unless Jon is a millionaire who wants to spend all his money on this idea, he needs to raise money to make this new cryptocurrency a reality. He can go to a venture capitalist, a bank, or angel investors and ask for money. The problem with that approach is that he'll most likely have to give up part of his ownership of his company. So instead, he can listen to his friend Kiana and go for an ICO.

REMEMBER

Here are the general steps to take to initiate an ICO (see the later section "So You Want to Start an ICO: Launching an ICO Yourself" for more information):

1. **Create a white paper.**

   A *white paper* is a detailed document explaining a business model and the reason a particular coin may really take off. The more use cases Jon has in his white paper for WEAR Coin to show it can actually become a popular and high-volume coin, the better.

2. **Add a tab to your website dedicated to ICO funding.**

   In this example, Jon puts a tab on his WindowsWear site dedicated to WEAR Coin ICO funding.

3. **Spread the word to your connections and ask for funding.**

4. **Sell a quantity of your crowdfunded coin in the form of *tokens*, which means digital assets.**

   Normally ICOs ask for Bitcoin or Ethereum in exchange for the tokens. But you can also accept *fiat* (traditional government-backed) currencies such as the U.S. dollar.

5. **Send the investors coin tokens.**

   In this example, Jon sends his investors WEAR Coin tokens.

If WEAR Coin really hits, starts getting used a lot, and is listed on a ton of crypto exchanges, the early investors can see a significant return on their investments.

WARNING

People who invest in ICOs normally don't have any guarantee that the new cryptocurrency will increase in value in the future. Some ICO investments have been incredibly profitable in the past, but future ICOs may not be. Unless you really trust the management, the company's dedication to success, and its knowledge of the business model and the industry, investing in an ICO is very much comparable to gambling. Flip to the later section "Investing in an ICO" for more details.

ICOs versus IPOs

A lot of people experience a bit of a confusion about the difference between initial coin offerings (ICOs) and initial public offerings (IPOs, which is the first time a company sells its stocks to the public). These concepts sound similar, and in many ways, they are similar. Here are the main differences:

» **In theory, anyone can do an ICO.** At the time of writing, ICOs aren't regulated in many countries. That means literally anyone can launch an ICO. All you need is a white paper, a pretty website, and a ton of rich connections who are willing to give you money. By contrast, only established private companies that have been operating for a while are allowed to carry out IPOs. (See the nearby sidebar "Watching ICOs in the United States" for more information.)

» **You don't even need to have a product to launch an ICO.** Most of the companies that are doing ICOs don't have anything concrete to present to the public; some of them have *proof-of-concept* (which demonstrates the idea is workable), and others have proof-of-stake. Starting an ICO is even easier than starting a crowdfunding for a proper start-up. For start-ups to get funded, they normally need something called *minimum viable product* (MVP), which is a product with enough features to satisfy the early investors and to generate feedback for future developments. In the ICO process, you can reduce the MVP to documents like white papers, partnerships, and media relations.

» **ICOs are easier to invest in — until they're not.** The only thing you need to start investing in ICOs is access to the Internet. You don't need brokers to carry out your investment. At the time of writing, you can buy any tokens of any company in most countries. However, the list of countries that started adding regulations or banning ICOs altogether started to increase in 2018. In the United States, it's even more complicated because the ICO rules vary from state to state.

WARNING

Many ICOs block investments from their country of residence because regulatory bodies consider ICO tokens to be securities. These strict regulations limit the ICO participation only to accredited investors and severely limit the investor pool, making it difficult to participate in ICOs. That being said, people have been found to use a virtual private network (VPN) to bypass the geo-blocking (geographical blocks), thus making it look like they're coming from an authorized country so they can invest anyway and creating a lot of legal issues.

TIP

You can view ICO regulations by country at `www.bitcoinmarketjournal.com/ico-regulations/`.

» **ICOs don't grant you ownership of the project.** When you invest in an IPO, you technically become a partial owner of that company. That's why they call the investors shareholders. This designation doesn't really matter if all you're looking for is to sell the stock as its value rises. ICO investors may benefit in many ways in the future, but they have nothing to do with the company itself. All they're getting are a bunch of digital coins (tokens) that may or may not rise in value in the future.

WATCHING ICOs IN THE UNITED STATES

The Securities and Exchange Commission (SEC) is watching the ICO space in the United States very closely and shuts down most of the ICOs that it thinks pose a huge risk to the public investing. The presale option of the ICO can *only* be open to accredited investors (thus not the general public). The ICO for the public can be problematic if the token is considered a security by the SEC as opposed to a platform token (it's absolutely needed to run the platform). Most ICOs launching new cryptos of Ethereum, for example, can't make the case for a platform token (as there is no new platform that requires its own token), so they fall into the securities category.

Also, for U.S.-based companies launching ICOs, there is a lockout period for investors buying in the presale stages, usually 12 months, in which they can't trade the new crypto they invested in. This is done to prevent a pump-and-dump operation, and it's watched very closely by the SEC.

Companies launching ICOs also have to comply with the U.S. federal KYC and AML regulations, which include not accepting or sending cryptos to a large list of wallet addresses that are on the Financial Crimes Enforcement Network's blacklist as either money laundering operators or terrorism financing.

Investing in an ICO

REMEMBER

ICO investing involves a lot of risk. You shouldn't invest money you can't afford to lose in an ICO. If your risk tolerance is low, you can consider many alternative investment assets, as I overview in Chapter 3.

Note also that some ICOs aren't even meant to be investments. They're a tool you can use for a specific product. In the real estate sector, you can use the Propy token to buy properties internationally. Unikrn's CEO Rahul Sood noted in 2017 that "buying a token is buying a product that we're selling that can be used on the Unikrn platform. People should not be looking at this as an investment. If they are looking at this as an investment, they're making a mistake. Tokens are not investments."

But this is an investing chapter in an investing book, and perhaps you've decided to give it a try. Here are some tips on how you can go about it.

Finding ICO listings

You may find out about upcoming ICOs through word of mouth, at a financial event, or through an online ad. If you don't have any specific ICO in mind and just want to search for one from scratch, you can get help from ICO listing websites. But finding the right ICO listing website can also be a challenge because more than 100 of them are already out there, and more are popping up every day.

Here are some tips to keep in mind when searching for an ICO listing website:

>> Start out by comparing two or three ICO listing websites at a time. Are they all featuring the same ICOs on top? This strategy can help you figure out which website is giving you the verified ICO listing.

>> Make sure a site has features such as an ICO calendar, ICO rating, and ICO description.

>> Offering market statistics about the ICO, filters, and scam warning features is a plus.

TIP

At the end of the day, using your everyday search engine may be your best bet to find an ICO listing website. You can consider search terms like "ICO listings," "top ICOs 2019," or "best ICO listing websites." Here are a few to get you started:

>> Coinschedule: www.coinschedule.com

>> ICO Market Data: www.icomarketdata.com/

» ICObench: https://icobench.com/

» ICOindex: https://icoindex.com/

Analyzing an ICO listing

After you pick your ICO listing website, you're now ready to evaluate and choose the upcoming ICOs you're interested in investing in. With hundreds of ICOs popping out every month, this step can be lengthy, but it's a crucial process. The steps to take when researching an ICO can be similar to those I talk about in Chapter 9 for selecting cryptocurrencies. The following sections give you some research points to keep in mind.

Who's behind the ICO?

The team of developers and management behind the ICO is the most important thing you need to find out about. Who are they? What are their credentials? The ICO website should give you background on the team; otherwise, I would move on to the next ICO listing that provides such crucial information readily on its website. Try to find the team members on LinkedIn to verify their backgrounds (or even existence). In addition, try finding ICOs' boards of advisors and financial backers. Are these people you can trust your money with? Are they dedicated to take their idea to the next step?

WARNING

I've been to many ICO pitching conferences where the team just kept on name-dropping — things like "the prince of Dubai is investing millions in us" or other unverifiable blabs. In these cases, I normally run, not walk, and never look back.

What's the cryptocurrency for?

You want to familiarize yourself with the idea behind the crypto as much as possible. Sure, anyone can start a cryptocurrency and list an ICO. The question is why these people have chosen to do so. What specific value does their token have that other cryptocurrencies already in existence don't offer? Who's their competition? How are they better than the competition? What type of technology are they using? Who is their target market, and how large is it?

WARNING

The idea behind the cryptocurrency is important, but beware of unrealistic promises. Scam projects often make bold claims about their products but have nothing new or disruptive in their technology. If someone claims a new cryptocurrency will replace Bitcoin, end world poverty within a year, fix global warming, or increase in value by 10,000 percent, you can add that project to your scam list.

Does the team have a prototype or a code?

As I mention in the earlier section "ICOs versus IPOs," you don't necessarily have to have a prototype to launch an ICO. But those with a minimum viable product can show you that the team is serious about the idea and is able to hit future milestones. If a project has no working code whatsoever prior to an ICO, that's a major red flag.

Does the team have a blockchain?

The majority of ICOs don't have a blockchain (flip to Chapter 4 for an introduction to blockchain technology). The founders simply pitch the idea for the utility their tokens can provide. Personally, I prefer to search among those that are based on solid blockchain technology that solves a solid problem rather than those that are glorified apps that can be built without creating a brand-new cryptocurrency.

What's the plan to drive prices higher after the ICO?

The main reason you invest in an ICO is in speculation that its price will go higher in the future. That's why the team behind the ICO should provide you with a road map on how it's planning to do so. This part of the analysis can be similar to that of any already-trading cryptocurrency I talk about in Chapter 8. Here are some key features to watch out for:

» The crypto has a high enough network volume.

» The crypto is better than the competition.

» The ICO gives investors an incentive to hold rather than quickly spend the tokens.

» The new tokens will have sufficient liquidity.

» The team is proactive in getting the token listed in multiple exchanges.

Many teams seek to create their own exchanges in order to generate the liquidity and volume needed to take off. But I wouldn't view that as sufficient evidence for the token's future success. Getting listed on various exchanges can be tough, which is why it's an important indicator of the token's success down the road.

Does the team have a wide, supportive community?

You don't want to be a sheep who simply follows others, but reaching out to the ICO community can give you a sense about the token. How many supporters does a given ICO have on sources like Reddit, Twitter, and Facebook? Do the supporters appear to be robots, or are they real people and crypto enthusiasts? Beware of paid "community members" whose job is to say positive things about the ICO on social media. Also look for proper media coverage, press releases, and the team's presence on the social media.

Outlining the ICO investment process

When you've found your unicorn ICO, you normally need to have a legit cryptocurrency to invest in it, although sometimes ICOs accept fiat currencies as well. Most importantly, you also need to have a cryptocurrency wallet. Flip to Chapter 7 to identify different types of wallets that can work for you.

Most ICOs are built on the Ethereum blockchain. That's why in many cases you specifically need Ethereum cryptocurrency and an Ethereum wallet to invest in an ICO. See Chapter 8 for more about this crypto.

Not all ICOs are created the same. Therefore, I can't show you the exact steps to take when buying into an ICO. Regardless, here are some general guidelines:

1. Make sure you check the official page of the ICO.

2. If the ICO requires you to pay by another crypto, such as Ethereum or Bitcoin, you must first acquire those coins on an exchange (see Chapter 6) and store them in your crypto wallet (see Chapter 7).

3. After completing your due diligence on the ICO's nature (see the earlier section "Analyzing an ICO listing"), register for the ICO based on its website's instructions.

4. Wait for the launch date and follow the instructions. This step normally consists of transferring your cryptocurrency assets from your crypto wallet to the ICO's public address. This step may also cost a transaction fee.

5. After the ICO is launched, the team sends the new tokens to your crypto wallet.

Because of the risky nature of ICOs and the difficulty in selecting the best ones, you may consider skipping the ICO and waiting until the token/cryptocurrency is launched before buying it. Though many ICOs see an immediate and rapid surge right after launch, more often than not they come crashing down shortly after. The crash doesn't necessarily mean that the token isn't worthy of holding. Historically, these types of price changes happen in the tech industry quite often, providing an excellent post-launch buying opportunity. When things settle down and more people have analyzed the new token, its price can move back up slowly, giving you an opportunity to invest at your own pace. An ICO is rarely too good to pass up it (although it does happen).

Holding your tokens after your purchase

The method you choose to monitor your ICO purchase highly depends on the reasons you bought in the first place. Although not all ICOs are investment vehicles, most teams behind ICOs prefer that you don't buy and dump their tokens after the ICO, so they do whatever it takes to convince you to hold onto the tokens. And doing so may just pay off in the long run.

REMEMBER

If you invested in the ICO for capital gain purposes only, be prepared to hold onto your investment for a while. At first, your investment may turn negative with a loss, or it may consolidate at the same price with no real returns for a while. Often these periods of losses and consolidation are followed by a massive surge, which may give you the opportunity to take profit. Keep in mind that sometimes the big surges are the beginning of an uptrend (or more gains) in the market, so by selling too rapidly you may miss out on more profit. Other times, the surge can be a simple pump-and-dump. Therefore, you need to continuously monitor and conduct the Invest Diva Diamond Analysis (IDDA; see Chapter 9) to create the best exit strategy.

REMEMBER

If you make money on your ICO investment, you have to report it as capital gains. See Chapter 21 for more on taxes.

So You Want to Start an ICO: Launching an ICO Yourself

In 2017, everyone seemed to be launching an ICO. But after a number of scams, failed ICOs, and a general buzzkill in the cryptocurrency world, the hype around ICOs cooled down somewhat. By February 2018, 46 percent of the 2017 ICOs had failed, despite the fact that they had raised over $104 million. People realized that in order to be taken seriously and have long-term success, they must give it their all. At the end of the day, integrity wins.

One key debate is whether ICOs will replace the traditional start-up fundraising process. After all, over 50 percent of start-ups also fail within the first five years, so the statistics aren't that far off when comparing ICOs to venture capital.

The following sections give you a few things to keep in mind before deciding to go the ICO route.

Understanding the challenges

Throughout this chapter I talk about how anyone can start an ICO (see the earlier section "How an ICO works and how to start one" for specifics). Launching a *successful* ICO, on the other hand, is a different story. Here are a few things you need right off the bat:

» A minimum of $60,000 to launch an initial campaign

» Six months to one year of a pre-public engagement phase

» A "dream team" to join your project

» A product that uses your token

» A meaningful reason to integrate the digital token into your product

Taking a few steps before the launch

If you're A-OK with the challenges in the previous section and want to become the next ICO success story, here are some steps to get you started. Just a heads-up: These steps are overly simplified.

Create a product that needs an ICO

The only thing that can increase the demand for your token is having a real utility. If a decentralized token doesn't really impact the value of your product, then forget about it. People are becoming increasingly smart about ICO investments. To become one of the success stories in the field, you need to have a thorough understanding of your market and your target audience. Most importantly, you must know what people will be willing to give you their money for. You can run a survey on a site like SurveyMonkey or BitcoinTalk Forum (check out https://bitcointalk.org/) to see the market reaction to your idea. Make sure you also find out about your competition in the space.

Get legal advice

Are ICOs legal in your country? Are you legally covered if things go wrong? ICOs are becoming more regulated. That's why you must do your due diligence to comply with all relevant laws and regulations in the field. You can find attorneys who are experienced with ICOs using your search engine or LinkedIn; search for terms like "ICO lawyers near me" or "ICO lawyers [enter your country]."

Create a token

This step is actually the easiest step of the process, especially if you're not planning on creating a blockchain from scratch. You can simply use platforms such as Ethereum and Waves. If you follow their instructions, it can literally take less than 20 minutes to issue your own token on Ethereum. Creating a token is outside the scope of this book, but you can see a detailed road map at https://medium.com/ bitfwd/how-to-issue-your-own-token-on-ethereum-in-less-than-20-minutes-ac1f8f022793.

Write a white paper

As I explain earlier in this chapter, white papers are essential for analyzing an ICO or a cryptocurrency. So you can imagine that your investors are likely to demand a thorough, clear one before they give you their money. Search for white paper templates online, and make sure you're up-to-date with what investors are looking for.

Create a launch buzz

This step is also very similar to launching any new product or start-up. As a start-up owner myself, I've been studying launching techniques throughout my entrepreneurial journey, and I'm still learning. Launching an ICO has other additional marketing requirements unique to its nature, including the following:

>> Getting listed on hot ICO listing websites

>> Reaching out to ICO journalists and bloggers

>> Creating your own Reddit, Twitter, Facebook, and LinkedIn pages

>> Considering doing an *airdrop,* which means distributing your token for free to the masses to gain attention and media buzz

>> Considering a global road show and participating in well-attended blockchain events/conferences or partnering with an influencer

TIP

Creating a successful marketing campaign around your ICO is well beyond the scope of this book. So if you're not a natural marketer, make sure you hire the right marketing team to help you along the way! Hiring a great marketing team is yet another challenge that is well beyond the scope of this book, but you can start by searching on your favorite search engine, looking on LinkedIn, or attending local networking events you may find on www.eventbrite.com.

Get your token listed on exchanges

Creating your own exchange can certainly help boost your token's liquidity and volume, but you must be proactive in getting your token listed on as many exchanges as possible. Exchanges will potentially become the main place people will buy and sell your token, so getting it accepted on the strongest and most established ones is critical — and something that requires a heck of a lot of hustling, networking, and proving your coin is worth it. See Chapter 6 more about exchanges. If you do want to create your own exchange, companies such as Shift Markets (www.shiftmarkets.com/) can help with that sort of thing.

Chapter **12**

Cryptocurrency Mining

When I first heard of Bitcoin mining, I immediately imagined a hot guy with a ripped body, wearing a helmet with a flashlight on it, getting dirty inside a mountain. However, I soon learned cryptocurrency miners don't have to have any of these qualities. All you need is access to high-speed Internet and a high-end computer. In this chapter I explore the basics of crypto mining.

REMEMBER

As I explain in Chapter 5, not all cryptocurrencies require mining. Bitcoin, the granddaddy of all coins, started the mining craze in 2009, setting up the concept of blockchain technology (see Chapter 4). However, many new coins out there can't be mined and use alternative methods to generate value.

Understanding How Mining Works in a Nutshell

Bitcoin and other minable cryptocurrencies rely on miners to maintain their network. By solving math problems (see Chapter 5) and providing consent on the validity of transactions, miners support the blockchain network, which will otherwise collapse. For their service to the network, miners are rewarded with newly created cryptocurrencies (such as Bitcoins) and transaction fees.

To really understand mining, you first need to explore the world of blockchain technology in Chapter 4. Here's a quick overview: If you want to help update the *ledger* (transaction record) of a minable cryptocurrency like Bitcoin, all you need to do is to guess a random number that solves a math equation. Of course, you don't want to guess these numbers all by yourself. That's what computers are for! The more powerful your computer is, the more quickly you can solve these math problems and beat the mining crowd. The more you win the guessing game, the more cryptos you receive as a reward. If all the miners use a relatively similar type of computing power, the laws of probability dictate that the winner isn't likely to be the same miner every time. But if half of the miners have regular commercial computers while the other half use supercomputers, then the participation gets unfair to the favor of the super powerful computers. Some argue that those with supercomputers will win most of the time, if not all the time.

Cryptocurrency networks such as Bitcoin automatically change the difficulty of the math problems depending on how fast miners are solving them. This process is also known as adjusting the difficulty of the proof-of-work (PoW) that I talk about in Chapter 5. In the early days of Bitcoin, when the miners were just a tiny group of computer junkies, the proof-of-work was very easy to achieve. In fact, when Satoshi Nakamoto released Bitcoin, he/she/it intended it to be mined on computer CPUs. (The true identity of Satoshi is unknown, and I'm adding "it" because there are even discussions that Satoshi can be a government entity.) Satoshi wanted this distributed network to be mined by people distributed around the world using their laptops and personal computers. Back in the day, you were able to solve rather easy guessing games with a simple processor on your computer.

As the mining group got larger, so did the competition. After a bunch of hard-core computer gamers joined the network, they discovered the graphics cards for their gaming computers were much more suitable for mining. My husband was sure among those people. As a gaming geek, he had two high-end computers with Nvidia graphic cards sitting in his game room, collecting dust after we got married. (For obvious reasons, he had to trade his gaming time up for dating time.) When he saw my passion for cryptos, he had to jump in and turn on his computers to start mining. But because he joined the mining game rather late, mining Bitcoin wasn't turning out to be that profitable. That's why he turned to mining other minable cryptos. (I talk about finding the best cryptocurrencies to mine later in this chapter.)

Mining isn't a get-rich-quick scheme. To mine effectively, you need access to pretty sophisticated equipment. First you need to do the math to see whether the initial investment required to set up your mining assets is going to be worth the cryptos you get in return. And even if you choose to mine cryptocurrencies instead of buying them, you're still betting on the fact that their value will increase in the future.

As Bitcoin became more popular, mining it became more popular, and therefore more difficult. To add to the challenge, some companies who saw the potential in Bitcoin value started massive data centers, called *mining farms*, with ranges of high-end computers whose jobs are only to mine Bitcoins. Figure 12-1 shows an example of a mining farm setup.

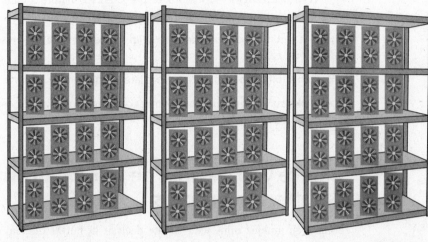

FIGURE 12-1:
High-end computers in a mining farm.

So next time you think about becoming a Bitcoin miner, keep in mind who you're going up against! But don't get disappointed. You do have a way to go about mining: mining pools, which I talk about later in this chapter.

Discovering What You Need to Mine

Before getting started with mining, you should set yourself up with a few mining toys. When you've got everything up and running, mining becomes rather easy because everything happens automatically. The only thing left to do is pay your electric bills at the end of each month.

REMEMBER

First things first — here's a brief to-do list to get you started:

>> Get a crypto wallet (flip to Chapter 7 for details).

>> Make sure you have a strong Internet connection.

- **Set up your high-end computer in a cool location.** By *cool,* I literally mean "low temperature" and not "stylish."
- **Select the hardware to use based on the cryptocurrency you want to mine.** I explain more about this in the next two sections.
- **If you want to mine solo (not recommended), download the whole cryptocurrency's blockchain.** Be prepared; for mature cryptos, downloading the whole blockchain may take days.
- **Get a mining software package (flip to the later section on software for more).**
- **Join a mining pool.** I explain more later in this chapter.
- **Make sure your expenses aren't exceeding your rewards.** I explain more later in this chapter.

Before you begin: The mining profitability of different cryptos

Some tech junkies mine just for the heck of it, but at the end of the day, most people mine cryptos with profit in mind. But even if you fall in the former group, you may as well get a reward out of your efforts, eh? Mining profitability can change drastically based on cryptocurrency value, mining difficulty, electricity rates, and hardware prices at the time you're setting up your mining system. You can go to websites like `www.coinwarz.com` to see which cryptos are best to mine at a given time. As of September 2018, for example, that site indicates the most profitable cryptocurrency to mine is Verge (XVG), while Bitcoin is ranked number seven, as you can see in Figure 12-2.

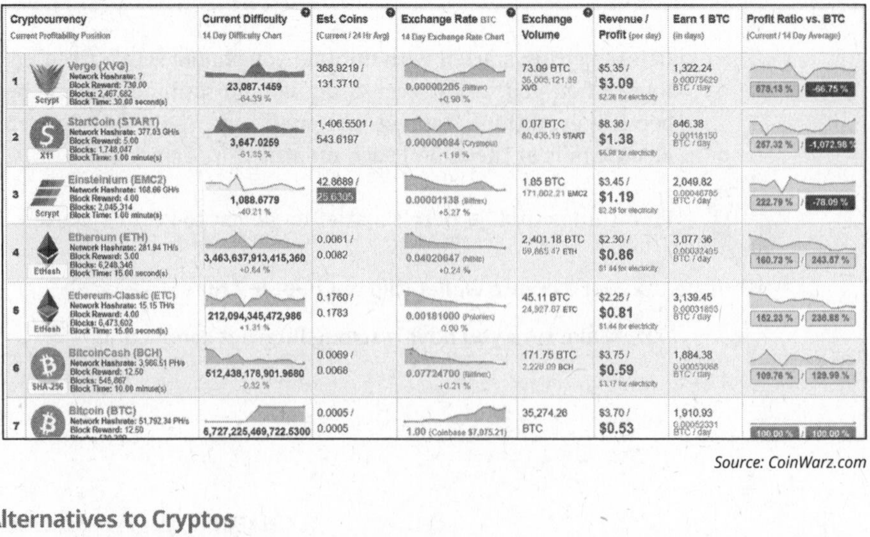

Cryptocurrency (Current Profitability Position)	Current Difficulty (14 Day Difficulty Chart)	Est. Coins (Current / 24 Hr Avg)	Exchange Rate BTC (14 Day Exchange Rate Chart)	Exchange Volume	Revenue / Profit (per day)	Earn 1 BTC (in days)	Profit Ratio vs. BTC (Current / 14 Day Average)
1 Verge (XVG) Network Hashrate: ? Block Reward: 730.00 Blocks: 2,467,682 Block Time: 30.00 second(s) Scrypt	23,087.1459 -84.39 %	368.9219 / 131.3710	0.00000205 (Bittrex) +0.90 %	73.09 BTC 35,005,121.39 XVG	$5.35 / $3.09 $2.26 for electricity	1,322.24 0.00075629 BTC / day	878.13 % / -66.75 %
2 StartCoin (START) Network Hashrate: 377.03 GH/s Block Reward: 5.00 Blocks: 1,748,047 Block Time: 1.00 minute(s) X11	3,647.0259 -61.35 %	1,406.5501 / 543.6197	0.00000084 (Cryptopia) -1.18 %	0.07 BTC 80,436.19 START	$8.36 / $1.38 $6.98 for electricity	846.38 0.00118150 BTC / day	267.32 % / -1,072.98 %
3 Einsteinium (EMC2) Network Hashrate: 108.66 GH/s Block Reward: 4.00 Blocks: 2,045,314 Block Time: 1.00 minute(s) Scrypt	1,088.6779 -40.21 %	42.8689 / 25.6305	0.00001138 (Bittrex) +5.27 %	1.85 BTC 171,802.21 EMC2	$3.45 / $1.19 $2.26 for electricity	2,049.82 0.00048785 BTC / day	222.79 % / -78.09 %
4 Ethereum (ETH) Network Hashrate: 281.94 TH/s Block Reward: 3.00 Blocks: 6,248,346 Block Time: 15.00 second(s) EtHash	3,463,637,913,415,360 +0.64 %	0.0081 / 0.0082	0.04020647 (hitbtc) +0.24 %	2,401.18 BTC 59,865.47 ETH	$2.30 / $0.86 $1.44 for electricity	3,077.36 0.00032495 BTC / day	160.73 % / 243.87 %
5 Ethereum-Classic (ETC) Network Hashrate: 15.15 TH/s Block Reward: 4.00 Blocks: 6,473,602 Block Time: 15.00 second(s) EtHash	212,094,345,472,986 +1.31 %	0.1760 / 0.1783	0.00181000 (Poloniex) 0.00 %	45.11 BTC 24,927.87 ETC	$2.25 / $0.81 $1.44 for electricity	3,139.45 0.00031853 BTC / day	152.23 % / 236.88 %
6 BitcoinCash (BCH) Network Hashrate: 3,986.51 PH/s Block Reward: 12.50 Blocks: 545,667 Block Time: 10.00 minute(s) SHA-256	512,438,178,901.9680 -0.32 %	0.0069 / 0.0068	0.07724700 (Bitfinex) +0.21 %	171.75 BTC 2,228.09 BCH	$3.75 / $0.59 $3.17 for electricity	1,684.38 0.00053068 BTC / day	109.78 % / 129.99 %
7 Bitcoin (BTC) Network Hashrate: 51,792.34 PH/s Block Reward: 12.50	6,727,225,469,722.6300	0.0005 / 0.0005	1.00 (Coinbase $7,075.21)	35,274.26 BTC	$3.70 / $0.53	1,910.93 0.00052331 BTC / day	100.00 % / 100.00 %

FIGURE 12-2: Snapshot of mining profitability list in September 2018.

Source: CoinWarz.com

Even if mining isn't profitable at the moment, your cryptos can be worth a lot in the future if the coin value surges. By mining cryptos that have low profitability at the moment, you're taking an investment risk. For more on risk, flip to Chapter 3.

Mining hardware

Different types of cryptocurrencies may require different types of hardware for best mining results. For example, hardware (such as ASICs, which stands for application-specific integrated circuits) has been customized to optimize cryptocurrencies like Bitcoin and Bitcoin Cash. But for cryptocurrencies without dedicated hardware, such as Ethereum, Zcash and BitcoinGold, graphics processing units (GPUs) are good enough to process the transactions. Of course, GPUs are still slow at mining compared to mining farms. If you decide to mine Bitcoin with a GPU, for example, you may wait years before you can mine one Bitcoin! You can find GPUs at any store that sells computer hardware equipment.

As mining became more difficult, crafty coders started exploiting graphics cards because those provided more *hashing power,* which is the rate at which you mine (flip to Chapter 5 to explore hashing). They wrote mining software (in other words, developed mining algorithms) optimized for the processing power of GPUs to mine way more quickly than central processing units (CPUs). These types of graphics cards are faster, but they still use more electricity and generate a lot of heat. That's when miners decided to switch to something called an *application-specific integrated circuit,* or ASIC. The ASIC technology has made Bitcoin mining much faster while using less power. (You can search "where to buy ASIC miner" on your favorite search engine.)

During crypto hype, mining equipment such as ASICs becomes incredibly expensive. At the beginning of 2018, for example, they were priced at over $9,000 due to high demand. That's why you must consider your return on investment before getting yourself involved in mining; sometimes simply buying cryptocurrencies makes more sense than mining them does.

Cryptocurrency mining may make more sense to do in winter because it generates so much heat in the hardware. You may be able to reduce the cost of your electricity bill by using nature as your computer's natural cooling system. Or using your computer as your home's heating system! Of course, the cost of the electricity used by mining computers far exceeds the cost of heating or cooling the house.

Mining software

Mining software handles the actual mining process. If you're a solo miner, the software connects your machine to the blockchain to become a mining node or a miner. If you mine with a pool (see the next section), the software connects you to the mining pool. The main job of the software is to deliver the mining hardware's work to the rest of the network and to receive completed work from the other miners on the network. It also shows statistics such as the speed of your miner and fan, your hash rate, and the temperature.

Again, you must search for the best software at the time you're ready to start. Here are some popular ones at the time of writing:

>> **CGminer:** CGminer is one of the oldest and most popular examples of Bitcoin mining software. You can use it for pools like Cryptominers to mine different altcoins. It supports ASICs and GPUs.

>> **Ethminer:** Ethminer is the most popular software to mine Ethereum. It supports GPU hardware such as Nvidia and AMD.

>> **XMR Stak:** XMR Stak can mine cryptocurrencies like Monero and Aeon. It supports CPU and GPU hardware.

REMEMBER

These options are just examples and not recommendations. You can go about selecting the best software by reading online reviews about their features, reputations, and ease of use. This market is evolving, and navigating your way to find the best options may take time. Personally I rely heavily on my search engine to find a number of resources, and then I compare the results to choose the one I feel most comfortable with.

Mining pools

Mining pools definitely bring miners together, but luckily you don't have to get into your beach body shape to join one. (But if I had stuck to my hot miner guy image, a mining pool would've just made that picture perfect. A bunch of hot guys, wearing helmets, sipping cool drinks in a pool. . . .)

Simply put, a *mining pool* is a place where regular miners who don't have access to gigantic mining farms (described earlier in this chapter) come together and share their resources. When you join a mining pool, you're able to find solutions for the math problems faster than going about it solo. You're rewarded in proportion to the amount of work you provide.

WARNING

Mining pools are cool because they smooth out rewards and make them more predictable. Without a mining pool, you receive a mining payout only if you find a block on your own. That's why I don't recommend solo mining; your hardware's hash rate is very unlikely to be anywhere near enough to find a block on its own.

To find a mining pool that's suitable for you, I recommend doing an online search at the time you're ready to jump in. That's because this market changes rapidly, and so do the infrastructure and the participants. Here are some features to compare when selecting the best mining pool for you:

>> **Minable cryptocurrency:** Make sure the pool is mining the cryptocurrency you've selected.

>> **Location:** Some pools don't have servers in all countries. Make sure the one you choose is available in your country.

>> **Reputation:** This factor is an important one. Don't get in the pool with nasty people.

>> **Fees:** Some pools have higher fees than others. Make sure you don't prioritize fee over reputation, though.

>> **Profit sharing:** Different pools have different rules for profit sharing. One thing to consider is how much of the coin you need to mine before the pool pays you out.

>> **Ease of use:** If you're not tech-savvy, this feature can be important to keep in mind.

A mining setup example

Figure 12-3 shows what my husband's mining setup looked like at the beginning of 2018 to mine Ethereum. Keep in mind that he already had these systems sitting in his game room, so he didn't really make much investment with mining in mind. He did invest in the hardware wallet, though. (Head to Chapter 7 for more on wallets.)

>> Two custom-made, high-end gaming computers from boutique PC builders (one from Maingear and the other from Falcon Northwest)

>> Two Nvidia GTX 1070 Tis in his first PC; two Nvidia Titan X Pascals in the second PC

>> Two Ledger Nano S hardware wallets

>> Ethermine.org pool to mine Ethereum

FIGURE 12-3:
High-end gaming
rigs that can be
used for mining.

Diving in and making sure mining is worth your time

After you have all your tools together, you then need to set up and start mining. It can certainly be challenging to do so, and the dynamic of the mining community changes regularly, so you must make sure that you are up-to-date with recent changes and have acquired the latest tools for your mining adventure. You can always do so by researching the key elements I mention in the previous sections on your search engine.

TIP

If you're looking to mine Bitcoin, keep in mind that your profitability depends on many factors (such as your computing power, electricity costs, pool fees, and the Bitcoin's value at the time of mining), and chances are very high that you won't be profitable at all. You can check whether Bitcoin mining is going to profitable for you by using a Bitcoin mining calculator (check out `www.investdiva.com/mining-calculator/`). Mining calculators take into account all the relevant costs you may be paying to mine and show you if mining a certain cryptocurrency is profitable for your situation. Simple mining calculators ask you questions about your hash rate, the pool fees, and your power usage, among others. Figure 12-4 shows you a sample mining calculator powered by CryptoRival. Once you hit the "Calculate" button, it shows you your gross earning per year, month, and day.

By doing the mining calculation ahead of time, you may realize that mining other cryptocurrencies may make more sense.

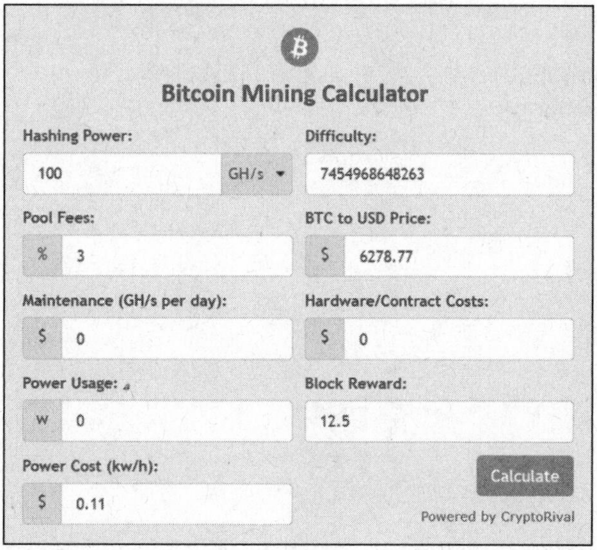

FIGURE 12-4:
Example of a
simple mining
calculator.

Source: CryptoRival.com

blockchain technology

» Keeping an eye on blockchain and cryptocurrency ETFs and other indexes

Chapter **13**

Stocks and Exchange Traded Funds with Cryptocurrency Exposure

Even if you're a hard-core fan of cryptocurrency investing, getting some indirect exposure to the industry rather than diving directly headfirst into the market is always a good idea. In this chapter, I overview some methods to find stocks and exchange traded funds (ETFs) that can get you just the right amount of exposure to the crypto market while diversifying your portfolio in other fields as well.

REMEMBER

Stocks, ETFs, and all other investment assets carry a certain amount of risk. To create an investment portfolio that is unique to your financial situation and goals, make sure you calculate your risk tolerance by checking out Chapter 3 and attending my *Make Your Money Work for You PowerCourse:* https://learn.investdiva. com/free-webinar-3-secrets-to-making-your-money-work-for-you. If you're looking for one-on-one consultations, I recommend a dear friend and author of multiple *For Dummies* books, Paul Mladjenovic. You can check out his services here: www.ravingcapitalist.com/.

To buy stocks and ETFs, you likely must open an account with a broker in your area, which is different from your cryptocurrency exchange or broker. While some brokers like Robinhood (http://share.robinhood.com/kianad1) offer cryptocurrencies as well as stocks and ETFs, at the time of writing the number of such brokers is limited in the United States. See Chapter 6 for more information on brokers and exchanges.

Looking for Stocks with Exposure to Cryptos

When I want to start the process of strategy development for any asset, I make sure I check all the points of the Invest Diva Diamond Analysis (IDDA), as I explain in Chapter 9. That includes analyzing the markets from fundamental, sentimental, and technical points of view and then adding my risk tolerance and portfolio diversity to the mix to achieve a perfect, personalized strategy that works for me. The same works for picking stocks. But if you're looking specifically for stocks with exposure to the cryptocurrency/blockchain industry, you need to do the analysis on both ends — the stock itself and its crypto side. The following sections cover how you can conduct the analysis on your own.

If you're interested in getting my up-to-date stock picks and the latest investment strategies, consider joining Invest Diva's Premium Investing Group at https://learn.investdiva.com/join-group.

Fundamentals

Blockchain and cryptocurrencies are related, but not all companies who are investing in blockchain technology have direct exposure to the cryptocurrency market. And even though the cryptocurrency market took a hit in 2018, for example, major public companies continued their rapid investments in blockchain technology. In fact, when PricewaterhouseCoopers (PwC) surveyed 600 executives from 15 territories in August 2018, 84 percent of them indicated their companies were "actively involved" with blockchain technology.

As I discuss in Chapter 4, blockchain is the underlying technology for cryptocurrencies such as Bitcoin and Ethereum. In 2018, companies who were reorganizing their structure to incorporate blockchain included IBM, Accenture, Deloitte, J.P. Morgan, and HSBC, to name a few. I can only imagine more big names will have jumped on the blockchain wagon by the time you have this book in your hands. On the other hand, research from Cowen suggests blockchain won't experience widespread adoption before 2022. Therefore, doing up-to-date research when conducting fundamental analysis on this topic is crucial.

Enough about companies that are investing in blockchain. How about cryptocurrencies? How can you get indirect exposure to this byproduct of blockchain technology? You need to think outside the box. The following sections give you some points to search for before you select stocks with crypto exposure. (For more information on fundamental analysis, check out Chapter 9. You can also visit https://learn.investdiva.com/free-webinar-3-secrets-to-making-your-money-work-for-you.)

Companies can get involved with the cryptocurrency market in so many ways. Make sure to stay on top of the news on websites such as https://crypto briefing.com/ and https://pro.benzinga.com/?afmc=2f/ to be in the know.

Crypto mining exposure

Some major cryptocurrencies are minable. And to be able to mine, you need high-end computers with sophisticated hardware, as I cover in Chapter 12. When cryptocurrency mining is at its peak, such companies' stock value also skyrockets. One example of this trend was Advanced Micro Devices stock (AMD) in 2017 and 2018. My Premium Investing Group members and I saw over 1,000 percent return over the two-year period that we held onto our AMD stocks. More specifically, we started buying AMD shares when it was $1.84 per share at the beginning of 2016 and sold throughout 2018 as it reached $25 and above. Of course, cryptocurrency mining was only one of the drivers behind AMD's price surge. But for sure, as more people got into cryptocurrency mining, the demand for AMD graphics processing units (GPUs) went higher, and so did AMD's share value.

Many other companies are now focusing on this area and may potentially do a better job than AMD in the future. Media websites such as www.hardocp.com/, www.guru3d.com/, and www.anandtech.com/ often track the latest tech news, so following them can give you an edge in knowing which companies can give you crypto mining exposure.

Crypto payment exposure

Another way to get indirect exposure to the cryptocurrency market through public companies is to go after those that accept altcoins as a payment method for their services. Some pioneers in this area include Overstock.com (stock symbol: OSTK) and Microsoft (stock symbol: MSFT) in 2017 and 2018. You can find out which companies accept cryptos as payment through news sources such as Mashable (https://mashable.com/), NewsBTC (http://newsbtc.com), and MarketWatch (www.marketwatch.com/).

WARNING

If crypto payment exposure is the *only* reason you're investing in these types of stocks, you must remember that their price volatility can be directly correlated to the cryptocurrency market itself and therefore may not give you the diversification you're looking for. For example, Overstock's OSTK shares saw massive gains after it started to accept Bitcoin at the end of 2017 and throughout the beginning of 2018. However, as the Bitcoin price crashed, so did OSTK's share price, as you can see in Figure 13-1.

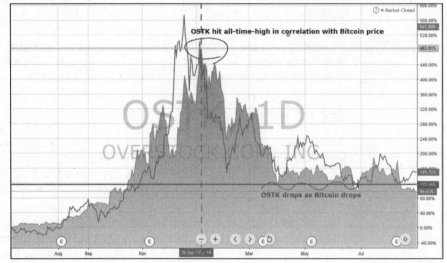

FIGURE 13-1: OSTK share prices throughout 2018 show correlation to Bitcoin prices.

Source: tradingview.com

Crypto trading exposure

While the government authorities were trying to figure out regulations around cryptocurrencies, many public trading companies, brokers, and traditional exchanges got ahead of the crowd to offer cryptocurrency trading opportunities for the masses. For example, when Interactive Brokers Group (stock symbol: IBKR) announced on December 13, 2017, that it will allow its customers to *short* Bitcoin (sell it in speculation that its value will drop), its stock price actually dropped. The reason for that may have been that at the time, Bitcoin's price was at its peak, and most people didn't like the idea of shorting Bitcoin. Of course, Bitcoin prices ended up falling a few months later, and IBKR saw a boost in its stock price value, as you can see in Figure 13-2. It then dropped again due to factors other than its Bitcoin exposure.

Source: tradingview.com

FIGURE 13-2:
The stock price of Interactive Brokers (IBKR) dropped on December 13 following the announcement of a Bitcoin speculation service.

WARNING

Speculative trading based on rumors and news can be very risky. When analyzing a stock from a fundamental point for a medium-to-long-term investment strategy, you must consider other factors, such as the company's management, services, industry outlook, financial statements, and financial ratios. See Chapter 17 for more on short-term trading strategies and Chapter 18 for more on long-term investing strategies.

Market sentiment factors

The second point of the IDDA (Invest Diva Diamond Analysis) focuses on market sentiment. As I indicate in Chapter 9, *market sentiment* is the general behavior and "feeling" of market participants toward a specific asset such as cryptos or stocks. When searching for stocks with crypto exposure, you must measure the market sentiment not only toward that stock but also toward the cryptocurrency industry. This approach gives you an idea about the direction you can take with your investment.

For a very simplified example, say all other IDDA points, including fundamental and technical analyses, are showing that you can expect the price of a given stock to go lower in the future. (The technical term for this move is a *bearish reversal* in a stock price.) But if you want to complete your IDDA analysis, you must also measure the market sentiment, using shorter time frames and indicators such as Ichimoku Kinko Hyo, which I talk about in Chapter 20.

Other market sentiment indicators include the following:

>> Moving average convergence divergence (MACD) (www.investdiva.com/investing-guide/macd/)

>> Relative strength index (RSI) (www.investdiva.com/investing-guide/relative-strength-index-rsi/)

>> Bollinger Bands (BOL) (www.investdiva.com/investing-guide/bollinger-bands-bol/)

Other considerations

At the end of the day, if you're looking to create a well-diversified portfolio by getting indirect exposure to cryptocurrencies, you may want to avoid *double dipping* (investing in the same category/industry twice). Stocks with exposure to cryptos should only be a proportionate piece of your overall portfolio, as categorized by industry. If you're looking to get an idea of how much you'll make on your investment with the amount of risk you're taking, and how much you should value the company's stock price, you must analyze the industry properly from all points of the IDDA. Then you can focus on picking the best stock in that category.

Here are some questions to ask before picking the top crypto related stocks for your portfolio:

>> Is the company working on any new developments in its technology?

>> What impact are potential breakthroughs likely to have?

>> Is the demand for the crypto related services related to key economic variables? If so, which ones?

>> How much is the company planning to spend on crypto related services? How is it planning to fund that spending?

>> Is the company rapidly employing and opening new crypto/blockchain-related jobs?

You can find the answers to these questions by researching the company's press releases and public reports. Your broker may also help you get your hands on the most recent developments. Of course, at Invest Diva, we also try to stay on top of all the developments, so make sure you subscribe free to my updates at https://learn.investdiva.com/start. Then you can move on to the next IDDA points, such as technical analysis (see Chapters 9 and 16) and risk management (as I explain in Chapter 3).

Considering Cryptocurrency and Blockchain ETFs

If you're having a hard time picking the right stock, then you may want to consider another option. One of the easiest ways to get exposure to a specific industry without having to pick the top assets in that category is trading an exchange traded fund, or ETF.

An ETF is similar to a mutual fund in that they're both "baskets" of assets in the same category. But ETFs are becoming more popular for reasons such as the following:

» They're more tax efficient than mutual funds.

» They have lower trading expenses compared to those of mutual funds.

» They're simpler/more flexible than mutual funds.

» They're more accessible than mutual funds to an average investor.

In the following sections, I introduce you to ETFs and other indexes that provide exposure to cryptocurrencies and blockchain technology.

Getting an overview of blockchain ETFs

In 2018, a handful of blockchain-related ETFs were accessible to individual investors. However, Bitcoin ETFs or cryptocurrency ETFs didn't have much luck getting regulated, even though many of them were in line to get approval from the Securities and Exchange Commission (SEC). That's why investors who really wanted exposure to the crypto industry through an ETF had to look for the next best thing, which was a blockchain ETF.

The first blockchain ETFs to hit the markets were BLOK and BLCN, both of which launched on January 17, 2018 (right at the time when Bitcoin was taking a hit). On January 29, 2018, another blockchain ETF, KOIN, showed its face in the competition. Here's a brief introduction to these three ETFs:

» BLOK's full name is the Amplify Transformational Data Shearing ETF. Its basket holds 52 assets, including Digital Garage, Inc. (stock symbol: DLGEF), GMO Internet, Inc. (stock symbol: GMOYF), and Square, Inc. (stock symbol: SQ). You can find the most recent updates to this ETF at www.marketwatch.com/investing/fund/blok.

» BLCN's full name is the Reality Shares Nasdaq NexGen Economy ETF. Its top holdings have more attractive stocks with blockchain exposure, including Advanced Micro Devices, Inc. (stock symbol: AMD), Intel Corporation (stock symbol: INTC), Microsoft Corporation (stock symbol: MSFT), and SBI Holdings, Inc. (stock symbol: SBHGF). You can find the most recent developments in this ETF at https://finance.yahoo.com/quote/BLCN/holdings/.

» KOIN's full name is Innovation Shares NextGen Protocol ETF. This one didn't get as much love as the other two ETFs at the beginning. Its top holdings include Taiwan Semiconductor Manufacturing Co. Ltd. ADR (stock symbol: TSM), Amazon (stock symbol: AMZN), Nvidia (stock symbol: NVDA), Microsoft, and Cisco Systems (stock symbol: CSCO).

This option, to me, looks like a pretty good selection because of its focus on artificial intelligence. But perhaps the reason investors weren't as lovey-dovey with this ETF at the beginning was that it appears to have the least amount of direct exposure to the blockchain industry when compared to the other two. However, as you can see in Figure 13-3, its returns surpassed that of BLOK and BLCN by September 2018. You can find out about the most recent developments in KOIN at www.morningstar.com/etfs/ARCX/KOIN/quote.html.

Disclaimer: I personally own AMD, INTC, NVDA, AMZN, and MSFT in my portfolio as of 2018.

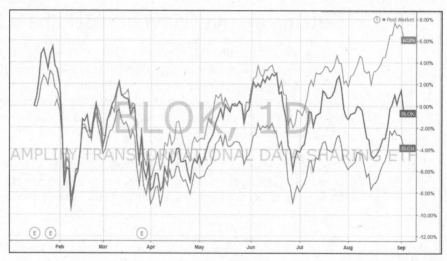

FIGURE 13-3: BLOK, BLCN, and KOIN ETF comparison in 2018.

Source: tradingview.com

REMEMBER

These three ETFs had the early-arrival advantage for some time, but that doesn't necessarily mean they're the best in the game.

Investing in ETFs makes the stock-analysis process a bit easier, but you still need a general understanding of the ETF's holding companies in order to be able to pick the one that best suits your portfolio. If various ETFs' holdings are widely different even in the same industry, you may want to consider investing in multiple ETFs, as long as their prices aren't correlated.

Keeping an eye on other indexes

While cryptocurrency ETFs take their time to get regulatory approval, you can look for other indexes in the industry that can give you exposure to the crypto market. For example, in March 2018, Coinbase — one of the largest crypto exchanges in the United States — announced that it was planning to launch its own index fund. The index aimed to follow all the digital assets listed on Coinbase's exchange, GDAX, which at the time included Bitcoin, Litecoin, Ethereum, and Bitcoin Cash. However, in October 2018 the exchange had to shut down the index due to lack of industrial interest. Instead, it's shifting its focus to a new retail product. Stay ahead of these types of announcements by subscribing to my mailing list (`https://learn.investdiva.com/start`). Here are some other cryptocurrency news sources in alphabetical order:

>> `https://www.cnbc.com/`

>> `https://www.coindesk.com/`

>> `https://www.forbes.com/crypto-blockchain/`

>> `https://www.investing.com/news/cryptocurrency-news`

>> `https://www.nasdaq.com/topic/cryptocurrency`

>> `https://www.newsbtc.com/`

Chapter **14**

Cryptocurrency Futures and Options

Futures and options are two forms of a general financial instrument called *derivatives.* They derive their value from the price action of something else — traditionally, from financial assets like stocks, commodities, *fiat* (government-backed) currencies, and other market indexes. As the cryptocurrency market becomes more popular, different cryptocurrency derivatives have been popping up and are accessible to individual traders.

In this chapter I first overview the basics of futures and options trading, and then I explore how they work in the crypto market.

TIP

At the time of writing, many regulations exist around such assets, so you can invest in them through a handful of brokers and exchanges around the world. In the United States, Bitcoin futures trading is available on a handful of brokers and exchanges such as these:

>> **Cboe:** http://cfe.cboe.com/cfe-products/xbt-cboe-bitcoin-futures

>> **CME Group:** www.cmegroup.com/trading/bitcoin-futures.html

>> **E*TRADE:** https://us.etrade.com/knowledge/education/events/ trading-bitcoin-cboe-xbt-bitcoin-futures

>> **Interactive Brokers:** www.interactivebrokers.com/en/home.php

>> **TD Ameritrade:** www.tdameritrade.com/investment-products/futures-trading/bitcoin-futures.page

TIP

In countries such as the United Kingdom, Japan, and Korea, you may be able to trade cryptocurrency options and futures on Deribit: www.deribit.com/. However, at the time of writing, the company doesn't offer their services in the United States.

Focusing on the Fundamentals of Futures

Here's a hint: Futures have something to do with the future! For example, when you buy a sack of coffee from your local supermarket, you pay for it right then and there at the market price. But what if you think the price of coffee will go down in the future? You can't buy coffee now at its "future" price in your local market, but you sure can in the futures market. If you think the price of coffee per pound is going down from $5 to $4 by June of next year, you can create a futures contract to buy a certain amount of coffee at $4 next June.

In the following sections, I explain the features of commodity futures (the most common type) and discuss other types of financial futures.

Futures' features

Traditionally, futures are most popular among commodities like grains, coffee, metals, wood, and meat. When you buy coffee in the futures market, you don't receive your coffee until a date in the future that you've agreed on with the seller. That's why your transaction isn't complete for some time. During this time, you own a highly liquid *futures contract* that you can hold or trade in the futures market. No matter what you do with the contract, as long as it's outstanding, the seller has a legally binding obligation to deliver your coffee on that specified date in the future. You have a similar obligation to take the coffee delivery. No return policy!

Two of the most important futures trading features are *hedging* and *speculating*. In fact, the futures market can't exist and operate efficiently without either one. Another characteristic of futures is *margin trading*. Here's how they work:

>> **Futures hedging:** Traditionally, the hedgers are businesses that either produce a commodity or use it as an input to their production process. As an investor, you can use hedging as a type of risk management to prevent losses and not necessarily to make capital gains. You can hedge one investment by making another investment to offset the risk of the first investment — it's something like investing in an insurance policy to offset the risk of something happening to you in the future.

>> **Futures speculating:** The speculators are quite the opposite of the hedgers. They trade futures simply to earn a profit on expected price swings. They have no inherent interest in the commodity or its financial future other that its price action. For example, if you think the price of a commodity will increase in the future, you may be able to make a profit by purchasing the asset in a futures contract and selling it at a higher price later on. Regardless, the futures market depends on them because their trades help make the market more liquid.

>> **Margin trading:** You can take advantage of something called *leverage* when trading futures, just like in the foreign exchange or forex market (covered in Chapter 15). The difference is that *all* futures contracts are traded on a margin basis. You can't opt out of this feature. When you buy a futures contract *on margin,* it means you need to put only a fraction of the total price in cash. When trading futures contracts, you usually need a margin of about 2 percent to 10 percent of the contract value. The good news is that you don't have to borrow money to finance the balance of the contract, which makes it less risky than how margin trading works in forex.

The margin deposit is simply a security or a guarantee to cover any losses that may occur. It is *not* a partial payment for your purchase.

Financial futures

Although commodities make up for a big segment of the futures market, financial futures are another popular dimension of it. *Financial futures* use a different type of underlying asset than commodities do, and they offer a speculating vehicle for many markets such as forex, interest rates, and stock indexes. They have similar advantages to commodity future trading and have become a major hedging tool for institutions and individual traders alike. One key difference is the way the price of each type of financial futures contract is quoted:

>> Currency futures in the United States are quoted in U.S. dollars per unit of the underlying foreign currency — for example, U.S. dollar per Canadian dollar or U.S. dollar per Japanese yen.

>> Interest rate futures contracts are priced as a percentage of the *par value* (face value) of the underlying debt instrument. For example, the par value of most Treasury-based interest rate futures are $100,000, and therefore each contract trades in whole-dollar bids of $1,000.

>> Stock index futures are quoted in terms of the actual underlying index. Such indexes include the S&P 500 and Nasdaq.

Just like commodities, financial futures can expose you to a ton of profit and loss. But you must thoroughly understand your investments as well as the risks involved in order to be a successful futures trader.

WARNING

Speculating each type of futures can be very a specialized task. If you don't know much about each industry, you may as well be gambling in Las Vegas.

Introducing the Basics of Options

Options help you enter a contract with someone else to buy or sell something of value. If you're the option buyer, you have the right to buy an underlying asset (like coffee) within a given period of time at a price that was agreed upon at the time of the contract. If you're the seller, you must be ready to sell that underlying asset within the contract's instructions.

The following sections compare options to futures, describe types of options, and explain the risks.

Futures versus options

REMEMBER

Futures and options are very similar. They both involve the future delivery of something at a specific price. The big difference between a futures contract and an options contract comes down to the date of buying and selling. Here are some important points to keep in mind:

>> When trading a futures contract, you must buy/sell on or before an agreed-upon date.

>> With options, you can buy/sell over a specified period of time.

>> Put and call options (see the next section) specify the price at which you can buy or sell.

>> Futures prices aren't spelled out on the contract. Instead, the price on a futures contract is established through the trades among traders on the exchange. This means the delivery price is set at whatever price the contract sells for.

Puts and calls

The two basic kinds of options are called puts and calls, which are basically a version of selling and buying:

>> With a *put,* you can sell an underlying security at a specific price over a period of time.

>> With a *call,* you get the right to buy that security at the agreed price within a certain period of time.

Why don't they just call it buying and selling and save trouble? One key benefit of using a different name is that you're forced to remember that with puts and calls, you get no ownership privileges and gain no interest or dividend income. All you get are gains and losses from the price movements of the underlying assets. Just like futures, you can take advantage of the leverage puts and calls offer.

TIP

Paul Mladjenovic, author of a number of *For Dummies* investing books, has a great education course on options investing. You can check it out at www.raving capitalist.com/home/ultra-investing-with-options/.

Risks

WARNING

Options trading comes with a couple of notable risks:

>> One of the major risks with options puts and calls trading is that you can't make time your friend. Puts and calls have limited lives; the market may not have enough time to move favorably in your direction before the option expires, and you may end up losing money right before the prices move to your advantage.

>> Another major risk is that you can lose 100 percent of your initial investment if the markets move a tiny bit in an unfavorable direction at a wrong time. Though with normal investing you can wait it out, puts and calls options are totally worthless when they expire.

Understanding Cryptocurrency Derivatives Trading

Derivatives trading may very well be the next big boom in the cryptocurrency market. In 2018, many financial organizations in the United States, such as Goldman Sachs and TD Ameritrade, started exploring cryptocurrency trading derivatives:

» In June 2018, Goldman Sachs COO David Solomon said that the company is already helping its clients invest in Bitcoin futures and that it's "very cautiously" considering "some other activities" in the field.

» In October 2018, TD Ameritrade joined a group of financial corporations to back a new, regulated, crypto-related derivatives exchange, ErisX (https://erisx.com/). ErisX filed to register as a derivatives clearing organization with the Commodity Futures Trading Commission (CFTC) in 2017 and plans to apply its services, such as futures contracts, to digital assets in 2019 and onward.

At the time of writing, crypto derivatives trading, including options and futures, is still in its infancy. However, with many leading investment organizations already jumping in, you can expect such trading services to be accessible to the masses in no time, perhaps even by the time you have this book in your hands. The following sections give you the scoop.

The advantages of crypto derivatives trading

With crypto derivatives trading, you're betting on the price of specific coins (like Bitcoin or Ethereum) either on a future date or within a certain range of time. Derivatives trading may be more complex than simply buying and selling crypto-currencies on an exchange, but a quick advantage is that you don't have to worry about storage security. If you're concerned about the risk of losing your crypto wallet or assets in a hacking attack, crypto derivatives have you covered. Because you don't actually own coins when trading options and futures, you don't have to worry about things like a crypto wallet, storage, and security (see Chapter 7 for an introduction to wallets).

The advantages of crypto derivatives for the industry

Even if you choose not to trade crypto derivatives, the existence of such trading options may be good for the crypto industry as a whole. Why?

>> First and foremost, crypto derivatives may be able to boost the liquidity and trading volume across digital assets other than Bitcoin, which makes them easier to trade. Higher liquidity helps traders buy and sell more quickly and avoid risk of sudden, massive movements in the price at the time they're placing their trading orders.

>> Another advantage of having regulated crypto derivative exchanges is that more people may become interested in the cryptocurrency market and put pressure on regulators to advance their views on the industry.

Trading resources

TIP

To stay up-to-date with the latest advancements in the crypto derivatives market, consider checking in regularly with financial news and cryptocurrency update providers such as those in the following list:

>> Benzinga Pro (https://pro.benzinga.com?afmc=2f)

>> CCN (www.ccn.com/)

>> CoinDesk (www.coindesk.com/)

>> Cointelegraph (https://cointelegraph.com/)

>> Crypto Briefing (https://cryptobriefing.com)

>> Cryptonews.com (https://cryptonews.com/)

>> Medium (https://medium.com/topic/cryptocurrency)

>> NewsBTC (https://newsbtc.com)

TIP

If you like to browse your Facebook stream for news, consider "liking" these news providers. In that case, make sure you change the setting of the news pages you follow to see them first on your feed. Otherwise, the news updates will get lost among the thousand baby picture updates you get from your friends.

Chapter **15**

Dealing with the Dollar and Other Fiat Currencies

Calling typical currencies "fiat" isn't something I was used to before cryptocurrencies became a thing. I simply used to call them "currencies." If I wanted to get specific, I'd talk about "major currencies" like the U.S. dollar, the euro, and the Japanese yen or "exotic currencies" like the Mexican peso and the Iranian rial.

Currency trading, also known as the *foreign exchange market (forex)*, is the art of predicting the future value of fiat currencies against one another. Technically, a *fiat* currency is a legal tender that your local government supports through the central bank. The advent of cryptocurrencies has worried some fiat currency issuers (that is, central banks). Some believe that the cryptocurrencies may replace fiat currencies in the future. But for now, one of the ways to get your hands on cryptocurrencies is to exchange your fiat currencies for them. That's why understanding the basic movements in the world's fiat currencies may come in handy in your cryptocurrency investing endeavors.

In this chapter, I take a look at the U.S. dollar (USD) as the world's reserve currency along with other major currencies and their relationships with the cryptocurrency market. (I introduce trading cryptocurrencies versus fiat currencies in Chapter 10.)

Considering the World's Reserve Currency: The U.S. Dollar

If you live in the United States, your first cryptocurrency investment is likely an exchange between the U.S. dollar and a digital asset like Bitcoin. Bitcoin prices can be incredibly volatile, but you also must consider the fluctuations of the U.S. dollar, which may lead to a better or worse trading deal for you. For example, if the U.S. dollar is incredibly strong, you can buy more bits of Bitcoin with it. I explore some key factors that affect the value of the U.S. dollar in this section.

A LIFETIME FASCINATION WITH CURRENCY FLUCTUATIONS

As a child, I was fascinated by currency fluctuations. I always heard my parents worry about the value of our Iranian currency diminishing versus the U.S. dollar (USD). You see, after the Iranian revolution, most of my relatives, including my brother, left Iran for the United States in fear of the new government. In order for my brother to be able to go to school in the United States, my parents had to send him money from Iran, converting the ever-devaluing Iranian rial to the USD. The stronger the U.S. dollar got, the tougher it was for my parents to hit the $1,000 minimum per month to send to my brother. I always wondered who was behind all the currency fluctuations. I remember asking my dad when I was 10 years old, "Is there a guy in the government who decides the value of the USD every morning and announces it to the world?" My dad answered, "No, there are a whole lot of people behind the pricing, especially the central banks." I still didn't really get it then.

When I went to Japan to study electrical engineering, I started paying attention to currency fluctuations again. I was getting paid a scholarship in Japanese yen by the Japanese government. So I always wondered how my 20,000 yen per month would convert to the Iranian rial and the U.S. dollar if I were to exchange and save some of it in a foreign bank account.

I got into currency trading in 2008, when the stock market and the U.S. dollar crashed. In a bet against the U.S. dollar, I traded $10,000 worth of Japanese yen in September 2008 using a forex broker margin account. Within a month, my initial investment was doubled as the USD dropped like a rock. That was the most I had ever made in a month. Naturally, I decided to quit my electrical engineering career path, jump on a plane to the financial district on Wall Street in New York, and work in the currency trading industry.

Focusing on factors that affect the U.S. dollar

The U.S. dollar (USD) is one the most popular currencies globally. If you travel to any country in the world, that country likely accepts the U.S. dollar in return for its local currency. This clout gives the United States a great privilege. Many people simply pile up on U.S. dollars in their savings account. Often when the demand for USD goes higher, the dollar becomes even stronger. But when the U.S. economy takes a hit, or when the *Federal Reserve* (the United States's central bank, also called the *Fed*) makes pessimistic remarks about the future of the U.S. economy, the U.S. dollar is normally one of the first financial assets to go down.

Uncle Sam has been on watch because China's been ramping up to become a threat to the USD as the world's reserve currency. And now, Bitcoin enthusiasts think the USD and Chinese yuan won't stand a chance against cryptocurrencies in the future.

TIP

If you're buying cryptocurrencies by using the U.S. dollar, you get a better deal if the USD is strong. You can buy more units of a digital coin if its value is low against the USD.

REMEMBER

Many factors affect USD price action. Even though I've studied the U.S. dollar's market movements for over a decade now, I still can't say for sure where its price is headed next. However, by conducting the Invest Diva Diamond Analysis (IDDA; see Chapter 9), you can stack the odds in your favor. Market sentiment, crowd psychology, and supply and demand can all contribute to the strength and weakness of the U.S. dollar the same way they impact other financial assets. The fundamental points can be different, though. Some of the fundamental factors that impact the U.S. dollar value include the following:

>> **Interest rates:** The *interest rate* is the price those who borrow money pay. It refers to the percentage of the borrowed amount of money that the borrower pays to the lender. When the U.S. Federal Reserve increases interest rates or is expected to do so, the U.S. dollar often gets stronger versus other fiat currencies and cryptos alike. While all economic calendars on websites such as Bloomberg (www.bloomberg.com) or Yahoo! Finance (https://finance.yahoo.com/) track upcoming and previous interest rate decisions, you can also keep track of the changes directly on the Federal Reserve website in the United States: www.federalreserve.gov/monetarypolicy/fomccalendars.htm.

>> **Inflation:** *Inflation* is the reason why your grandmother paid less for a dozen eggs than you do. It refers to the general increase in the prices of goods and supplies. When inflation gets high, the Fed tries to control it by raising interest rates. Because of the way inflation affects interest rates, an increase in inflation usually has a positive impact on the USD. Inflation data is measured by something called the Consumer Price Index (CPI), which is

also tracked on most economic calendars. In the United States, you can also track inflation on the Bureau of Labor Statistics website: www.bls.gov/schedule/news_release/cpi.htm.

>> **Gross domestic product (GDP):** *Gross domestic product* reflects a country's yearly production and revenue. The U.S. dollar grows stronger when the GDP is high. To get direct access to GDP data, you can check out the Bureau of Economic Analysis website: www.bea.gov.

>> **Unemployment rate:** The U.S. unemployment rate in particular is a huge forex gossip topic. A decline in the unemployment rate means that the economy is doing well and more jobs have been created, which results in a stronger dollar in the United States. You can find the unemployment rate announcement schedules for the United States here: www.bls.gov/schedule/news_release/empsit.htm.

>> **Nonfarm payrolls (NFP):** The *nonfarm payrolls* figure shows the total number of paid U.S. workers in every business, excluding employees of places like farms, private households, and general government. An expanding nonfarm payroll is a good indication that the economy is growing and therefore can lead to a stronger USD. You can find the event schedule and data here: www.bls.gov/schedule/news_release/empsit.htm.

Looking at Bitcoin versus the U.S. dollar

REMEMBER

Even the biggest Bitcoin enthusiasts don't believe Bitcoin can replace the U.S. dollar anytime soon, if ever. Bitcoin must overcome way too many hurdles before it can claim to be the world's reserve currency. Plus, even though Bitcoin is the celebrity of all cryptocurrencies, other, "better" versions of Bitcoin may climb up the digital currency ladder and replace Bitcoin even before it can replace the USD. A few more reasons why Bitcoin likely won't ever replace the USD include the following:

>> Unknown miners all over the world pose a major security threat. We don't know where some of those massive mining farms are located and how they are planning to spend their Bitcoins.

>> In cryptocurrencies like Bitcoin that can be mined, a group of miners hypothetically can get together to control over 50 percent of the network, preventing the normal transaction process and possibly leading to security issues and hacking.

>> There is a very limited supply of coins ever to be created (21 million coins).

>> Forty percent of the world's Bitcoins are held by 1,000 people, so the financial inequality has already begun, putting the power in the hands of a small portion of the world's population. This doesn't sit well with one of the main reasons for blockchain technology (see Chapter 4) and the idea of cryptocurrencies, which is to fix the financial inequality issue around the globe.

>> There is a lack of security, as I talk about in Chapters 3 and 7.

One of the main differences between Bitcoin and the U.S. dollar is price fluctuations. As you can see in Figure 15-1, even when Bitcoin (BTC) was considered to have calmed down in the period between June and September 2018, its price action was way crazier than that of the U.S. Dollar Index, DXY. The DXY measures the value of the USD relative to a basket of foreign currencies. This relative stability gives the USD an edge in terms of security.

FIGURE 15-1:
U.S. Dollar Index (DXY) price action compared to BTC/USD.

Source: tradingview.com

Even though the forex market is known for its price volatility and unpredictable nature, Bitcoin certainly beats the USD at its own game.

REMEMBER

While the mainstream media usually follows only Bitcoin, other cryptocurrencies such as Ethereum (ETH), Litecoin (LTC), and Bitcoin Cash (BCH) can also be traded versus the U.S. dollar on cryptocurrency exchanges such as Coinbase (`www.coinbase.com/join/59d39a7610351d00d40189f0`). However, at least at the time of writing, the majority of other cryptocurrencies, even some of the famous ones like Ripple (XRP) and Stellar Lumens (XLM), can only be traded versus other cryptocurrencies on exchanges such as Binance (`www.binance.com/?ref=18381915`), as they aren't available on exchanges that support the U.S. dollar.

On the other hand, if you're only speculating on cryptocurrency price actions, you may be able to track other cryptocurrencies' values versus the U.S. dollar on websites like the following:

>> **AVATrade:** `www.avatrade.com/?tag=87597&tag2=~profile_default`

>> **eToro:** `http://partners.etoro.com/A75956_TClick.aspx`

Examining the Euro and Other Major Currencies

REMEMBER

You can technically trade any country's currency in the forex market, but seven specific currencies are the most popular. Investors call these currencies the *majors.* They're popular not only because they're more accessible worldwide but also because their movements are more predictable. Moreover, their countries' economies are considered more stable (although this can be debatable). And importantly, transaction fees for trading them are lower compared with other, less popular currencies. Here's the list of majors:

>> Euro (EUR)

>> British pound (GBP)

>> Swiss franc (CHF)

>> Japanese yen (JPY)

>> Canadian dollar (CAD, also known as the loonie)

>> Australian dollar (AUD, also known as the Aussie dollar)

>> New Zealand dollar (NZD, also known as the Kiwi dollar)

TECHNICAL STUFF

When you trade the majors against the U.S. dollar, they're called the *major currency pairs.*

I explain a bit more about each currency in the following sections. I compare the general forex market versus the cryptocurrency market later in this chapter.

The euro and the British pound

The euro is a shared currency among 19 out of the 28 members of the European Union. If the U.S. dollar is the king of the forex market, the euro is queen; it's the second most traded currency in the world after the USD.

The British pound is that black sheep in the family that didn't get on with the euro after the United Kingdom became a member of the eurozone. The British pound was more valuable than the euro, and the UK government didn't want to give it up. Other countries had to give up their national currencies in favor of the more powerful euro. But having a stand-alone currency may be considered a lucky move because when the United Kingdom voted in 2016 to leave the eurozone (in an act called *Brexit*), the separation became a tad less complicated because the currencies were already separate. *Note:* At the time of writing, the Brexit talks are still ongoing, and there's a chance the eurozone will take the United Kingdom back. Regardless, both the EUR and the GBP have been exposed to a ton of volatility ever since the split talks began. Many investors lost money, and many made some.

TIP

Though the long-term view of the EUR and GBP remains unclear, some of my medium-term strategies have worked out in making my students and me richer. For example, I traded the GBP/JPY pair (the British pound versus the Japanese yen) multiple times, as you can see in Figure 15-2. I used a combination of technical analysis, fundamental analysis, and sentimental analysis to develop these trading strategies based on IDDA, which I introduce in Chapter 9. I share the majority of my trading strategies in my Premium Investing Group (`https://learn.investdiva.com/join-group`), but sometimes I also publish them on my blog, like this in this entry: `www.investdiva.com/investing-guide/eurjpy-ichimoku-cloud/`.

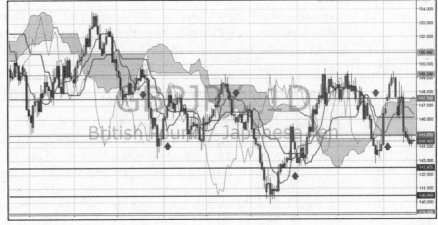

FIGURE 15-2: Trading GBP/JPY between key support and resistance levels of 144.85 and 147.50.

Source: tradingview.com

Safe havens: The Swiss franc and the Japanese yen

The Japanese yen and the Swiss franc are some forex traders' go-to currencies when the U.S. dollar and euro are doing poorly and getting weaker in value. That's why they're often called *safe havens*. I saw this effect firsthand in 2008 when the USD's value was dropping and JPY became one the biggest winners, allowing me to double my first-ever forex trade within a month (check out the sidebar in this chapter for details). The Japanese yen is considered more of a safety zone than the Swiss franc, especially because of a sudden move by the Swiss National Bank (SNB) in 2015 that shocked the financial markets and therefore created a ton of volatility in the CHF on January 15, 2015.

TECHNICAL STUFF

January 15, 2015, was a dark day in the forex community. Many traders, including myself, had parked our bets on the Swiss franc, thinking the Swiss are too neutral to do anything sudden and outrageous to endanger our investments. Boy, were we wrong! On that day, out of nowhere the Swiss National Bank made a change in its currency valuation policy that resulted in a sudden 30 percent increase in the franc's value against the euro. That also meant that my bullish position on the USD/CHF got in trouble. But I was actually lucky, considering I only lost a trade. Many companies actually went bankrupt because of this! You can read about the Swiss franc history and the day that's now remembered as Black Thursday here: www.investdiva.com/investing-guide/swiss-franc-trading-history-future/.

Regardless, both the JPY and the CHF remain safe havens for traders because many investors expect them to keep their value in the times of global financial crisis.

The Aussie, Kiwi, and Canadian dollars

Forex traders consider the Australian dollar, New Zealand dollar, and Canadian dollar *commodity currencies*. The reason is that they're highly correlated to commodity price fluctuations, among other things. For example, Australia has a lot of natural resources like iron, gold, and aluminum. It also has large farms and a ton of cows that produce milk and other dairy products. Australia's economy depends on these commodities, and that's why the Australian currency, the AUD, often takes cues from commodity prices and the state of imports and exports in the country.

TIP

Being China's trading buddy, Australia's economy is also correlated to changes in the Chinese economy. For example, if the Chinese economy is doing poorly or getting hit by tariffs from the United States (as seen in 2018), then the Australian dollar gets weaker. Like its Aussie neighbor, New Zealand is also big on agriculture, so the Kiwi can be impacted by things like the price of grains and dairy products. The Canadian dollar, on the other hand, is often viewed as highly correlated to oil prices. In other words, if the price of oil plummets, then you can expect the Canadian dollar to go down with it. Keep in mind, though, that these correlations aren't absolute, and sometimes other factors such as geopolitical risk events can take over price action.

Comparing the Forex Market and the Crypto Market

People rarely view Bitcoin and other cryptocurrencies as currencies when they invest in them. Most investors and market participants alike treat cryptos like securities such as common stocks. But the fact of the matter is that to buy any cryptocurrency, you have to trade it versus another currency — fiat or crypto — as I explain in Chapter 10. Because of this need, many forex brokers have started offering cryptocurrency services to their forex trading crowd. (Flip to Chapter 6 to explore how you can trade cryptos by using a forex broker.) The following sections spell out some similarities and differences between the forex and the crypto markets.

REMEMBER

Despite a few similarities, comparing forex with cryptocurrencies is like comparing apples and oranges. They're two different financial instruments and require a different type of approach when you're developing investment strategies around them.

The similarities

One of the key similarities between forex and cryptocurrency trading is that they both carry a huge amount of risk. If you choose to trade cryptocurrencies on a short-term basis versus other digital or fiat currencies, you may need to study their price actions by using the technical analysis methods I introduce in Chapter 16. However, as the cryptocurrency market becomes more mainstream, you can expect its movement to become more predictable.

The crazy amount of day-to-day volatility can also be viewed as a similarity. Day traders may benefit from the price fluctuations in both markets. In most cases, liquidity is high enough for major cryptocurrencies and forex pairs to make it easy for trading orders to go through pretty easily.

The differences

Now this point is a lot easier to write about! Here are some of the main differences between the forex and cryptocurrency markets:

WARNING

- » **Size:** The forex market is by far the largest market in the world, and no crypto, no matter how large its market cap is, comes even close to forex. To give you an idea, the forex market has a daily trading volume of around $5 trillion USD. The cryptocurrency market, on the other hand, has a daily volume close to that of the New York Stock Exchange at around $50 billion USD. It's not bad, but forex is the clear winner. (Chapter 8 has more on cryptos and market cap.)

    The fact that the forex market is ultra large doesn't mean you can make more profit in it. If anything, the daily fluctuations make it riskier and harder to predict.

- » **Variety:** You can choose from a ton of cryptocurrencies, but only seven major fiat currencies are actively traded. This range makes the *choosing* part easier for forex traders, while you have to analyze hundreds of cryptos to find yourself a catch. Head to the earlier section "Examining the Euro and Other Major Currencies" for more on the seven most popular fiat options.

- » **Purpose:** Forex is more suitable for day traders. Although short-term trading isn't exactly my cup of tea, most forex traders get in and out of positions a lot more quickly than any other types of investors. By contrast, most crypto investors hold on to their assets for longer period of times.

- » **Money supply:** Money supply is perhaps the key difference between forex and crypto. A country's central bank plays a massive role in determining its major currency's future. But Bitcoin and other cryptocurrencies are products of the blockchain industry; they aren't regulated by a central bank. So the fundamental analysis I talk about in Chapter 9 is entirely different for forex and cryptocurrencies.

Resources for forex trading

Forex was my first love. I made my first trade in forex, wrote my first book about forex, and named my first company Forex Diva. With that, I like to think I'm pretty resourceful when it comes to forex. Here are some quick tips to get you started in forex trading if you're planning to mix things up a little bit with the crypto world.

- » **Forex brokers:** Finding a forex broker that suits your needs is no easy task. You must make sure the broker is safe to carry your investments, complies with your local financial guidelines, has enough money supply and liquidity to execute your trading orders fast, and has reasonable fees for its services, among other things. I explain all about forex brokers and the steps you need to take in choosing one in my education courses, but here's a place you may be able to find the right one for you: `https://forestparkfx.com/?id=UU1U ckhZSVN30W1WNnNuNHIxaH1qUT09`.

WARNING

>> **Your forex account:** Though many brokers offer you an option to start with as little as $50, keep in mind that in order for you to really make profit in the forext market, you must have at least $10,000 of disposable money in your account, as well as superior knowledge about how the market works. Otherwise, you're just gambling and likely to lose your initial investment within months, if not days.

>> **Economic calendar:** To know what's going on in the forex market, you must follow the economic calendars of the countries whose currencies you're about to trade. Many websites offer the forex economic calendar for free, such as the following:

- `www.forexfactory.com/`
- `www.investing.com/economic-calendar/`
- `www.fxstreet.com/economic-calendar`

>> **Forex news:** Besides the economic data, other factors — such as geopolitical tensions, supply and demand of commodities like oil and gold, and speeches by important political figures in a country — influence currency fluctuations. You can find out about these news items on websites such as these:

- `www.dailyfx.com/`
- `www.fxstreet.com/`
- `www.reuters.com/finance/currencies`

WARNING

Forex news outlets often create false hype around the market, which leads to emotional trading decisions. Make sure you don't fall in the trap of clickbait headlines like "The Number One Currency You Should Be Trading Right Now."

>> **Education:** Okay, now I have to toot my own horn. My *Forex Coffee Break* education course has won a bunch of awards and is known as one of the easiest and most fun ways to learn all about forex. Check it out at `https:// education.investdiva.com/forex-coffee-break-with-invest- diva-education-course`.

>> **Strategies:** As a part of my portfolio, I invest in the forex market on a medium-term basis, using the IDDA technique I introduce in Chapter 9. If you're not a day trader, then you may find my Premium Investing Group helpful (`https://learn.investdiva.com/join-group`). It's where I offer not only forex strategies but also cryptocurrency and stock investing signals as well.

4

Essential Crypto Strategies and Tactics

Find out whether technical analysis is a good technique for developing an investment strategy or nothing more than voodoo.

Explore the differences between short-term trading and long-term investing, and decide which one is the right route for you.

Dig into different investment strategy development methods, and incorporate your risk tolerance into your plan for minimizing losses and maximizing gains.

Get introduced to Ichimoku and Fibonacci techniques, and find out how you can use them to enhance your investment strategy.

Make sure you're not getting burned by taxes, and find out different ways you can reduce your crypto-related taxation.

Chapter **16**

Using Technical Analysis

S ome people believe that the financial markets, crypto or otherwise, are just another form of legalized gambling. They believe that the markets move randomly and have no connection to market psychology or to the fundamentals, such as the state of the economy or the people behind a blockchain technology.

I'm not one of those people. Over years of observing and investing in many different markets, I (along with many other fellow investors) have come to see history repeating itself in the markets over and over again. The markets move as a result of a combination of the three top points of the Invest Diva Diamond Analysis (IDDA), which I showcase in Chapter 9:

» Fundamental analysis

» Market sentiment analysis

» Technical analysis

Flip to Chapter 9 for basics of fundamental and market sentiment analysis in the cryptocurrency market. In this chapter, I show you how technical analysis can help you identify the best buy and sell price levels, whether you're a long-term investor or an active trader.

Many cryptocurrency exchanges and brokers offer charting services to make it easier for you to trade directly from their platform. Some of these charts are sophisticated, and some aren't. Personally, I like using TradingView (www.tradingview.com/) for all my technical analysis, from foreign exchange (forex) to stocks and cryptocurrencies. You can use its free service for almost all assets, or you can choose to upgrade to its paid services to access charts without ads and to get some other perks.

Beginning with the Basics of Technical Analysis

In short, *technical analysis* is the art of studying the history of an asset's price action to predict its future. The reason it often works is the result of a bunch of factors, including the following:

>> **Investor behavior:** Research in behavioral finance shows that investors make decisions based on a number of psychological biases that repeat themselves.

>> **Crowd psychology:** Many market participants use the same technical analysis methods, therefore strengthening the key price levels.

When the price movement patterns repeat themselves, investors who spot them early can get an edge in their strategy development and get better-than-average returns. Even though the cryptocurrency market is relatively new, the patterns are already forming in short- and medium-term time frames. The following sections give you basics on chart types, time frames, and psychological factors.

Past performance doesn't guarantee future results. Technical analysis helps only stacking the odds in your favor and doesn't guarantee profit. Therefore, you must conduct proper risk management, as I discuss in Chapter 3.

I talk a great deal about technical analysis in my *Make Your Money Work for You PowerCourse.* Check it out at https://learn.investdiva.com/free-webinar-3-secrets-to-making-your-money-work-for-you.

The chart art

So you want to get down and dirty with the historical price movements of your favorite cryptocurrency. As technical as this type of analysis sounds, you often find yourself using the creative side of your brain when you do it; the chart is your canvas. You can use different types of charts to plot the behavior of any crypto-currency's price against other currencies, *fiat* (government backed) or not. Technical analysts love charts because they can visually track an otherwise number-oriented activity. Charts have evolved in the past decades as an increasing number of investors have used them to develop their strategies across different markets, including the stock, foreign exchange (forex), and cryptocurrency markets.

Some charts are simple and track only the price at the end of a session. Other charts are more complex and track every price movement during the session. Some of the most popular charts include these:

>> **Line charts:** Line charts display only the closing prices of the market. That means for any given time period, you can know only what the crypto's price is at the *end* of that time period and not what adventures and movements it's had *during* that time period. A line is drawn from one closing price to the next closing price, and you can see the general movement of a currency pair over a period of time. Figure 16-1 shows an example, featuring Bitcoin versus the U.S. dollar (BTC/USD) over a one-day time frame.

FIGURE 16-1:
Line chart
of BTC/USD
over one day.

Source: tradingview.com

>> **Bar charts:** No, this option isn't a list of the local drinking establishments. At any given time frame, a *bar chart* shows you the opening market price, the price action during that time frame, and the closing price, as you can see in Figure 16-2. The little horizontal line to the *left* shows the price at which the market opened. The little horizontal line to the *right* is the closing point of the time period. Watch this fun video where I explain about bar charts: https://www.youtube.com/watch?v=RghwgzNgZ64.

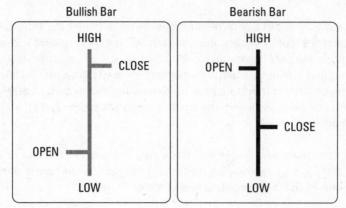

FIGURE 16-2: Bullish and bearish bars.

© John Wiley & Sons, Inc.

>> **Candlestick charts:** *Candlestick charts* look like bar charts, but the area between the open and close prices is colored to show you the general movement of the market during that time period. If the market generally moved up during the time period (known as *bullish* market sentiment), the area is normally colored green. If the market goes down (*bearish* market sentiment), the area is normally colored red. Of course, you can choose any colors you like; I normally like to use green for a bullish market movement and purple for a bearish market movement, as you can see in Figure 16-3. A candlestick chart also shows the low and high price of the asset during the time period.

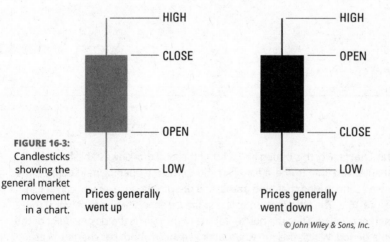

FIGURE 16-3: Candlesticks showing the general market movement in a chart.

© John Wiley & Sons, Inc.

This type of chart is my favorite not only because it's the most visually appealing but also because it was developed by a Japanese rice trader. I lived in Japan for seven years, so I love anything that has Japanese roots or sounds Japanese, like Bitcoin's anonymous founder(s)! Even though no one really knows who started Bitcoin, the anonymous founder(s) at least pretended to be a Japanese guy named Satoshi Nakamoto. Regardless of the fact that there is no proof for this, the smallest unit of Bitcoin is called a Satoshi, and I get a kick out of it whenever I hear it.

The time factor

Depending on the type of investor you are, you can choose different time frames to conduct technical analysis. For example, if you're a day trader and want to take advantage of the crypto markets' fluctuations, you can study the market prices in the past 30 minutes, hour, or four hours. On the other hand, if you're a long-term investor and want to let the markets find their way toward your buy/sell limit orders, then you can analyze the price actions in the past days or months to find repetitive patterns and key psychological price levels. (Hint: That's how I develop my own strategies.)

All types of charts can be used in different time frames. A one-hour line chart shows you the closing price at the end of every hour. A daily candlestick chart shows you the open, close, low, and high prices during one-day periods as well as the general market movement over a longer time frame, as you can see in Figure 16-4. That figure shows Ethereum's price action versus the U.S. dollar (ETH/USD) plotted on a daily candlestick chart.

FIGURE 16-4: Daily candlestick chart of ETH/USD.

Source: tradingview.com

The psychology factor: Trends

As you study market movements, you may start finding patterns and prices that keep showing their faces on the chart. A lot of this repetition has to do with market psychology and the crowd's general feeling about the cryptocurrency.

One of the most eye-catching formations on a chart is a trend. A trend on a chart has nothing to do with trends on Twitter or in the fashion world, but the idea behind it is similar. When you notice that a cryptocurrency's price keeps going up on a chart, that movement means the market participants are feeling good about the crypto. They keep buying it and therefore pushing its price higher. You may even say that the crypto is trending.

REMEMBER

You may have heard the famous investing phrase "the trend is your friend." If you spot the trend early enough, you may be able to take advantage of the rising prices and make some money. Same goes for when the crypto's price is moving down, or is on a *downtrend*. If you spot a downtrend early enough, you may be able to either sell your cryptocurrency or set a limit order (see Chapters 17 and 18) to buy more at a lower price.

Spotting the Key Levels

The whole point of technical analysis is to identify the best prices at which to buy and sell. Ideally you want to buy at the lowest price the cryptocurrency can drop to in the foreseeable future. And you want to hold on to it and sell at the highest price it can reach within your preferred time frame. In well-established markets with a ton of historical data, you can identify these prices by spotting key price levels that have created some sort of restriction for the market movements in the past. In the following sections, I break down some of these important levels.

Support levels

REMEMBER

A *support level* is a barrier that prevents the prices from going lower. It's always below the current market price on your chart. Market participants who spot the support generally wait at that level to buy the cryptocurrency. One of the popular ways to spot a support level is to study the cryptocurrency's past performance on the chart. If a price level keeps "supporting" the cryptocurrency's value from dropping lower, you can mark it as a support level.

As you can see in Figure 16-5, one of Bitcoin's key support levels is around $6,000. Bitcoin's price tested around this psychological level multiple times in 2017 and 2018. But each time, the support level prevented Bitcoin from dropping lower.

FIGURE 16-5:
Bitcoin's key
support level at
around $6,000.

Source: tradingview.com

REMEMBER

Notice I say "around." Support levels aren't always a concrete number. Even though most news outlets say things like "Bitcoin dropped below the $6,000 psychological level," key supports are often a zone rather than a round number.

TIP

The support level becomes stronger the more it's tested. But after strong support is broken, the market sentiment runs a good chance of shifting to bearish and starting to drop lower toward the next support levels.

Resistance levels

REMEMBER

Resistance is a barrier that prevents the prices from going higher. It must be above the current price on your chart, and you can use it as a point to sell your crypto assets. You can identify a resistance level with your naked eye by looking for *peaks* on the chart. Every peak can be considered a resistance level as long as it's above the current market value.

Check out Figure 16-6 for some of Bitcoin's key resistance levels when it was trading around $6,620 in September 2018.

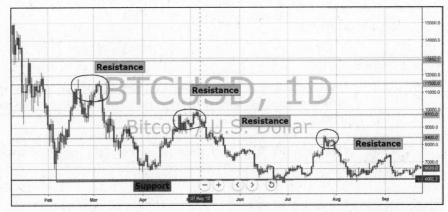

FIGURE 16-6:
Bitcoin's key
resistance levels
in September
2018.

Source: tradingview.com

I personally prefer to use Fibonacci retracement levels to identify support and resistance levels. By applying Fibonacci to a past trend, you can immediately see a number of support and resistance levels without having to apply them one by one on your own. Of course, Fibonacci levels aren't always completely accurate, and you may need to play around with your application a bit to get it right. Check out Chapter 20 to see how.

Trends and channels

Earlier in this chapter, I explain how trends can be formed based on market psychology. Some trends are very easy to spot. For example, the period between July and December 2017 was a period of an extreme *uptrend* in Bitcoin and many other cryptocurrencies when the prices just kept going up. Of course, this strong uptrend caught the attention of many people, investor or not, which led to the crypto bubble that came down crashing in 2018. But spotting trends isn't always as easy.

Drawing trend lines is an art. And just as with any other type of art, everyone has a unique opinion on them. Here are two basic methods to draw an uptrend and a downtrend:

» To draw an uptrend line, when you've casually identified a bullish momentum on the chart, simply click on the trend line instrument on your trading platform and connect two or more major valleys (bottoms) as shown in Figure 16-7.

» To draw a downtrend, connect two or more major peaks (tops).

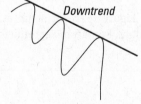

FIGURE 16-7: How to draw uptrends and downtrends.

Uptrend

Downtrend

© John Wiley & Sons, Inc.

If the trend lines are above the current price, you can also consider them *angled* resistance levels. If the line is below the current price, you can use it as a support level.

TIP

Check out this fun, short video where I explain the art of drawing trend lines: `https://www.youtube.com/watch?v=aHOnBcnDumQ&t=1s`.

Now what if the market is moving between two parallel support and resistance levels? Technical chartists call this formation a *channel*. You can use lengthy channels for short-term trading strategies that I talk about in Chapter 17. For example, a common strategy is buying at the lower band of the channel and selling at the upper band. Figure 16-8 shows basic channels you can identify on your chart.

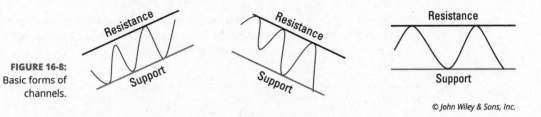

FIGURE 16-8:
Basic forms of channels.

© John Wiley & Sons, Inc.

When the trend is no longer your friend

Unfortunately, trends never continue forever. All good things must come to an end. What goes up must come down. And many other clichés. Identifying the exact time a trend ends is one of the hardest jobs of technical analysts. Oftentimes, the market just teases the crowd with a sudden but short-lived change of direction. Many investors panic. But then the price gets back on track with the long-term trend.

Though key support and resistance levels can help you predict when a trend may end, you must back up your discoveries with fundamental and market sentiment analysis, as I explore in Chapter 9.

Picking Out Patterns on a Chart

Technical analysts are constantly looking for ways to identify key support and resistance levels. This job is no easy task, but chart formations can help you with your observations. Becoming an expert technical chartist can take time, and many analysts go through years of studying for degrees such as the Charted Market Technician (CMT). But for now, here's the gist of some important chart patterns.

In my award-winning education course, *Forex Coffee Break*, I aim to make technical analysis as easy and as fun as possible even for newbies. You can check it out at https://education.investdiva.com/forex-coffee-break-with-invest-diva-education-course.

Bullish reversal patterns

When a *bullish reversal* formation is confirmed, it normally indicates that the trend of the market price will reverse from a downtrend into an uptrend. It reverses the market into a bullish position. Some well-known bullish reversal chart patterns (shown in Figure 16-9) include the *double bottom* (when the price tests a key support level twice, creating two valley shapes at the support level), *the head and shoulders bottom* (when the price tests approximately the same support level three times), and the *saucer bottom* (when the price gradually reaches a key support level and gradually moves up, forming a shape of a bowl).

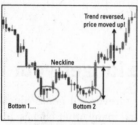
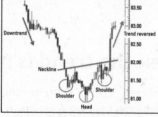
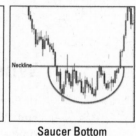

FIGURE 16-9: Examples of bullish reversal chart patterns.

Double Bottom   Head and Shoulders Bottom   Saucer Bottom

© *John Wiley & Sons, Inc.*

TIP

A popular trading strategy that uses bullish reversal patterns is to buy when you identify the pattern at its so-called *neckline* (which is a key resistance level) and sell at the next key resistance levels.

Bearish reversal patterns

As its name suggests, a *bearish reversal* formation is the exact opposite of a bullish one (see the preceding section). With a bearish reversal, the prices normally hit a resistance during an uptrend and can't go any higher. Therefore, they're forced to reverse into a bear market. Some famous bearish reversal patterns (shown in Figure 16-10) include the *double top* (a formation of two mountain-like shapes on the chart as the price tests a key resistance level), the *head and shoulders* (when the price tests approximately the same resistance level three times, but the second time it goes a bit higher, making it look like a peaking head), and the *saucer top* (when the price gradually reaches a key resistance level and then gradually moves back down).

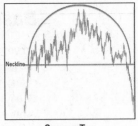

Double Top   **Head and Shoulders**   **Saucer Top**

FIGURE 16-10:
Examples of
bearish reversal
chart patterns.

© John Wiley & Sons, Inc.

TIP

Some typical strategies using bearish reversals include the following:

>> Take profit of assets you've been holding after you identify the pattern.

>> Short-sell at the neckline and take profit at the next support levels.

Smoothing Charts Out with Moving Averages

If you find price charts and all the information they contain too complicated, you're not alone! Likeminded investors and chartists often turn to tools categorized as moving averages (MAs) to identify those trends more easily.

By definition, a *moving average* is a mathematical procedure that records the average value of a series of prices over time. You have a ton of ways to calculate moving averages and use them based on your trading needs. Some are basic, and some are more sophisticated. Personally, I like to mix and match MAs with technical chart patterns and, of course, Fibonacci retracement levels. The following sections have more on MAs; flip to Chapter 20 for details on Fibonacci retracement levels.

WARNING

You may have gotten used to the idea that trading signals and indicators are often just full of it. The cryptocurrency market often acts in an arbitrary fashion, ignoring all the supposed rules. That's why you should never rely on only one method of analysis and should *always* confirm your decisions with other tools and points of the Invest Diva Diamond Analysis (IDDA) in Chapter 9. On top of that, you should never invest money you can't afford to lose.

Basic moving averages

On your trading chart, you can find basic moving averages (MAs) that smooth out the prices ranging from 10 to 200 time periods. For example, if you look at a daily chart, you can select a short-term moving average that calculates a series of 15 data points. This figure is called a *15-day moving average*, or a *fast MA*. If you want to see a longer-term average movement, you can use a longer period, such as 200 days, and call it a *slow MA*.

REMEMBER

Longer-term moving averages do a better job at picking up the major trends. On the other hand, shorter-term MAs are more sensitive to recent price actions. Technical analysts often use a combination of MAs and study their positioning versus one another.

Sophisticated moving averages

Geeky technical analysts like me often take their MA practice to the next level, using more complex combinations of moving averages to understand the market sentiment better. Here are some of the most widely used sophisticated MAs:

>> **Moving average convergence divergence (MACD):** MACD is an indicator that shows the difference between a short-term moving average and a long-term moving average. Click here for more information: www.investdiva.com/investing-guide/macd/.

>> **Bollinger Bands:** Created by Mr. Bollinger in the 1980s, this indicator includes two bands above and below the market price. Click here for more information: www.investdiva.com/investing-guide/bollinger-bands-bol/.

>> **Relative strength index (RSI):** RSI is a momentum indicator, or oscillator, that measures the relative internal strength of the cryptocurrency's price against itself. Click here for more information: www.investdiva.com/investing-guide/relative-strength-index-rsi/.

>> **Ichimoku Kinko Hyo:** This option is my personal favorite; it consists of five different MAs all on top of each other. It gives you all you need to know all at once (hence its name, which means "a glance at the chart in balance"). Head to Chapter 20 for more details.

Chapter **17**

Short-Term Trading Strategies

L et me set this straight: I'm not a big fan of short-term trading. It's a personality thing. Some traders thrive on the thrill of short-term trading adventures, or *speculative trading*. I sweat on speculations. I prefer to invest long term, sit back, relax, have nights of peaceful sleep, and let the markets do their thing. (You can discover some long-term investing strategies in Chapter 18.)

That being said, I have many students who ask me for short-term strategies. And being the awesome coach that I am, I deliver. In this chapter, I go through some methods I use to develop short-term strategies that have worked for my students in the past. Although the basics of short-term trading are similar across different assets, crypto trading requires you to consider some additional steps to stack the odds in your favor.

Distinguishing Three Short-Term Time Frames

Short-term trading can also be called aggressive trading. Why? Because you're taking more risk in the hope of making more profit. As I discuss in Chapter 3, investment of any kind requires a constant balancing and trade-off between risk and return. To earn more return, you must take more risk. When aiming to make money in the short term, you must be prepared to lose your investment (and maybe even more!) in that time frame as well, especially in a volatile market like cryptocurrencies.

Short-term trading can be divided into different categories within itself based on how quickly you realize the profits — hours, days, or weeks. Generally speaking, the shorter the trading time frame, the higher the risk involved with that trade. The following sections spell out the three most common short-term trading time frames for cryptocurrencies.

Profiting within hours

If you've ever wondered what a day trader does, this is it! *Day trading* is one form of aggressive short-term trading. You aim to buy and sell cryptos within a day and take profit before you go to bed. In traditional markets like the stock market, a trading day often ends at 4:30 p.m. local time. But the cryptocurrency market runs 24/7, so you can define your day-trading hours to fit your schedule. Pretty neat, right? With this great power comes great responsibility, though. You don't want to lose your shirt and get your spouse angry at you.

Here are a few questions to ask yourself to determine whether day trading is indeed the right crypto route for you:

>> Do you have the time to dedicate to day trading? If you have a full-time job and can't stick to your screen all day, day trading probably isn't right for you. Make sure you don't use your company time for trading! Not only you can get fired, but you also won't be able to dedicate the required time and energy to trading either. Double the trouble.

>> Do you have sufficient risk tolerance for day trading? Check out Chapter 3 for more on risk management, and attend this webinar to calculate your risk tolerance:https://learn.investdiva.com/free-webinar-3-secrets-to-making-your-money-work-for-you.

>> Even if you can financially afford to potentially lose money day trading, are you willing to do so? Do you have the stomach to see your portfolio go up and down on a daily basis? If not, perhaps day trading isn't right for you.

If you've made up your mind that day trading is the right crypto route for you, the following sections share some tips to keep in mind before getting started.

Define crypto trading sessions

Because cryptocurrencies are traded internationally without borders, one way you can define a trading day is to go by the trading sessions in financial capitals of the world like New York, Tokyo, the *eurozone* (made up of the European countries whose official currency is the euro), and Australia. Figure 17-1 shows these sessions. This method follows similar trading sessions as in the foreign exchange (forex) market.

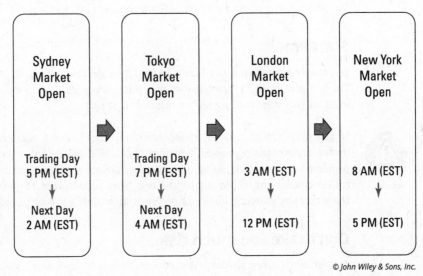

FIGURE 17-1: Cryptocurrency trading sessions based on international time zones.

Sydney Market Open	Tokyo Market Open	London Market Open	New York Market Open
Trading Day 5 PM (EST) ↓ Next Day 2 AM (EST)	Trading Day 7 PM (EST) ↓ Next Day 4 AM (EST)	3 AM (EST) ↓ 12 PM (EST)	8 AM (EST) ↓ 5 PM (EST)

TIP

Some sessions may provide better trading opportunities if the cryptocurrency you're planning to trade has higher volume or volatility in that time frame. For example, a cryptocurrency based in China, such as NEO, may see more trading volume during the Asian session.

Know that day trading cryptos is different from day trading other assets

When day trading traditional financial assets such as stocks or forex, you can follow already established fundamental market-movers such as a company's upcoming earnings report or a country's interest rate decision. The cryptocurrency market, for the most part, doesn't have a developed risk-event calendar. That's why conducting fundamental analysis (see Chapter 9) to develop a day-trading strategy is way harder for cryptos.

Set a time aside

REMEMBER

Depending on your personal schedule, you may want to consider scheduling a specific time of the day to focus on your trades. The idea of being able to trade around the clock is pretty cool in theory. You can just get on your trading app during a sleepless night and start trading. But this flexibility can backfire when you start losing sleep over it. Remaining alert during day trading, or night trading for that matter, is very important because you need to develop strategies, identify trading opportunities, and manage your risk multiple times throughout the trading session. For many people, having a concrete discipline pays off.

Start small

Day trading involves a lot of risk. So until you get the hang of it, start with a small amount and gradually increase your capital as you gain experience. Some brokers even let you start trading with a minimum of $50.

WARNING

If you start trading small, make sure you aren't using margin or leverage to increase your trading power. Leverage is one of those incredibly risky tools that's projected as an opportunity. It lets you manage a bigger account with a small initial investment by borrowing the rest from your broker. If you're trying to test the waters by starting small, using leverage will defeat that purpose.

Don't take too much risk

According to Investopedia, most successful day traders don't stake much of their account — 2 percent of it, max — with each trade. If you have a $10,000 trading account and are willing to risk 1 percent of your capital on each trade, your maximum loss per trade is $100 ($0.01 \times $10,000$). So you must make sure you have that money set aside for potential losses, and that you aren't taking more risk than you can afford.

Secure your crypto wallet

One major problem with day trading cryptocurrencies is securing your crypto wallet. As I explain in Chapter 7, the least secure cryptocurrency wallets are online wallets. Because you're going to need your capital handy throughout the trading day, you may have no choice but to leave your assets on your exchange's online wallet, which can expose you to risk of hacking.

TIP

One way to enhance your security here is to not actually buy and sell cryptocurrencies but rather to speculate the price action and crypto market movements by using brokers who facilitate such services, as I discuss in Chapter 6.

Stay away from scalping

Scalping is the shortest-term trading strategy some individual traders choose. It basically means jumping in and out of trades frequently, sometimes in a matter of seconds. If you're paying commission fees for every trade, not only are you exposing yourself to a ton of market risk when scalping, but you can also get burned out by the fees before you make any profit. Individual traders rarely make any profit scalping. Now, if you're part of an enterprise that has access to discount commission fees and huge trading accounts, the story may be different.

Profiting within days

If you want to trade short term but don't want to stick to your computer all the time, this time frame may be the right one for you. In traditional trading, traders who hold their positions overnight are categorized as *swing traders.* The most common trading strategy for swing traders is *range trading,* where instead of riding up a trend, you look for a crypto whose price has been bouncing up and down within two prices. The idea is to buy at the bottom of the range and sell at the top, as you can see in Figure 17-2. If you're using a broker who facilitates short-selling services, you can also go the other direction.

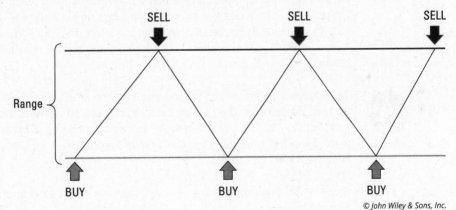

FIGURE 17-2:
A simplified range-trading strategy.

© John Wiley & Sons, Inc.

Of course, in real life the ranges aren't as neat and pretty as what you see in the example I put together for Figure 17-2. To identify a range, you must be proficient in technical analysis. A number of technical chart patterns (see Chapter 16) and indicators can help you identify a range. For more on technical analysis, check out my award-winning trading courses at https://learn.investdiva.com/services.

REMEMBER

If you choose swing trading rather than day trading, one downside is that you may not be able to get an optimized tax rate that's created for day traders in some countries. In fact, swing trading is in the gray area for taxation because if you hold your positions for more than a year (long-term investing; see Chapter 18), you also get an optimized tax rate. For more on tax optimizations, flip to Chapter 21.

TIP

If you're trading the cryptocurrency market movements without actually buying them, make sure you aren't paying a ton of commission fees for holding your positions overnight. Consult with your broker before developing your swing-trading strategy, or check out `https://forestparkfx.com/?id=UU1UckhZSVN3OW 1WNnNuNHIxaH1qUT09` to select a broker that suites your strategy.

Profiting within weeks

This time frame falls into the category of *position trading* in traditional markets. Still shorter than a long-term investing strategy but longer than day trading, this type of short-term trading can be considered the least risky form of short-term trading. But it's still risky. (Flip to Chapter 3 to read more about risks involved in trading cryptocurrencies.)

For this type of trade, you can identify a market trend and ride it up or down until the price hits a resistance or a support. As I explain in Chapter 16, a *resistance* level is a psychological market barrier that prevents the price from going higher. A *support* level is the opposite: a price at which the market has difficulty "breaking below."

WARNING

To hold your positions for weeks, you need to keep your crypto assets in your exchange's online wallet, which may expose you to additional security risk (as I explain in Chapter 7). You may be better off utilizing a broker that provides price-speculation services for this type of trading strategy so you don't have to own the cryptocurrencies.

One popular position-trading strategy involves the following steps, as you can also see in Figure 17-3:

>> Identify a trend (using technical analysis).

>> Wait for a pullback.

>> Buy at the pullback within the uptrend.

>> Take profit (sell) at a resistance.

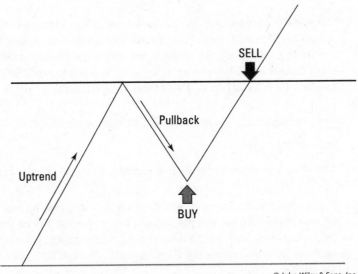

SELL

Pullback

Uptrend

BUY

© John Wiley & Sons, Inc.

FIGURE 17-3: Buying at the pullback in an uptrend market, taking profit at resistance.

TIP

In my Premium Investing Group, I often provide position-trading strategies for members by using the Ichimoku Kinko Hyo + Fibonacci combo technique. See Chapter 20 for more about this technique, and visit here to join the group: https://learn.investdiva.com/join-group.

Trying Short-Term Analysis Methods

You can't become a successful short-term trader just by reading the news. Short-term trading is an art that combines active risk management with a great understanding of crowd psychology and price actions that goes beyond the scope of this book. Also, the cryptocurrency market isn't as established as other markets, so trading the lesser-known cryptos on a short-term basis can be even riskier. You can compare that to trading penny stocks or gambling, which are almost sure ways to lose money. Regardless, the following sections present some analysis methods that professional traders with large accounts and a high risk tolerance can use.

WARNING

According to Medium.com, day trading the cryptocurrency market has brought some investors profits between 1 and 2 percent, while on other values they *lose* money. For most, day trading the crypto market has been a zero-sum game.

Deciphering chart patterns

You can use the majority of the chart patterns I talk about in Chapter 16 for short-term trading as well as medium- and long-term trading strategies (covered in

Chapter 18). All you need to do is to set your chart view to a shorter time frame. I normally check with three different time frames when developing a trading strategy. If I'm analyzing the markets for more rapid profit-taking, I look at three short time frames. For example, if you're looking to profit within hours, you can analyze the price action on these three time frames:

» 30-minute chart (to get a sense of the market sentiment)

» Hourly chart

» Four-hour chart (to get an understanding of the bigger picture)

If you see different forms of bullish reversal chart patterns (see Chapter 16) across all three time frames, you may have a higher probability of a new uptrend starting, which can lead you to a successful bullish trading strategy. The following sections show an example of the Bitcoin/U.S. dollar (BTC/USD) crypto/fiat pair on September 5, 2018.

TIP

I use `https://tradingview.go2cloud.org/aff_c?offer_id=2&aff_id=13497` for charting as they provide many technical analysis tools and customizable charts.

A 30-minute chart

You're looking at the 30-minute chart, and at 9:30 a.m., you suddenly see a massive drop that brings Bitcoin's price down from approximately $7,380 to $7,111, as you can see in Figure 17-4. This formation is called a *bearish engulfing candlestick pattern* among technical analysts. Is this the beginning of a new downtrend?

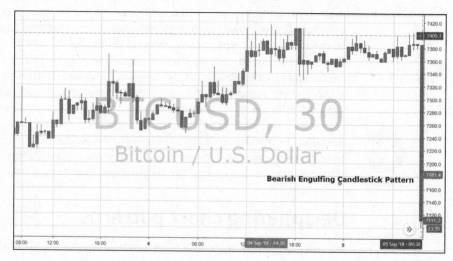

FIGURE 17-4:
BTC/USD
30-minute chart
on September 5,
2018.

Source: tradingview.com

An hourly chart

By switching from the 30-minute chart (see the preceding section) to the hourly chart, you notice the same drop (shown in Figure 17-5). But because now you can see the bigger picture, you discover that this drop was after a period of uptrend in the market, which may be a signal of a pullback during an uptrend. But how low can the pair go?

FIGURE 17-5:
BTC/USD hourly chart on September 5, 2018.

Source: tradingview.com

A four-hour chart

By switching from the hourly chart (see the preceding section) to the four-hour chart, you notice that the bearish engulfing pattern is formed in a much longer uptrend that has been moving up since the middle of August. By observing the four-hour chart, you can pinpoint the key support levels, shown at $6,890 and $6,720, that the price can pull back toward within this newly established bearish market sentiment. In Figure 17-6, I've used the Fibonacci retracement levels to identify the key price levels with higher accuracy. Flip to Chapter 20 for more on Fibonacci.

Following the technical analysis guidelines, you can expect a bit of a correction after this sudden drop, followed by more drops to key support levels on the four-hour chart. With this, a potential trading idea may be to sell at correction or at market price and then to take profit at one or two support levels.

FIGURE 17-6:
BTC/USD
four-hour
chart on
September 5,
2018.

Source: tradingview.com

After sudden drops in the markets, sometimes the market corrects itself before dropping more. Often, it corrects itself to key *pivot levels* (a level that's considered trend-changing if the price breaks below or above it), which in this case is the 23 percent Fibonacci retracement level at $7,090. The reward for waiting for a correction is that you may be able to take more profit short-selling at a higher price. The risk with it is that the market may not correct itself, and you may miss out. Personally, if I think the market is really going to shift into a bearish sentiment, I sell some at market price and set a sell *limit order* at the key pivot level just in case the market corrects itself before further drops. This way, you can distribute your risk. A sell limit order is a type of trading order you can set on your broker's platform, which enables you to sell your assets at a specific price in the future.

For a short-term profit-taking, I consider setting buy limit orders at both key support levels at 38 percent and 50 percent Fibonacci retracement levels. In this example, I aim to take partial profit at around $6,890, and then exit the trade completely at $6,720. Again, this approach may limit my gains if the market continues to drop, but it also limits my risk if the price doesn't fall as low as the second key support, so it gives me proportionate risk–reward ratio. Figure 17-7 shows how the market actually performed.

The BTC/USD price did correct a little bit, but it didn't go as high as the 23 percent Fibonacci retracement level. So if you had only waited for a correction to sell, you would've missed out on the trading opportunity. The market did drop to both key support levels at 38 percent and 50 percent Fibonacci retracement levels. So if you had sold at market price, you would've taken profit at both key support levels. On the other hand, the price continued to drop beyond the 50 percent Fibonacci retracement level, so that may represent a missed opportunity to maximize your returns.

Source: tradingview.com

FIGURE 17-7:
BTC/USD
four-hour chart
strategy
performance.

REMEMBER

However, in my opinion, it's always better to be safe than sorry. That's why I always recommend that my students avoid being greedy when it comes to strategy developments.

Using indicators

Another popular technical analysis method is to use indicators such as the relative strength index (RSI), Bollinger Bands (BOL), and Ichimoku Kinko Hyo (ICH). I call such indicators elements of a beauty kit. By adding them to your chart, you make it more beautiful and accent the important features just as you would by putting on makeup on your face!

Indicators are mathematical tools, developed over the years by technical analysts, that can help you predict the future price actions in the market. You can use these indicators in addition to chart patterns to get a higher analysis accuracy. But in short-term trading, some traders use only one or two indicators without paying attention to chart patterns. In fact, you can create a whole trading strategy by using only one indicator in short-term trading. Flip to Chapter 16 for more on indicators. To find out more about my signature Ichimoku-Fibonacci combo strategy, check out Chapter 20 and my book, *Ichimoku Secrets* (CreateSpace Independent Publishing Platform): https://learn.investdiva.com/ichimoku-secrets-trading-strategy-ebook.

Avoiding illegal pump-and-dump stuff

As a cryptocurrency trader, you need to be aware of what can happen among illegal group activities that manipulate the markets, take profit, and leave others shirtless. A *pump-and-dump* scheme happens when a group of people or an influential individual manipulates the market prices in its own favor. For example, in an unlikely illegal act, a highly influential person named Joe goes on TV and says, "I think Bitcoin is going to reach $60,000 tomorrow," while he already has an established buy and sell strategy to trade a ton of Bitcoin. The moment his speculation hits the news, everyone else who's watching TV gets excited and start buying Bitcoin based on this suggestion. The hype helps Bitcoin's price go up and Joe's strategy to go through. But before the rest of the market can catch up, Joe sells (dumps) his Bitcoins, taking a ton of profit but sending Bitcoin's price crashing down.

REMEMBER

Pump-and-dump schemes can happen in any market. But at least with traditional markets like equities, the Securities and Exchange Commission (SEC) actively tries to go after the bad guys. In the cryptocurrency market, the regulations have yet to be fully established. According to a study published by the *Wall Street Journal*, dozens of trading groups manipulated cryptocurrency prices on some of the largest online exchanges, generating at least $825 million between February and August of 2018.

On the other hand, websites like `https://pumpdump.coincheckup.com/` help traders identify potential pump-and-dump schemes in the market by tracking the cryptos that suddenly spike over 5 percent within five minutes.

Managing Short-Term Trading Risk

Managing your risk when short-term trading can be quite different from that of medium- and long-term investing. To avoid a major account meltdown trading short term, you must balance your risk and return more actively. Using a stop-loss order is one method to consider.

A *stop-loss* order is a price at which you tell your broker to "stop your losses" and get you out of your position. For example, say you think Bitcoin is going to go up from $6,000 to $6,100 in the next hour, so you enter a buy position. But instead, Bitcoin starts dropping below $6,000, putting you in a losing position. To avoid losing too much money, you can set a stop-loss order at $5,950. You can set a risk-reward ratio at any number that makes sense to your risk tolerance.

I famously don't use stop-losses when investing long term. (I talk about it in the free master class at https://learn.investdiva.com/free-webinar-3-secrets-to-making-your-money-work-for-you. I also discuss long-term strategies in Chapter 18.) Some traders argue that when you're trading short term, not using a stop-loss can result in your account getting completely wiped out.

WARNING

In medium to long-term trading, using a stop-loss can be riskier than not using it, especially if you're not a full-time trader. Make sure you have a complete understanding of your trading objectives and risk tolerance before using a stop-loss in crypto trading.

TIP

One easy way to calculate your risk-reward ratio is to divide your estimated net profit (the reward) by the price of the maximum risk you're willing to take. For example, if you want to have a 1:2 risk-reward ratio, that means you're willing to make double the amount of what you're willing to risk. But before you understand how much risk you can take, you must calculate your risk tolerance, which I discuss in Chapter 3.

Chapter **18**

Long-Term Investing Strategies

D o you know how long the first Bitcoin investors waited to see any type of return? Around seven years. Some Bitcoin miners and early investors actually forgot about their crypto assets and had to go on a treasure hunt to find their Bitcoin wallets during the 2017 bubble.

The point is that just like many other markets, time and patience can be your best friends. But you still need to have a plan based on your risk tolerance and financial goals in order to profit long term. In this chapter, I go over the basics of long-term investing in cryptocurrencies.

Time Is on Your Side: Getting Started with Long-Term Investing

When I talk about long-term investment strategies, I'm basically treating crypto-currencies as assets. And just like any other type of financial investment, you need to create a portfolio that goes along with your risk tolerance and financial goals. To do so, you can begin by examining the criteria for constructing your crypto portfolio (such as risk management, discussed in Chapter 3) and then use them to develop a plan for allocating different types of crypto assets in the various categories I explore in Chapter 8. In the following sections, I dig into a couple of things to keep in mind when getting started with your portfolio management.

Your personal goals and current situation

REMEMBER

You should consider a wide variety of issues when managing your portfolio long term. Factors like risk and return are some of the obvious ones that I cover in Chapter 3. But when it comes to long-term investment in risky assets like cryptocurrencies, you need to take it a step further. Here are some questions you should answer:

>> What's your income size now, and where can it go in the future?

>> Are you likely to change your job in the future? Is your current job secure?

>> What's your marital status now? Do you have any children? Where do you see yourself on this front in five years?

>> What's your investment experience?

>> Do you have any other investments in assets such as equities or real estate? How diversified is your overall portfolio?

These questions may sound cliché, and you may already have the answers in your head. But investing long term is a logical process, and actually writing down the most basic elements of your personal goals and characteristics always pays off. When you've assessed your own financial situation and goals, you can have a better understanding of how to move forward with your crypto portfolio. Your needs may even determine the avenue you choose.

For example, if you're retired and your income depends on your portfolio, long-term cryptocurrency investing may not be suitable for you. You may want to consider a lower-risk, current-income-oriented approach. If you're young and willing to take the risk in the hope of getting high returns, you may even consider the short-term trading strategies I cover in Chapter 17. Personally, as a married person with a secure job and one little baby (Jasmine), I allocated 15 percent of my portfolio to cryptocurrencies in 2017 and gradually increased it as the markets fell. For my parents, I chose a different approach. They're retired and need current income to survive. That's why I recommended that they allocate only 5 percent of their savings to cryptocurrencies in 2018 with the goal of capital gains in the next few years.

REMEMBER

To sum it up, build your portfolio around your needs depending on the following variables:

>> Your current income

>> Your age

>> The size of your family

>> Your risk preferences

TIP

For more on risk management and calculating your risk tolerance, check out Chapter 3 and this free master class: `https://learn.investdiva.com/free-webinar-3-secrets-to-making-your-money-work-for-you`.

Your portfolio's objectives

REMEMBER

Assessing your personal goals and life situation brings you one step closer to creating your own portfolio (see the preceding section). When creating a long-term portfolio, you generally want to consider these objectives:

>> **Generating current income:** These investments can generate a regular payment, which can be at odds with high capital appreciations.

>> **Preserving capital:** This low-risk, conservative investment strategy generates moderate returns.

>> **Growing capital:** Focusing on capital growth requires you to increase your risk tolerance and reduce your need for a current-income-based investment strategy.

>> **Reducing taxes:** If you're in a high tax bracket, you may consider a portfolio that generates capital gains. If you're in a lower tax bracket, you have lower incentive to defer taxes and earn high investment returns, so a portfolio with higher-current-income assets may be suitable for you.

>> **Managing risk:** You should always consider the risk-return trade-off in all investment decisions.

They get tied together with your personal goals and other investments. For example, current income and capital preservation are good objectives for someone with a low risk tolerance who has a conservative personality. If you have medium risk tolerance and don't need to depend on your investment for current income as much, you can select capital growth as your portfolio objective. In many countries, including the United States, taxes also play a major role in your investment goals. For example, if you're in a high tax bracket, focusing on capital gains may be a better option for you because you can defer taxes, as I explain in Chapter 21. Last but not least, you should consider your risk-return trade-off in all your investment decisions, whether long term or not.

TIME AND CRYPTOS: THE FAMOUS PIZZAS

To truly understand the significance of time in holding your assets, consider this true story. On May 22, 2010, a Bitcoin miner named Laszlo Hanyecz spent 10,000 Bitcoins to buy (hold your breath) two large pizzas from Papa John's. At the time, the 10,000 Bitcoins were worth about $30. This transaction is widely believed to be the first time anyone used Bitcoins to buy something tangible. He even posted about his purchase on a popular Bitcoin Forum at the time, Bitcoin Talk, as you can see here: `https:// bitcointalk.org/index.php?topic=137.0`.

By May 22, 2018, a mere eight years later, the amount he paid in Bitcoin for the two pizzas was the equivalent of $83.7 million. That's about $42 million per pie. Now May 22 is known as Bitcoin Pizza Day.

What's the moral of this story? Every time you get impatient with your long-term crypto investments, remember poor Laszlo kicking himself on Bitcoin Pizza Day, knowing he could've been a millionaire had he just sat on his Bitcoins for a few years instead of getting the instant gratification those two pizzas brought him.

Creating Long-Term Strategies

Any type of investment can be summed up in four words: Buy low, sell high. But of course no one can get it perfectly right every time. With cryptocurrencies in particular, the market is still testing out new psychological levels, so predicting the highs and lows can be that much more difficult. The following sections introduce some methods I've been using to expand my long-term cryptocurrency portfolio.

Observing psychological levels

In 2018 the crypto market still isn't mature enough to enable thorough long-term technical analysis. Besides Bitcoin, many cryptocurrencies are so new that they haven't even formed a full cycle on the trading charts. But as time goes by, key psychological support and resistance levels have started to develop. I've found Fibonacci retracement levels (see Chapter 20) very helpful in identifying key levels even in the newer cryptocurrencies.

The reason psychological levels are already appearing in the crypto market may be that many crypto investors are using traditional technical analysis methods (see Chapter 16) for their cryptocurrency investment strategies. With that, you can expect the crypto crowd psychology to form similar chart patterns to those of other markets, such as equities and the foreign exchange market (forex), in longer time frames like weekly and monthly charts. Crowd psychology is the constant battle between the sellers (the bears) and the buyers (the bulls) in the market that leads to price movements in an asset. Psychological levels are those that the prices have difficulty breaking, due to the strength or weakness of the bears and bulls in the market.

TIP

You can find a great deal about investing crowd psychology in plain (and funny) videos in my *Forex Coffee Break* education course at `https://learn.investdiva.com/forex-coffee-break-with-invest-diva-education-course`.

After you identify the psychological levels, you can use them to develop different types of strategies based on your current portfolio, your risk tolerance, and your financial goals. Here are some examples:

>> Buy at a key support level and sell at a key resistance level.

>> Buy at current market price and sell at a key resistance level.

>> Wait for a pullback when the price reaches a key resistance level and buy lower. Then sell at the next key resistance level.

>> Buy at a key support level and hold long term.

You can use the techniques in Chapters 16 and 20 to identify such support and resistance levels for your investment strategy.

Selling when you reach your goal

A cryptocurrency's price may continue going higher after it reaches a key resistance level. But how long do you wait? Which resistance level do you choose? Does using resistance levels even make sense for your financial goals? One realistic way to approach your investment strategy is to sell when you've reached your investment goal. (You can use a sell limit order, which I talk about later in this chapter, to do this.) The key here is that you shouldn't look back and regret your decision after you've made the sale, even if the price continues going up after you sell.

REMEMBER

Markets may continue to go up after you sell. Don't let your emotions take over your logical decision to sell. If you need the money and have already achieved your investment goal, you have no reason to regret an early sale. If anything, you can always get back in the market with a brand-new investment strategy.

Keeping tax consequences in mind

TIP

Tax laws change all the time, and they vary in different countries. However, in most cases taxes affect nearly all investment actions. As of 2018, in the United States a maximum of $3,000 of capital losses in excess of capital gains can be written off against other income in any one year. If you have a loss position in an investment and have concluded that selling it is wise, the best time to sell is when you have a capital gain against which you can apply the loss.

Before starting to invest, you must understand the basics of taxes in your country. Flip to Chapter 21 for an overview of how you should consider taxes before making investment decisions.

Considering Limit and Stop-Loss Orders

Cryptocurrency exchanges and brokers alike allow you to use various types of orders to buy and sell altcoins. Most active traders use *market orders* to buy or sell at the best available price, but long-term investors can use other types of orders such as limit orders and stop-loss orders.

TIP

Long-term investors can also use market orders in abnormal circumstances if they need to make a quick investment decision. Market orders are normally filled quickly at a price close to the current market price.

WARNING

Using market orders can sometimes involve risks, especially in volatile markets such as cryptocurrencies. Sometimes the price of cryptocurrencies drops or skyrockets in a matter of seconds. If you happen to use a market order on those occasions, you may get blindsided by the actual price at which your order is executed. That's why using a limit order is always safer than using market orders.

Limit orders

A *limit order* is a type of transaction order that allows you to buy or sell at your preferred price. For example, if the current Bitcoin market price is at $6,434, you can set a *buy limit order* to buy at $6,000 or even below that level if you think the price has the potential to drop.

Then you can set a *sell limit order* to take profit when you reach your investment goal, say at $7,000. I love using limit orders because they allow me to go about my life without worrying about prices too much while the markets do their usual movements.

REMEMBER

Always double-check your limit orders before putting them through. Make sure your buy limit order isn't above the current market price and your sell limit order isn't below the current market price. Traditional brokers often send you a warning if you make a mistake in setting limit orders, but at the time of writing, most crypto exchanges don't offer such courtesies. Personally, I've been the victim of setting a careless buy limit order that was way above the current market price, and it immediately went through without a warning from my exchange.

Just like in other markets, cryptocurrency limit orders have different options for how long they stay in effect. The most common types are good til canceled and fill-or-kill:

>> A *good til canceled* (GTC) order normally stays in effect for six months. If it's not executed within that time frame, your broker/exchange may cancel it. If you still want to keep the position in effect, you may need to renew it after six months.

>> A *fill-or-kill* order is canceled if it's not immediately executed. Therefore, it may be a better fit for short-term trading strategies (like those in Chapter 17).

Other types of limit orders offered by your trading platform may include *good til time* (your order stays in effect until a specific time you select) and *immediate or cancel* (your order is canceled if it's not immediately fulfilled by your broker). You can set more than one limit order for your cryptocurrencies. You can also choose to buy fractions of a cryptocurrency, especially when those like Bitcoin are so expensive. For example, in one account, I've set a buy limit order for Bitcoin versus U.S. dollar (BTC/USD) to purchase 0.4 Bitcoins when the price reaches $6,000. On the order form, I've also added a good til canceled buy limit order to buy 0.2 Bitcoins at $5,851. By having multiple limit orders, I eliminate the risk of missing out and avoid going all in at one price.

Stop-loss orders

You can use *stop-loss orders* to limit the downside loss exposure of your crypto investment. Stop-losses are basically a form of limit orders (see the preceding section), where you ask your broker to close your position and take losses at a specific price. I'm not a big fan of stop-losses, but for some investors cutting the losses short in case of a rapid decline in the market may make sense. Just like limit orders, stop-loss orders have different types like good til canceled.

WARNING

Volatile markets such as cryptocurrencies normally bounce back up from the lows as rapidly as they fall. That's why by using a stop-loss order, you may end up getting out of your position prematurely and miss out on potential gains. If you're looking to use a stop-loss order, you must analyze the market carefully and choose an appropriate level for your stop-loss. To get the latest cryptocurrency investment strategies and buy/sell limit order ideas, consider joining Invest Diva's Premium Investing Group at `https://learn.investdiva.com/join-group`.

Chapter **19**

Minimizing Losses and Maximizing Gains

D epending on whether you're a short-term trader or long-term investor, you can manage your portfolio either actively or passively. If you're a long-term investor (see Chapter 18), you may find yourself managing your portfolio passively by buying and holding a well-diversified portfolio over a set amount of time. If you're a short-term trader, you can use the tools I present in Chapter 17 to manage and obtain your desired objectives in a more active way.

I'm a big fan of long-term investing, but that doesn't mean I'm against active portfolio management. In fact, I've seen over and over again that you can get better returns, whether they're long term or short term, by actively managing your portfolio. Now, by *active*, I don't mean sticking to your screen all the time and covertly checking your investment apps throughout the day during conversations and meetings. This chapter explains some management strategies that can help you find a sweet balance to do it all and still maintain an outside life.

Keeping the Losses Down

A phenomenon called *loss aversion* occurs in behavioral finance when investors keep the losing assets in their portfolios while actively selling the "winners." This tendency is why going against the crowd is one way to curtail your losses. In the following sections, I explain some techniques you can use to keep your crypto investing losses down.

Measuring returns

Managing your cryptocurrency investments can be challenging because your assets may be scattered over different exchanges and cryptocurrency wallets. Additionally, you may have purchased some altcoins by using Bitcoin, some others by using the U.S. dollar (USD), and more by using cryptos such as Ethereum or Litecoin. That's why I recommend you keep a log of your investments and ink any changes you make to your portfolio. Here are the three steps in determining your portfolio returns:

>> Measuring the amount you've invested

>> Measuring capital gains, which is the profit you make through buying and selling cryptos

>> Measuring income, which is the payment you get by holding some cryptos (if applicable)

To calculate the amount invested, you can create a list similar to the one in Figure 19-1. The table shows numbers of coins, buying date, cost (both total and per coin), and current value.

My Crypto Portfolio as of September 1, 2018

Coin	Full name	Number of coins	Date bought	Total cost (including commission) (USD)	Cost per coin (USD)	Current price per coin (USD)
BTC	Bitcoin	0.5	6/29/2018	2,965	5,900	7,155
ETH	Ethereum	8	8/14/2018	2,250	275	293
XLM	Stellar Lumens	200	8/07/2018	44	0.200	0.2257
EOS	EOS	50	8/16/2018	225	4.45	6.55

© John Wiley & Sons, Inc.

FIGURE 19-1: An example of a cryptocurrency investment log.

Now, because you may be purchasing different coins by using either *fiat* (government-backed) currencies, such as the U.S. dollar, or other cryptocurrencies, you may need to convert your investment value to one type of currency to keep it simple and easier to track. In Figure 19-1, I converted all my purchasing value to the U.S. dollar (USD). Another way to track your investment is to create separate logs depending how you purchased your altcoins. For example, you can have a separate log for your investments with BTC and another one for those you purchased with USD.

You can create such logs on a monthly, quarterly, or annual basis depending on your investing time frame. For example, if you're a short-term trader, you may need a monthly log. If you're a medium-to-long-term investor, you can use quarterly and annual logs. You can normally find the return on your investment calculated by your brokerage or exchange services (see Chapter 6 for more on brokerages and exchanges).

Many crypto enthusiasts have given up measuring returns against fiat currencies like the USD altogether. If you believe Bitcoin is king and Ethereum is queen, you may end up buying most of your altcoins by using the king and queen anyway. Converting your crypto purchase to its USD value can be time-consuming. Also, most of the time you can't cash out in fiat currencies on your exchange anyway. USD, Bitcoin, and Ethereum all have fluctuations of their own versus other currencies, so a conversion may give you a false gain or loss impression. By converting to USD, it may look like you've gained profit on your initial investment, while in reality you may be in a losing position versus Bitcoin.

If you purchased your coins on an exchange by using another cryptocurrency such as Bitcoin, you can find the relevant USD value by searching your coin and the date you purchased it on websites like `https://tradingview.go2cloud.org/aff_c?offer_id=2&aff_id=13497`.

To measure your capital gains and income, you can simply check your account information with your broker and exchange. With cryptocurrency exchanges, your capital gain information is normally under tabs labeled "Wallet" or "Funds." Most exchanges provide the estimated value of your whole account either in Bitcoin or USD. If you have more than one account, you can add up these estimated numbers in your investment log and monitor them on a regular basis.

Monitoring exchange fees

To buy and sell cryptocurrencies, you need services like crypto exchanges and brokers. These companies mainly make money through transaction fees, as I discuss in Chapter 6. Although I don't recommend choosing an exchange based only on low fees, sometimes fees can become an important decision-making factor, especially for active traders. The fees can get even larger if you're looking to convert a fiat currency to a cryptocurrency like Bitcoin and then send it to another exchange to buy another cryptocurrency by using Bitcoin, and so on. Fees can be the biggest downside to short-term trading strategies for cryptocurrencies.

TIP

Here are some tips for keeping your exchange fees minimal while keeping your investment secure:

>> Buy your lump-sum major cryptos on more secure exchanges, which may have higher transaction fees. For example, when I need Bitcoin and Ethereum to trade other cryptocurrencies, I buy a large amount of both on an exchange with higher fees that allows using the U.S. dollar.

>> For active trading, choose exchanges that offer lower rates for your specific cryptocurrency pair, but make sure to periodically store your profit on a hardware wallet (see Chapter 7 for more on wallets).

>> Consider active trading with the exchange's native cryptocurrency. It may have a lower transaction fee than trading other cross-cryptos. For example, the Binance exchange offers cheaper trading options for its cryptocurrency, Binance Coin (BNB).

>> Always include the transaction fee when calculating your profit to be on top of your game. For example, if you buy 1 Ethereum coin for $200 but you pay $1.50 in transaction fees, you have spent $201.50 for your investment. While this amount doesn't make a great impact for long-term investments, active traders can feel the accumulative fees over time.

Understanding the art of getting out

I normally like to stay true to two of Warren Buffett's most famous investing rules:

1. Never lose money.

2. Never forget rule number one.

But no matter how thoroughly you conduct your analysis, at times you may find that getting out of a bad investment is better than holding onto it. The following sections give a few of my general strategies when it comes to getting out of an investment. Check out Chapter 9 for information on my Invest Diva Diamond Analysis (IDDA) system.

Don't be greedy

If you're using one of the technical chart patterns I present in Chapters 16 and 20, always set your profit taking limit order at the price level that's consistent with the technique. You may get a feeling that the market will continue going up after your profit target (PT) is triggered, and you may be tempted to readjust your PT prematurely. Sometimes the market will continue to rise. Sometimes it won't. Personally, I prefer to be safe rather than sorry, so I refrain from readjusting the PT orders way too often (unless I have a valid fundamental reason to do so besides just gut feeling).

Take partial profits

I simply love this rule and swear by it! You can call me a hoarder, but I can never let go of all my coins (or any other assets, for that matter) all at once. I set up strategic, partial profit taking prices depending on my (or my students') investment goals and let the markets handle the rest.

For example, if I buy 10 Ethereum coins (ETH) at $200 and I'm looking to take partial profit at key levels, I may sell 2 of my Ethereum coins at $470, sell 2 more at $591, and keep the rest long term. This way, I gain some profit along the way but don't let go of all my coins, so I still feel happy when the Ethereum price continues going up after I sell. Of course, calculating those key levels needs thorough analysis.

To view more information on my partial profit taking strategies, join my Premium Investing Group at `https://learn.investdiva.com/join-group`.

Let go of bad investments

Every once in a while, you find yourself holding onto a coin that's just not worth it. With worthy long-term investments, I tend to buy more coins as the price drops, but sometimes the cryptocurrency, its community, and its management simply don't have a future. This point is when reexamining your fundamental analysis (see Chapter 9) becomes important. When it becomes evident that this coin just ain't gonna bounce back, you may as well just bite the bullet and get out before your losses get bigger. If you're too scared to do so, you can always take losses in parts, using the partial profit method I talk about in the preceding section.

By letting go of your bad investments and taking losses, you may receive tax credits you can use to offset the taxes you must pay on your capital gains. Flip to Chapter 21 for more on taxes.

Letting the Profits Rise

I have to deal with two emotions when the markets start to rise. One is regretting not buying more when the prices were down. The other is the temptation to sell and take profit before reaching my carefully analyzed profit target limit order. What I need to keep reminding myself (and my students and fellow investors alike) is that emotions rarely lead to maximizing profit. At the end of the day, discipline is what makes your bank. The following sections detail some tricks I use to avoid emotional investing.

Buying at the bottom

Being able to purchase at the lowest price every time you invest is highly unlikely. But studying the market psychology and historical price patterns can help you get close. One of my go-to technical analysis tools to identify the bottom is the Ichimoku-Fibonacci combo.

As I explain in Chapter 20 and in my book *Ichimoku Secrets* (CreateSpace Independent Publishing Platform), you can use the Ichimoku-Fibonacci combination to gauge crowd psychology and identify key support and resistance levels. (*Support* is a price level where the market has difficulty breaking below; *resistance* is a price level where the market has difficulty breaking above.) For longer-term investing, I generally use the daily chart for Ichimoku analysis. As you can see in Figure 19-2, after the price of Ripple's XRP dropped below $0.70 on May 15, 2018, it then broke below the daily Ichimoku cloud. Following the Ichimoku Kinko Hyo's guidelines, I had an indication that the price of XRP may drop further toward key Fibonacci retracement and support levels at $0.57 and $0.47. By conducting this analysis, I was able to set a buy limit order at these levels ahead of time and aim to purchase at lower prices instead of buying immediately. This way you can maximize your profit and lower your net purchasing price.

TIP

Because the cryptocurrency market doesn't have enough historical data to rely on, sometimes the price continues to drop below the all-time-low levels, creating new lows. If you're confident enough in the fundamentals of the cryptocurrency, the new lows can give you an opportunity to buy more at lower prices. You can use Fibonacci's extended levels to identify new lows. To use these levels, you must first identify a trend where the price went either up or down for an extended period of time recently. Then drag the Fibonacci tool on your charting platform from the top to the bottom of the trend (if it's a downtrend) and from bottom to the top (if it's an uptrend). By doing so, the Fibonacci levels magically appear on your chart. Check out Invest Diva's Premium Investing Group where I routinely share my Ichimoku-Fibonacci strategies: `https://learn.investdiva.com/join-group`.

FIGURE 19-2:
Using the
Ichimoku-
Fibonacci combo
to identify
bottoms.

Source: tradingview.com

Knowing that patience is a profitable virtue

"Patience is a profitable virtue" is my main mantra in all the education courses at Invest Diva! My students say repeating this mantra has changed the way they invest and has increased their profit returns by a fair bit. Whenever I feel the adrenaline rushing through my head from looking at a chart, I take a step back. I change the time frame and look at the big picture. I do more fundamental research. If all five points of the IDDA (see Chapter 9) aren't aligned, I simply log off my trading account and go about my day. Getting nervous is very easy when the markets take a dip and you've invested a bunch of money in an asset. Being patient can often be the ultimate path to making tangible returns.

Identifying the peaks

"Buy low and sell high" is the name of the game! Again, you've got to be either Nostradamus or Lucky Luke to take profit at the highest price every time you invest. But if you use historical data and technical chart patterns, you can stack the odds in your favor. For active trading and medium-term investing in the cryptocurrency market, I still find the Ichimoku-Fibonacci combo pretty useful, as I explain in Chapter 20. Other tools include technical chart patterns and key psychological resistance levels.

Using Ripple's XRP as an example, in September 2018 I identified a double bottom chart pattern in the process of formation on the daily chart, as you can see in Figure 19-3. A *double bottom* is a popular formation on charts, where the price has difficulty breaking below a support level twice, forming two valley-shaped bottoms. When confirmed, it can be interpreted as a bullish reversal pattern, meaning that the prices may start going up.

FIGURE 19-3:
A double bottom chart pattern forming on XRP/USD daily chart.

Following the double bottom chart pattern guidelines (see Chapter 16), medium-term investors can expect the market to take profit when the price has moved up from the neckline ($0.3666 in Figure 19-3) the same distance from the bottom to the neckline, or the next available Fibonacci retracement levels (0.4273 and 0.5314). To be safe, I normally recommend taking partial profits at each level to distribute risk.

As you can see in Figure 19-4, on September 21, XRP reached both levels and then some before dropping back down. A medium-term investor would've taken profit at these levels, while a long-term investor would've stayed in his or her position.

For long-term investors, timing the profit taking can be a bit more challenging. The crypto market is an exciting new investment opportunity that a majority of people are just discovering. Just like with the dot-com bubble, the hype can lead to extreme volatility. You saw the results of the hype in 2017 when Bitcoin price surged over 1,000 percent and Ripple's XRP gained a whopping 36,018 percent. I personally know investors who sold right at the peak and became millionaires and others who bought at the peak and had to sit on their losses until the next surge. In this case, most investors who were able to sell at the peak are those who went against the hype and against the majority of the crowd.

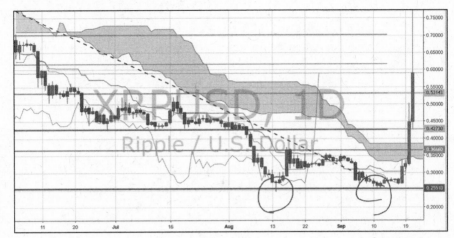

FIGURE 19-4:
A double bottom
chart pattern
confirms, and
XRP reaches
profit target
levels.

Source: tradingview.com

WARNING

Technical chart patterns such as double bottoms, indicators such as Ichimoku, and going against the crowd don't guarantee optimal results. These items are simply tools that increase the probability of identifying the best price to buy and sell. At the end of the day, you must conduct thorough risk management that applies to your personal financial goals and risk tolerance, as I discuss in Chapter 3.

Finding peaks and bottoms with a few trading tools

TIP

Here are some cheat sheets of the trading tools I use to identify peaks and bottoms:

» **Bearish reversal chart patterns:** These patterns form on the chart during a period of surging prices and indicate that the market sentiment and price action may turn bearish and start dropping. Find out more at www.investdiva.com/investing-guide/bearish-reversal-patterns-list1/.

» **Bullish reversal chart patterns:** These patterns form during a downtrend and indicate the prices may start to turn bullish and rise. Check out www.investdiva.com/investing-guide/bullish-reversal-patterns-list/.

» **Ichimoku Kinko Hyo:** This Japanese indicator consists of five different moving averages, helping you get a better view of the current market sentiment and predict the future price action. See www.investdiva.com/investing-guide/ichimoku-kinko-hyo-explained/.

CHAPTER 19 **Minimizing Losses and Maximizing Gains** 247

Chapter **20**

Using Ichimoku and Fibonacci Techniques

In Chapter 16, I talk about how you can use technical analysis to develop cryptocurrency trading strategies. Though a ton of moving averages and chart patterns can help you with your strategy, one of my favorite techniques is combining Ichimoku Kinko Hyo and Fibonacci retracement levels. In this chapter, I overview the basics of these two technical indicators and show you how you can use them for trades.

TIP

Advanced Ichimoku-Fibonacci methods are beyond the scope of this publication; you can discover more about them in my book *Ichimoku Secrets* (CreateSpace Independent Publishing Platform): https://learn.investdiva.com/ichimoku-secrets-trading-strategy-ebook.

Getting a Handle on Ichimoku Kinko Hyo

Its name may sound intimidating, but let me reassure you that Ichimoku Kinko Hyo is here to make your technical analysis easier, not harder! It's a Japanese phrase that roughly translates to "one-piece balanced table." In cryptocurrency investing, Ichimoku Kinko Hyo allows you to find out everything you need to know about the price action in "one glance": Ichimoku.

The components of Ichimoku Kinko Hyo

This indicator consists of several different moving averages (MAs). Each of these MAs serves a specific purpose, and their positioning versus each other and the price can help you understand the current market sentiment and predict its future direction. Here are some of the components you see when you add the Ichimoku Kinko Hyo (ICH) to your chart:

>> The Ichimoku cloud (Japanese name: Kumo)

>> The base line (Japanese name: Kijun)

>> The turn line (Japanese name: Tenkan)

>> The delay span (Japanese name: Chiko)

Your charting provider may use different colors for each of these components, but in Figure 20-1 I use a thick pink line for Kijun, a thick blue line for Tenkan, and a thin green line for Chiko. The Ichimoku cloud is actually the space between two other moving averages, Senkou (leading) span A and B. Depending on the direction of the cloud, this space is normally colored green for bullish and red for bearish market sentiment. (A *bullish* market sentiment means the price is expected to rise. A *bearish* market sentiment is when the prices drop.)

Name	Kumo	Kijun	Tenkan	Chiko
Meaning	Cloud	Base	Turn	Delayed
Image				

FIGURE 20-1: Ichimoku Kinko Hyo components.

© John Wiley & Sons, Inc.

If you're looking for an easy charting service that helps you with technical analysis including Ichimoku and Fibonacci, I recommend TradingView (www.tradingview.com/), which I personally use as well. You can use this charting service for almost any asset, including cryptocurrencies, foreign exchange (forex), and stocks.

Figure 20-2 shows the Ichimoku Kinko Hyo components in action on a chart that displays the price action of Ripple (XRP) versus Bitcoin (BTC) on a four-hour (or 240-minute) basis. That means each of the candlesticks (see Chapter 16) shows the price movements of XRP versus BTC in four hours. The Ichimoku components dance around the prices, crossing above and below the price action depending on the calculations. You can take these movements as indications about the future price direction.

FIGURE 20-2: Ichimoku Kinko Hyo applied to the XRP/BTC four-hour chart.

Ichimoku interpretations

You can use the Ichimoku components' positioning against each other as well as versus the price to predict where the price may go next. The following sections present some basic interpretations of Ichimoku Kinko Hyo.

REMEMBER

Past performance is never an indication of future results. Therefore, all these indications are merely an addition to your thorough research on your investments; you shouldn't treat them as guaranteed strategies. For technical analysis, you must study other chart patterns (see Chapter 16) to further strengthen your Ichimoku strategy. Additionally, always conduct all points of the Invest Diva Diamond Analysis (IDDA; see Chapter 9) before making a final investment decision.

Buy signals

If you identify one or more of the following signals on a chart, chances are that the price may continue higher and therefore it's a good time to buy:

» If the price is moving above the Ichimoku cloud, this movement may indicate a bullish momentum in the market and is therefore a buy signal.

» When the Chiko (delayed) line moves above the cloud, it can be considered a buy signal.

» When the Tenkan (turn) line crosses above the Kijun (base) line, that crossing may indicate a shift in the market sentiment from bearish to bullish and therefore be a buy signal.

Sell signals

The following represent sell signals:

>> When the price moves below the Ichimoku cloud

>> When the Chiko (delayed) line crosses below the cloud

>> When the Tenkan (turn) line crosses below the Kijun (base) line

Other common interpretations

Besides pure buy and sell indications, Ichimoku Kinko Hyo can also help you identify support and resistance layers as well as provide a general understanding of market conditions. Here are some of the interpretations:

>> As long as the five lines are parallel, the trend will continue in that direction.

>> When the prices are inside the Ichimoku cloud, that means that the market is in the process of consolidating, which isn't a good time to buy or sell.

>> You can use the lower band of the prevailing cloud as a layer of support, which is a level that the price has difficulty breaking below.

>> You can use the upper band of the prevailing cloud as a layer of resistance, which is a price that the market has difficulty breaking above.

TIP

You can use Ichimoku as an entry level for both buy and sell positions. You can also combine two or more of the interpretations to adjust your strategy based on your risk tolerance.

Introducing Fibonacci Retracement Levels

Using Ichimoku Kinko Hyo all by itself gives you just a partial view of the markets and doesn't help you with an exit strategy. (Head to the earlier section "Getting a Handle on Ichimoku Kinko Hyo" for more on that indicator.) The next step is to identify key support and resistance levels that the market may have difficulty moving below (in case of a support level) and above (in case of a resistance level). You can search for support and resistance levels in many ways. My favorite is to use Fibonacci retracement levels.

Some background on Fibonacci

Fibonacci is the nickname for Italian mathematician Leonardo Pisano Bigollo, who some refer to as "the most talented Western mathematician of the Middle Ages." Some of his most famous contributions to science include introducing the positional decimal numeral system, also known as the Hindu-Arabic numeral system, to the Western world and popularizing the Fibonacci sequence.

Mathematically, the *Fibonacci sequence* is the series of numbers where each number in the sequence is sum of the two numbers before it. So if you add the numbers 0 and 1, the result is 1, and you add that digit to the sequence. Then add up 1 and 1 and add the result, 2, to the sequence. Now add 1 and 2 — you get the idea. You can continue this way forever: 0, 1, 1, 2, 3, 5, 8, 13, 21, 34, 55, 89, 144 . . .

REMEMBER

The Fibonacci sequence has applications in technical analysis, but the sequence itself isn't exactly what you use. The *Fibonacci retracement levels* you use in technical analysis are a result of calculating the alternate ratio between the numbers in the sequence. By applying the ratios to an uptrend or a downtrend, you can identify support and resistance levels easily.

TECHNICAL STUFF

Here's how the ratios are calculated: After the first few numbers, if you divide any of the numbers by the succeeding number, you get approximately 0.618. For example, 34 divided by 55 rounds to 0.618. If you calculate the ratio between alternate numbers, you get 0.382. The ratio between every third succeeding number is 0.235. The sequence used in technical analysis consists of these ratios: 0.78, 0.618, 0.5, 0.382, and 0.236.

How to insert Fibonacci retracement levels into your chart

The good news is that you don't have to do any math calculations at all! All you have to do is to find the Fibonacci tool on your charting service and apply it to the price action. Here are the specific steps you need to take:

1. **Find a trend in the prices.**

   It can be an uptrend or a downtrend. Flip to Chapter 16 for an introduction to trends.

2. **Find the Fibonacci retracement tool on your cart and click on it.**

3. Click to apply the Fibonacci tool to the bottom of the trend (if it's an uptrend) or to the top of the trend (if it's a downtrend).

4. Drag the Fibonacci tool to the other end of the trend and then click again to drop the Fibonacci retracement levels on the chart.

   The Fibonacci retracement levels appear. Figure 20-3 shows an example.

FIGURE 20-3: Fibonacci retracement levels applied to an uptrend on the XLM/BTC chart.

Figure 20-3 shows the price action of Stellar Lumens (XLM) versus Bitcoin (BTC) in a four-hour chart. The bottom of the trend for the XLM/BTC pair is at 0.00003309, and the top of the trend is at 0.00003901. By dragging the Fibonacci tool from the bottom to the top, you can see the Fibonacci retracement levels marked as 0.78, 0.618, 0.5, 0.382, and 0.236.

Combining Ichimoku and Fibonacci Techniques

When you've got your eyes used to having Ichimoku and Fibonacci indicators on your charts separately (see the preceding sections), you can apply both of them to the chart and let the fun begin. Seeing so many lines on the chart may give you a headache at the beginning, but after a while you may even think that a chart without Ichimoku and Fibonacci is totally naked.

REMEMBER

Sometimes you have so many options to choose from when selecting a trend (up or down) for Fibonacci. More often than not, most trends give you the same Fibonacci retracement levels. The key Fibonacci resistance and support levels also often coincide with Ichimoku layers of support and resistance because Fibonacci is working to show you the key psychological levels that remain true across the board. This specifically is the beauty and magic of Fibonacci.

REMEMBER

You can use Ichimoku and Fibonacci in a number of ways to assist you with your technical analysis. I recommend that you use other technical analysis methods and chart patterns (see Chapter 16) as well to confirm your analysis. For example, you can use Ichimoku to spot a buy or sell signal, and then use Fibonacci levels to determine the price at which you can take profit.

Here's an example: You discover a double bottom bullish reversal chart pattern on a daily chart. (A *double bottom* pattern is a bullish reversal chart pattern that consists of two valleys at a key support level on the chart; turn to Chapter 16 to see examples.) You apply Ichimoku to the chart and notice an Ichimoku buy signal (as I describe earlier in this chapter). This discovery is a perfect opportunity to identify an entry point based on the double bottom chart pattern and the Ichimoku signal.

But where do you go from there, and where do you take profit? This point is when you can use Fibonacci. Depending on your risk tolerance (see Chapter 3), you can select a Fibonacci retracement level as your profit target and create a limit order through your broker account to sell at that level. (A *limit order* is a direction you put through your broker to buy or sell an asset at a specific price.)

Figure 20-4 shows a case study on the XLM/BTC four-hour chart where I've identified an Ichimoku-based bearish signal after the price broke below the Ichimoku cloud at 0.00003579.

Based on the Ichimoku strategy, you can create a *sell* limit order either at the lower band of the Ichimoku cloud (0.00003579) or a bit higher at the 0.5 Fibonacci retracement level of 0.00003605.

For profit taking, you can consider the 0.786 Fibonacci level at 0.00003435. For traders who like using stop-losses, you can use the 0.382 Fibonacci level or higher, depending on your risk tolerance. (For simplicity, I'm not mentioning other bearish signals that you can find on this chart.) A *stop-loss* is an order you can put through your broker to get you out of a losing trade before the losses get out of hand; flip to Chapter 17 for more info.

Source: tradingview.com

WARNING

The preceding case study is conducted on the four-hour chart, which is considered medium-term and thus carries a high level of risk. If you're looking for more conservative investment strategies, consider using the daily and monthly time frames. I discuss the various time frames in Chapter 16.

TIP

You can always come visit me in our Premium Investing Group (https://learn. investdiva.com/join-group), where I use Ichimoku and Fibonacci combos left and right to develop investment strategies.

Chapter **21**

Taxes and Cryptocurrencies

Before the 2017 crypto hype, many people who got into cryptocurrencies (whether through mining or investing) probably didn't even think about its tax implications. But as cryptocurrency investing becomes more mainstream, its taxation guidelines have taken center stage. In this chapter, I review the basics of cryptocurrency taxation.

REMEMBER

Keep in mind that these guidelines are based on the U.S. tax laws as of 2018. Depending on your crypto investment time frame, type of profit, and personal financial situation, you may need to consult with an accountant to get ready for tax day.

Distinguishing Three Types of Crypto Taxes

The tax setup for cryptos is complicated, to the point that U.S. lawmakers submitted an open letter to the Internal Revenue Service (IRS) in September 2018 asking it to make cryptocurrency taxations simpler. (You can see the letter at `https://waysandmeansforms.house.gov/uploadedfiles/letter_irs_virtual_currencies.pdf`.)

In most cases, you treat your cryptocurrency assets as property rather than currency. That means you pay capital gain taxes on your cryptocurrency investments. In this case, you don't have any tax obligations until you sell your coins for a profit. But what if you got your coins by mining? Or what if your employer pays you in cryptocurrencies? To make it simple, I've divided crypto taxation obligations into three likely scenarios in the following sections.

Income taxes

If you've invested in all the expensive equipment I talk about in Chapter 12 and are getting crypto mining rewards as a result, then you may be considered a crypto business owner. You're technically getting paid in cryptos for your business operation, and therefore you're subject to income tax by the IRS. Needless to say, you're also subject to income tax if you work for a company that pays you in cryptocurrencies.

TECHNICAL
STUFF

Personally, I was offered to get paid in Bitcoin when I started to report for News-BTC back in 2016. You know how much I regretted not accepting that offer in 2017 when Bitcoin value surged to $20,000? A lot! But of course, if I had taken it, I would've had to pay the income tax on the Bitcoins I received; if I'd then chosen to trade my Bitcoins for the U.S. dollar (USD) at the 2017 peak, I also would've been subject to capital gain taxes on the profit I made on my transaction. I talk about capital gain taxes in the next section.

If you receive mining or income rewards in crypto worth over $400 in one year, you must report it to the IRS. If you've set up a mining operation at your home, you can report your mining income as self-employment income on Schedule C of your tax return. Personally, though, I've set up my mining activity through my Invest Diva business, which helps me get a more generous tax policy when my net income is high. I talk about minimizing your crypto income tax later in this chapter.

REMEMBER

Always make sure to keep a record of your mining activity and financial statements in case you get audited by the IRS. Also, if you're filing as a business entity, make sure to consult with a tax professional to discover the best options for your particular scenario. Don't worry — you can even claim the accountant fees on your business!

REMEMBER

Even as a crypto miner and a business owner, you must understand the basics of cryptocurrency investing. If you sell or trade your cryptocurrencies for other alt-coins or any products, then you must pay capital gain taxes as I discuss in the next two sections (depending on whether they're long term or short term). Your mining activity profits often rely on the market value of the cryptocurrency as well as the amount of tax you'll be paying on them. To identify the best cryptocurrencies to mine, actively conduct the Invest Diva Diamond Analysis (IDDA) technique I introduce in Chapter 9, and swap to better cryptocurrencies if your mining strategy isn't making sense anymore. One point of IDDA is capital analysis, which includes your tax considerations.

Long-term capital gain taxes

In Chapter 2 I point to capital gains as one of the main reasons people invest in cryptocurrencies. That's how the IRS categorizes cryptocurrencies as well. Just like owning stocks and real estate, you must pay capital gain taxes after you sell your crypto assets for a profit. If you take a loss, you can lower your tax bill. Now, if you hold your crypto assets for over a year, you often get a better tax rate. This rate is called a *long-term capital gain tax.*

TIP

You can calculate your capital gains by doing simple math on the amount you gained or lost after you purchased your cryptos. For example, if you buy one Bitcoin for $5,000 and sell it for $10,000, then you've made $5,000 in capital gains minus the amount you pay for transaction fees.

INTRODUCING SOME CRYPTO TAX EXPERTS

The crypto investing market is a fairly new industry, and therefore many traditional tax folks may not have the necessary knowledge to help you with the best crypto tax decisions. Doing a search within my LinkedIn connections, I found a few U.S.-based crypto tax experts who may be able to help you out:

- **Camuso CPA:** Camuso CPA is a CPA firm that works with investors, businesses, and individuals nationwide and is a market leader in cryptocurrency tax advisory. In fact, Camuso CPA is the first CPA firm in the country to accept cryptocurrency payments in return for professional services. The firm caters to clients from Camuso CPA's network of investors, miners, and small businesses along with taxpayers who need help dealing with bitcoin and other cryptocurrencies. My point of contact here is the firm's founder, Patrick Camuso. You can reach him through the firm's website, www.CamusoCPA.com.

- **Jag CPAs & Co.:** My point of contact here is Shehan Chandrasekera, a certified public accountant in the states of Texas and New Jersey. He has broad tax knowledge of various industries including real estate, start-ups, blockchain, construction, e-commerce, healthcare, cannabis, and manufacturing and distribution. You can check him out through the company's website, www.jagcpastx.com.

Short-term capital gain taxes

A *short-term capital gain tax* is very similar to the mining and crypto income tax I mention earlier in this chapter. If you sell or trade your cryptos regularly and hold them less than a year, then your profit or losses may be categorized as income, which often has less favorable tax implications. Even if you don't officially cash out your cryptos, you may still be subject to short-term taxes if you use the cryptocurrency to purchase stuff, whether it's tangible products or other cryptocurrencies.

Active traders who make a few trades every now and then are subject to different tax laws than day traders who trade cryptos for a living. I discuss the difference in the later section "Reducing your trading tax."

Minimizing Your Crypto Taxes

Whether you've earned your crypto as income or have seen capital gains on your assets, the following sections show you some ways to cut the amount you owe the IRS.

Lowering your mining income tax

In the United States, you may get a better tax rate if you create a company or a business entity around your mining activities instead of mining as a self-employed individual. By doing so, you can take advantage of the tax breaks business owners get for paying for business-related stuff and get a better tax rate than individuals. Got that high-end computer to mine Bitcoin? Claim it on your business and lower your taxable income. Got your computer set up with mining equipment like the ASICs and expensive GPUs that I talk about in Chapter 12? Paying a ton on electricity when mining? Congrats, you can get a tax break on the rewards you got paid through mining.

That is, of course, if your coins are actually worth something. Even at a personal level, your mining operation can be very profitable, but it also can cost you a ton — way more than its rewards, especially if the crypto market isn't doing very well at the time. At the time of writing, if your overall net income is more than $60,000, filing as an S corporation, or an LLC that's taxed like an S corporation, may help you. Consult a tax professional for guidance.

REMEMBER

You can claim your expenses on your business only if the LLC, C corporation, or S corporation was created prior to earning the income from mining. Anything earned prior to the company formation won't be able to be included under the company for tax purposes.

Reducing your trading tax

Do you consider yourself a day trader? Then you may be eligible to pay way less in taxes than occasional traders. But first you must pass the IRS day-trading test by being able to answer "yes" to these three questions:

» Do you aim to make profit from the daily price changes in the crypto market instead of holding your positions long term or even overnight?

» Do you spend most of your day trading instead of having a full-time day job?

» Do you have a substantial and regular trading pattern and make a ton of trades on a daily basis?

If you do qualify as a day trader, you may be able to claim your rewards as a self-employed individual. This designation means you can deduct all your trading-related expenses on Schedule C like any other sole proprietor.

TIP

According to finance.zacks.com, your corporation will be taxed based on your profits and losses whether or not it's a one-owner corporation. You can also use the money you make from day trading to pay for your insurance, healthcare, and employee benefits, if you have any.

WARNING

Tracking your short-term crypto trading activities can be incredibly confusing. The industry has a ton of volatility and market fluctuation, and an exploding number of tradable cryptos are available to you 24/7. These situations make monitoring your resources manually almost impossible. Later in this chapter, I introduce some tracking resources you can use for your trading activities.

Bringing down your capital gain taxes

If you can't qualify as a day trader (see the preceding section), your best bet to reduce your crypto capital gain taxes is to be a long-term investor. That means holding your assets for over a year. Don't sell, trade, or buy anything with your cryptocurrencies within a year of your purchase.

As I mention earlier in this chapter, capital gain taxes on investments held for more than one year (long term) can be much lower than capital gain taxes on investments held for less than one year (short term). In 2018, long-term capital gains are taxed at 0 percent, 15 percent, or 20 percent, depending on your tax bracket. If you're in the high-income tax bracket, for example, your capital gains tax rate may be 20 percent. You can find out more about tax brackets here: www.irs.com/articles/2018-federal-tax-rates-personal-exemptions-and-standard-deductions.

REMEMBER

Trading one cryptocurrency for another may put you at risk of paying more taxes. To purchase certain cryptocurrencies at specific crypto exchanges, you have no choice but to convert your cryptos for one another in a shorter time frame, but if you make a huge profit on the initial crypto, you no longer fall into the category of long-term investor. Talk to a tax professional to ensure that you're paying the correct rate.

Checking the rate of your state

In the United States, different states have different state tax laws, and some states have better rates than others for specific groups of people or certain industries. Some states like Florida are considered a "retirement haven" because you don't have to pay individual income and death tax, and you'll also get a ton of asset protection and property tax benefits. When it comes to cryptocurrency investors, certain states like Wyoming have great tax incentives for crypto companies and investors because cryptocurrencies are exempted from property taxation altogether. In 2018, Wyoming became the first state to define cryptocurrencies as an entirely new asset class. Wyoming officials labeled it as the "utility token bill" and passed it into law in March 2018; it was designed to exempt specific cryptocurrencies from state money transmission laws.

TIP

As cryptocurrencies become more popular, you can expect more states to create such laws to incentivize businesses and individuals to bring their crypto talents and money there. That's why it's important that you're in the know with the latest developments in the industry. Websites like https://pro.benzinga.com?afmc=2f can help you get such information in a timely manner.

Evaluating Taxable Income from Crypto Transactions

REMEMBER

At the end of the day, reporting your crypto income and capital gains is on you. You must keep track of all your taxable events, which means every time you sell or trade your crypto assets for other stuff. At the time of writing, the IRS doesn't require third-party reporting for cryptocurrencies (meaning the entities you buy the cryptos from don't have to report the sales), which makes the tracking and reporting more complicated. Here are some tips and points to keep in mind when you're evaluating your crypto activities.

Tracking your crypto activity

TIP

The crypto market is expanding, and more monitoring resources are becoming available for traders, investors, and miners alike. Here are a few resources you can check out:

>> **CoinTracker** (https://www.cointracker.io/?i=eALc60xcyXpD): CoinTracker automatically syncs your crypto transactions with a growing list of exchanges such as Coinbase, Kraken, KuCoin, and more to generate tax forms. It also has an online support team.

>> **CoinTracking** (https://cointracking.info?ref=I248132): CoinTracking analyzes your investment activity and generates a tax report based on your profit and losses.

>> **CryptoTrader.tax** (http://cryptotrader.tax?fp_ref=behp6): This website connects you to a growing list of exchanges such as Coinbase, Binance, Bittrex, and more, and helps you calculate your crypto taxes in a few minutes. It has great online customer support that answers your questions immediately.

Handling crypto forks

In Chapter 5 I talk about how you can get free coins when a cryptocurrency is *forked* (where a portion of a crypto's community decides to create its own version of the currency). Of course, nothing is completely free, and you're likely required to pay taxes on the additional cryptos you receive through the fork. For example, if you own Ethereum and it undergoes a hard fork that pays you an equal amount of the new cryptocurrency in addition to your original Ethereum assets, you must pay ordinary taxes on the new free coins as opposed to long-term capital gain tax. You pay these taxes based on the U.S. dollar value of the new cryptocurrency the day you receive it.

REMEMBER

The IRS still offers little guidance regarding hard forks and taxation. Make sure you consult with a tax professional and stay ahead of the game by tracking all your crypto records using professional websites such as `http://cryptotrader.tax?fp_ref=behp6`.

Reporting international crypto investments

The cryptocurrency market and its rules are constantly evolving. That's why you must remain up-to-date about all your crypto transactions. But even if you invest in cryptocurrencies outside the United States, you must report the activity to the IRS.

REMEMBER

At the time of writing, you don't have to report your cryptocurrency on your Foreign Bank Account Report (FBAR). This guideline is based on a 2014 IRS statement that said, "The Financial Crimes Enforcement Network, which issues regulatory guidance pertaining to Reports of Foreign Bank and Financial Accounts (FBARs), is not requiring that digital (or virtual) currency accounts be reported on an FBAR at this time but may consider requiring such accounts to be reported in the future." Make sure you keep up-to-date with the IRS crypto regulations because they're subject to change every year; consult a tax professional. Also keep in mind that not having to report your cryptos on your FBAR doesn't mean you can hide your foreign cryptocurrency activities from the IRS.

WARNING

It bears repeating: You're responsible for knowing the tax ramifications of your crypto activity. The IRS has been going after cryptocurrency investments inside and outside the United States. It even forced Coinbase to turn over its customer records in 2017. So people who simply didn't know about the crypto tax implications got into trouble alongside those who were trying to hide their crypto investments.

5

The Part of Tens

Chapter **22**

Ten Considerations Before Getting Started with Cryptocurrencies

Are you ready to try cryptocurrency investing? In this chapter, I highlight some of the most important things to think about before starting your crypto investing journey, many of which I explain in detail in earlier chapters.

Don't Get Too Excited

REMEMBER

Starting to explore a whole new world is always exciting. Starting early can also sometimes get you ahead of the crowd. However, just like any type of investment avenue, cryptocurrency investing requires discipline, risk management, and a whole lot of patience. You shouldn't treat crypto investing as a get-rich-quick scheme. Even though your hopes may be up, especially since the market saw jaw-dropping returns in 2017, the likelihood of seeing such gains in such a short amount of time again is pretty low. The reason is simple: The bubble has burst. Investors are becoming more educated about the whole market, making more calculated investment decisions. So should you!

Measure Your Risk Tolerance

REMEMBER

Is crypto investing right for you? How much of your money should you invest in this market? Can you stomach high volatility? Do you have the patience to wait out potential storms? You can find the answer to all these questions by measuring your risk tolerance. This essential first step to any type of investment includes both your willingness to risk and your ability to risk. Flip to Chapter 3 for an explanation of different risk types and resources on measuring your risk tolerance.

Protect Your Crypto Wallet

A *crypto wallet* is where you store your digital assets like Bitcoin; you have to have one before you buy a cryptocurrency. So many different types of wallets are available, some of which come from the cryptocurrency exchanges that sell you the cryptos. But those aren't the most secure types of wallets, and they've often been the victims of hacking attacks that resulted in the loss of cryptos. Chapter 7 details different methods you can use to protect your cryptocurrency wallet before you start investing.

Find the Best Crypto Exchange/ Broker for You

Some of the most popular places to get your hands on cryptocurrencies are exchanges and brokers. Some of these marketplaces offer only a few cryptocurrencies, and some carry a wide range. Some have higher transaction fees. Some have better customer service. Some have a better security reputation. With some, you can exchange your *fiat* currency (which is the local currency of your country, like the U.S. dollar) for cryptocurrencies. With others, you must already have a cryptocurrency, like Bitcoin, and exchange it for other digital assets, like Ripple or Litecoin.

To find the best crypto exchange or broker, you must go through all these options and see which one fits your crypto needs most. In Chapter 6, I give a more thorough overview of different types of cryptocurrency exchanges and brokers out there.

REMEMBER

Oftentimes, you're better off using multiple exchanges for different purposes. Personally, I use three!

Determine Whether You Should Invest Short Term or Long Term

The time frame you invest in depends on your risk tolerance, your financial goals, your current financial situation, and the amount of time you have on your hands. For example, if you have a full-time job that requires most of your attention, you don't want to worry about short-term management of your crypto portfolio, or any other asset for that matter. You want to focus your energy on your main job (so you don't get fired) and manage your investment portfolio every few weeks or so to stay on top of things. Investing long term also requires less risk-taking.

TIP

In Chapter 3, I walk you through calculating your risk tolerance. In Chapters 17 and 18, I explore more about short-term and long-term investing. You can also check out my *Make Your Money Work for You PowerCourse* by attending this online webinar: https://learn.investdiva.com/free-webinar-3-secrets-to-making-your-money-work-for-you.

Start Small

If you're just testing the waters and don't have a solid financial plan, don't dump a whole chunk of money into the market. Start with a few hundred dollars, or whatever you can afford, and slowly grow your portfolio. Also, don't use your money to invest in only one type of crypto. If you're new to investing in anything, don't allocate all your investment funds to cryptos, either. Diversification is key until you find your sweet spot, especially for new investors.

Personally, I invest in stocks, exchange traded funds (ETFs), and foreign exchange (forex) as well as in cryptocurrencies. You can find at least ten different cryptos in my portfolio at any given time. For more on diversification within cryptocurrencies and other financial assets, check out Chapters 2 and 10.

Follow the Cause

TIP

Many cryptocurrencies are based on blockchain applications that aim to solve a specific problem in the world or in society (see Chapter 4 for the scoop on blockchain technology). Blockchain applications can provide a solution to almost any problem that's close to your heart, from banking the under-banked to preventing voter fraud to helping out farmers. By investing in the cryptocurrency of a blockchain application whose cause appeals to you, you support that cause in achieving its goals faster. This sense of accomplishment can make investing more meaningful and more fun for you. Focusing on causes also helps when you're picking cryptocurrencies out of the hundreds of options available. I talk about different crypto categories in Chapter 8.

Mull Over Mining

Mining is the backbone of many cryptocurrencies like Bitcoin. *Mining* cryptocurrencies refers to solving complex math equations by using powerful computers; successfully solving the problems earns you a reward in cryptos. Mining is normally considered very expensive because you have to invest in expensive computer gadgets and use up a lot of electricity while you run your computer for mining. But sometimes, especially depending on the cryptocurrency's value, mining may make sense. For example, if your electricity bill for mining is going to be lower than the cost of actually buying that cryptocurrency, you may want to consider mining instead.

TIP

Head to Chapter 12 for more on mining, its terminology, and the stuff you need to buy to do it. You can check out mining profitability by using mining calculators like the ones at www.investdiva.com/mining-calculator/.

Look into Investing in Other Assets First

If you've never invested in anything, you may find the whole cryptocurrency industry a bit overwhelming. Educating yourself about developing investment strategies while also learning about a financial sector you've never had any personal experience with can be difficult. In this case, you may consider starting by investing in things you know, like the stocks of a company you're already familiar with. After you become comfortable investing in things you know, you can then expand your portfolio to new vehicles like cryptocurrencies. See Chapter 2 for details on different types of assets.

TECHNICAL STUFF

For me, my first trading love was forex, which involves trading the currency of one country, like the U.S. dollar, for the currency of another country, like the Japanese yen. I was a student at a Japanese university when I traded for the first time ever. I was constantly checking the value of the Japanese yen versus the U.S. dollar, so getting a sense of the direction it was going at the time was easier for me.

Get a Support Group

Most people trade alone on their computers or smartphones. That can soon become a very lonely activity, especially if none of your friends are into it. When the markets are going against you, you can get frustrated, and when the markets are doing well, you may get overwhelmed, not knowing when to get out.

TIP

Though I explore strategy development methods to identify the best entry and exit points in this book, it always helps to have people who are in the same boat as you. Many cryptocurrencies have channels on the Telegram app or their very own rooms on websites like Reddit and BitcoinTalk where you can share information and commiserate with other crypto investors. Another resource is my Invest Diva premium investing group (https://learn.investdiva.com/join-group). Not only do I share my personal investment strategies across different asset classes like stocks, forex, and cryptocurrencies, but our very internationally diverse members also actively participate in the conversation, helping one another with things like finding the best exchanges in their local countries, asking questions you may not have thought of, and more.

Chapter **23**

Ten Possible Moves When Your Crypto Portfolio Is Down

Whether you're a short-term trader or a long-term investor, at times you find your crypto portfolio in the red zone with one or more of your holdings moving against you. Before you know it, you can find yourself in a FUD situation (crypto talk for fear, uncertainty, and doubt), which can become incredibly frustrating and can contribute to your making an emotional decision rather than executing a well-thought-out strategy. This chapter covers ten potential next steps when the market isn't on your side.

Do Nothing

In most cases, patience is a profitable virtue. If you got into a specific position after doing a thorough analysis from all points of the Invest Diva Diamond Analysis, or IDDA (see Chapter 9), chances are the current dip in the market is temporary. If you give it time, you may find yourself in positive territory again. Even the toughest markets find their way back up again if you wait long enough.

Of course, the cryptocurrency market is very new and hasn't shown enough evidence to prove that it follows the sentiment of other markets like the stock market. However, because most investors categorize cryptos as a capital gain asset just like stocks, the crypto market may well follow a market psychology similar to other such assets. *Capital gain assets* are those you invest in expecting a gain in their value to give you a positive return. Of course, waiting for a long time may not be suitable for all traders and investors.

REMEMBER

Depending on where you are in your life and what your financial goals are, you may be able to take advantage of making time your best investing friend. If you're on a ten-year plan to reach a financial goal — buying a house, for example — you shouldn't worry about the minor ups and downs in the markets.

Reevaluate Your Risk Tolerance

As I discuss in Chapter 3, measuring your risk tolerance is the very first step you need to take when you start investing in anything. But as life goes on, circumstances change in ways that may impact your risk tolerance. A down period for your portfolio may be a good time to reassess your risk tolerance to identify the best thing to do next.

For example, if you now have a higher risk tolerance than you did when you entered a position, you may consider adding to your losing position as I discuss later in this chapter. But if your financial situation has impacted your risk tolerance in a negative way and you don't have much time in your hands, you may consider cutting losses (also described later).

REMEMBER

The bottom line, however, is never make a rash decision based only on emotions and the *feeling* that your risk tolerance is high or low. By carefully calculating your tolerance, you may get a surprise to the contrary.

Look at the Big Picture

You can evaluate the bigger picture from both technical and fundamental viewpoints:

>> On the technical side (see Chapter 16), you may get a better idea of where the market is going by switching to longer-term time frames. For example, the market may be on a very long-term uptrend, where the price has been going

up for quite some time. In that case, the current dip may be a healthy correction, which can even be a good point to buy more of your crypto asset.

» On the fundamental side, you need to go back to the basic reasons you chose to invest in a specific cryptocurrency — things like the cause, the management and community, the technology, and everything else that can contribute to the long-term growth of the cryptocurrency's valuation. Flip to Chapter 9 for more on fundamental analysis.

Research the Fundamental Reasons the Crypto Is Down

When evaluating the big picture as I discuss in the preceding section, you may find that a core fundamental problem is driving the devaluation of your crypto asset. Perhaps the cryptocurrency is no longer backed by giant financial corporations, has gotten involved in a scam, or is running out of money and therefore not able to invest in its technology. You can use your favorite search engine to look into the fundamental details of any specific cryptocurrency. Simply search the crypto's name online and go through the most recent search results under the "News" category. If the fundamentals have changed for the worse and are the reason the value is down, you may need to reevaluate your position and potentially cut losses.

TIP

As a crypto enthusiast, I recommend that you keep up to date with the most recent crypto news anyway by following websites such as `https://cryptobriefing.com/`, `www.coindesk.com/`, and `www.newsbtc.com/`.

Consider Hedging

Hedging is a common investment practice to manage risk. By *hedging*, you basically go against your current position or industry to offset the risk it involves. I talk about hedging in derivatives like options and futures in Chapter 14, but you can also hedge by diversification (described in the following two sections) as well as by going against your current position. For example, if you've bought Bitcoin versus another cryptocurrency like Ethereum and Bitcoin's price is dropping, you can consider selling Bitcoin in a different trade and take advantage of the current downtrend.

TIP

Positional hedging is especially useful when you're trading cryptocurrencies on brokerages that allow short selling. For more on hedging strategies, consider joining Invest Diva's premium group at `https://learn.investdiva.com/join-group`.

Diversify within Crypto Assets

Adding other crypto assets that are exposed to a different type of risk than your losing cryptocurrency is another form of hedging (see the preceding section) that may help you balance out your portfolio. Identifying such cryptocurrencies can be very difficult, though, because at least at the time of this writing, most crypto assets are exposed to similar types of risk. See Chapter 3 to find out more about risk and Chapter 9 to identify top performing cryptos.

Diversify across Other Financial Assets

Until cryptocurrency investing becomes mainstream, you may find this strategy most helpful. If your analysis shows a longer doomsday period in the cryptocurrency market while other financial instruments like bonds are lucrative, you may consider diversifying away from cryptocurrencies to distribute risk. This approach is yet again a different form of hedging, which I discuss earlier in this chapter. Flip to Chapters 2 and 10 for more on diversification.

Exchange with a Better Crypto

After redoing the IDDA for your crypto assets that are down (see Chapter 9), you may realize that a particular crypto isn't worth holding onto. Unlike the stock market, where you have no choice but to take losses, in the crypto world you may have the option to exchange with a different, better cryptocurrency. For example, say you bought a bunch of a crypto called CrappyCoin at a high price, but its value has been plummeting with no signs of recovery. At the same time, you hear of a new, cheap cryptocurrency with a bright future. Though you may not be able to buy a ton of the new crypto with your devalued CrappyCoin, you still may benefit from cutting your losses on CrappyCoin early and exchanging with the better crypto.

Think about Adding to Your Current Position

Warren Buffett is a famous investor who adds on to his losing position — buys more of a falling stock at a cheaper price — when the markets drop. But of course, he does so only for assets that have strong fundamentals and are in the midst of a temporary, healthy pullback. He also can handle the risk.

This strategy has the potential to work for cryptos as well. Before you get too excited, keep in mind that the cryptocurrency market may act differently than the stock market (which is what Warren Buffett invests in) and may continue to be unpredictable and volatile in the coming years. That's why you must make sure you can afford a bigger prospective loss for a period of time until the crypto market gets back on track.

WARNING

Avoid using margin and borrowing money from your broker when adding to your losing position. Those approaches increase your investment risk.

REMEMBER

By adding on to your losing position, you can bring your average holding price lower and therefore profit more when the price eventually goes back up.

Contemplate Cutting Losses

Personally (and famously), I'm not the biggest fan of *stop-losses*, which are market orders you set to cut losses if the price of an asset like a crypto is going against your investment position. However, sometimes you have no other option for various reasons, including personal risk tolerance and market conditions. In that case, you may want to consider simply getting out of your losing position, calling it quits, and focusing on a different source of profit.

REMEMBER

Short-term traders are more likely to use stop-losses (see Chapter 17). Long-term investors (see Chapter 18) are supposed to have made the risk-management calculation ahead of time, making sure they have enough time to wait things out.

TIP

Using a stop-loss may become incredibly beneficial if you invested in a scam and learned about your mistake afterward because it will enable you to limit your losses before the value of the asset goes down to zero.

Chapter **24**

Ten Challenges and Opportunities for Crypto Investors

This chapter introduces you to ten opportunities and hurdles you may face during your cryptocurrency investing adventures. I bundle challenges and opportunities together because you can turn an obstacle into profit if you treat it the right way.

New Cryptos on the Block

Bitcoin, the first ever cryptocurrency, turned ten years old in 2018. But it's hardly the only cryptocurrency that investors are interested in anymore. For better or for worse, new cryptocurrencies keep popping up left and right, and you can expect that number to increase. Most likely, not all the 1,600 cryptocurrencies available in 2018 are going to make it big within five years. On the other hand, a single cryptocurrency that isn't even born yet may explode and replace Bitcoin for good in the future.

I mark this concept as both an opportunity and a challenge because you must remain open minded and have a vision for the future in order to screen through the newcomers and pick those with true potential. For more on selecting the best cryptocurrencies, flip to Chapter 9.

Finding Economic Data

Finding economic data is mainly a current challenge in the industry. Though many crypto-dedicated news organizations exist, finding the true economic data that drives the market can be difficult. Because the industry has no developed economic system for the industry, sometimes the media can create fear or greed in the market out of thin air, with no solid financial statement to back it up. To avoid falling into such traps, you may want to consider following more than one crypto news organization and then take what you read with a grain of salt.

Here are some financial and crypto news organizations (in alphabetical order) that you can follow for a better understanding of the markets:

>> AMBCrypto: https://ambcrypto.com/

>> Benzinga: https://pro.benzinga.com/?afmc=2f

>> Bitcoin Exchange Guide: https://bitcoinexchangeguide.com/

>> CCN: www.ccn.com

>> CoinDesk: www.coindesk.com/

>> CoinGape: https://coingape.com/

>> CoinGeek: https://coingeek.com/

>> Cointelegraph: https://cointelegraph.com

>> Crypto Briefing: https://cryptobriefing.com/

>> Crypto Daily: https://cryptodaily.co.uk/

>> The Daily HODL: https://dailyhodl.com/

>> Forbes: www.forbes.com

>> Global Coin Report: https://globalcoinreport.com/

>> MarketWatch: www.marketwatch.com/

>> NewsBTC: www.newsbtc.com/

Regulations

At the time of writing, cryptocurrency regulations are just in their infancy. Some countries are ahead of others in terms of regulations, creating an opportunity for their residents to take advantage of the crypto industry early. However, don't be disappointed if things take time. Lack of regulation is a big concern in the industry, but it may also give early investors the advantage of investing when the prices are low. As more countries regulate the cryptocurrency market and recognize it as a real financial instrument, the prices of the cryptos may go up.

Hackers

You may ask how a hacking incident can be an opportunity. Well, if you're a direct victim of a hacking incident, that's a clear challenge. (Flip to Chapter 7 for methods to protect yourself and your cryptos from getting hacked.) Hacking is a real issue in the industry, and unfortunately, it may not go away in the future. However, hacking incidents normally impact the crypto market price in a negative way only temporarily. That's when it can turn into opportunity for the rest of the market players to buy at lower prices.

WARNING

Taking advantage of a hacking incident doesn't mean you should invest in the company that was compromised. You must always do your research and analyze the circumstances. If a specific cryptocurrency or a crypto exchange is compromised in an irreversible way, you may want to stay away from it. However, the news may impact other cryptos in the market for no fundamental reason other than the fact that they're part of the same industry. When one player goes down, the negative wave impacts all others as well. You may consider focusing on those cryptos instead.

Bubbles

You may think that the crypto bubble has already burst and is now on its way to stabilization. But nothing suggests that yet another bubble won't pop up in new cryptocurrencies, or even in existing ones. With research and analysis, you can identify bubbles by rapid price growth that has no fundamental reason behind it — that is, growth based just on market hype. That's the best time to either sell your crypto assets at higher prices or simply stay away from it all until things calm down. The "stay away" part is the true challenge, because you've got to fight your FOMO (fear of missing out).

A Down Market

When your crypto portfolio is down, it may take your self confidence and positive attitude down with it. However, you must remember that a losing position isn't an insult of your intelligence, your family heritage, or anything else personal. It's likely just a natural movement of the market based on the market sentiment, and you shouldn't let it get to you. In fact, you may even be able to use it as an opportunity by expanding your investments and hedging as I discuss in Chapter 23.

REMEMBER

A losing portfolio isn't an indication that you're a bad investor and don't have what it takes to make profit in the market. Similarly, a winning investment doesn't prove that you're Einstein's (or Warren Buffett's) cousin, nor does it indicate that you've mastered the art of investing.

New Currencies and Projects

An undeniable wave of new economic systems is building, and it may or may not end with blockchain-backed cryptocurrencies. (See Chapter 4 for an introduction to blockchain.) Projects going on at the time of writing include Initiative Q, which started as a social experiment in June 2018. It bases its economic model on the fact that every currency has value simply because people have it and stores accept it as a payment system. The Initiative Q project claims to be "tomorrow's payment network." More specifically, it's doing a social financial experiment with a "future" currency called Q.

Early adopters (disclaimer: I'm one of them) can get free Qs by inviting others and encouraging them to invite more people. The project's philosophy claims that if enough people have Q, it may become a legit currency that can replace the U.S. dollar and be used globally.

REMEMBER

The reason I consider these types of projects to be an opportunity as well a challenge is that you may come across many wannabe future economic models that may contain a lot of risk or may just not have what it takes to get you there. For example, many people felt Initiative Q was a pyramid scheme and rejected the invitation to join, and I applaud those who are careful about giving away personal information. Initiative Q, in my opinion, has minimal risk because all it asks for is your name and email address, and its policy claims the company will destroy that data if the project doesn't succeed.

TIP

Here's what an Initiative Q invite looks like: `https://initiativeq.com/invite/BBCN_08hm`. The invitation links activate and deactivate periodically, so there is a chance that when you click the preceding link, it's in the deactivated period. But following the link, you can get access to Initiative Q's social media pages, where you may be able to find active links. Also, if you ask your friends and family members, they may have a link to share. Another possible event is that the project may be canceled by the time you read this!

Diversification

I talk about diversification in detail in Chapter 10. Though diversification is typically a golden risk-management strategy, too much diversification may be harmful to your portfolio. Why? Because by spreading too much of your investment fund across so many different assets, chances are you'll miss out on investing big in the top performers. And if you invest too little in the real winners, your returns will be little as well.

TIP

If you've done a thorough Invest Diva Diamond Analysis (IDDA; see Chapter 9) on a specific cryptocurrency and you believe it's going to make it big, you can consider allocating a bigger chunk of your portfolio to it rather than buying a ton of cryptocurrencies that you're not sure about. Sometimes only one or two great investments are all you need to get you to your financial goal.

Falling in Love with a Crypto

REMEMBER

Investing requires discipline and tough decisions. Cryptocurrencies may be charming, but getting too emotional over them may harm your investment account in the long run. If it's time to say goodbye to a crypto you considered to be a winner in the past, just do it. Falling in love with what you do is great, but you're in this business to make profit. Don't let emotions drive your investment decisions (too much; you can use a tiny bit of gut feeling when you've done all the logical analysis, though — see Chapter 9). But keep in mind that your cryptocurrencies likely won't love you back in a sentimental way.

Using Invest Diva Diamond Analysis

No matter what type of investor or trader you are, the Invest Diva Diamond Analysis, or IDDA for short, is there to guide you along the way. However, using IDDA (as I discuss in Chapter 9) requires patience and understanding of how the markets work. You can't just wing it. Even if a celebrity you love is promoting a specific cryptocurrency, that doesn't account for fundamental analysis. If you think you discovered a strong trend only on one time frame, you can't call it technical analysis without checking for other indicators. Make sure all elements of the IDDA are pointing in the same direction before making an investment decision.

TIP

When in doubt, you can always come visit me here for help: `https://learn.investdiva.com/start`.

6 Appendixes

Find the best places to check out if you're an active cryptocurrency trader.

Discover where you can get help for proper portfolio management.

Appendix **A**

Resources for Cryptocurrency Investors

In this book, I cover a great deal about how to pick a cryptocurrency and how to analyze the markets before investing. In this appendix, I give a little bit more detail for where you can find the things you need. Keep in mind that the information is as of the time of writing, and things may change by the time you get this book.

Exploring Top Cryptocurrencies

More than 2,000 cryptocurrencies exist as of 2019, and the number is increasing. One way of exploring cryptocurrencies is to compare them based on their *market capitalization*, which is calculated by multiplying the number of coins out there by their price. People pay attention to this number because the idea is that as investors gain confidence in a specific crypto, its price may go higher, resulting in a larger market cap. Market capitalization ranking is subject to change every single day. But for your reference, in this section I classify the top 200 cryptocurrencies by market cap as of the time of writing. (See Chapters 8 and 9 for more information on market cap, different types of cryptocurrencies, and identifying top cryptocurrencies for your needs.)

REMEMBER

You shouldn't analyze cryptocurrencies based on their market cap only. This section is just for your reference. Many other underlying factors can impact the future success of digital assets. For more, check out Part 2.

Top 100 cryptos by market cap

The top 100 cryptocurrencies by market capitalization are frequently subject to speculation by investors. The fact that they've made it to the top 100 indicates that the market has trust in them. However, always keep in mind that no cryptocurrency is too big to fail, and you may very well find a gem in lesser known cryptocurrencies. Here's the list of the top 100 as of the time of writing according to Crypto Briefing (https://cryptobriefing.com/). For more details on a particular crypto at Crypto Briefing, go to the homepage, choose "Coins and Caps" under "Live Data" at the top of the screen, and click on the name of the crypto in the table.

TIP

Each of the following coins has its own website that you can find by looking it up on your search engine. If the name of a coin is too generic (like Ark), consider typing its symbol or the keyword "crypto" next to it to narrow down your search results. Websites like Crypto Briefing (https://cryptobriefing.com/), CoinMarketCap (https://coinmarketcap.com/), and CoinGecko (www.coingecko.com/en) can provide more information in terms of the most recent rankings, prices, and market capitalization.

- » Bitcoin (BTC)
- » Ethereum (ETH)
- » Ripple (XRP)
- » Bitcoin Cash (BCH)
- » EOS (EOS)
- » Stellar (XLM)
- » Litecoin (LTC)
- » Cardano (ADA)
- » Tether (USDT)
- » Monero (XMR)

- TRON (TRX)
- Binance Coin (BNB)
- IOTA (MIOTA)
- Dash (DASH)
- Ontology (ONT)
- NEO (NEO)
- Tezos (XTZ)
- Ethereum Classic (ETC)
- NEM (XEM)
- Zcash (ZEC)
- VeChain (VET)
- DogeCoin (DOGE)
- Bitcoin Gold (BTG)
- 0X (ZRX)
- Maker (MKR)
- OmiseGo (OMG)
- ByteCoin (BCN)
- Decred (DCR)
- Lisk (LSK)
- Huobi Token (HT)
- QTUM (QTUM)
- Icon (ICX)
- Aeternity (AE)
- Zilliqa (ZIL)
- Basic Attention Token (BAT)
- Bitcoin Diamond (BCD)
- Nano (NANO)
- SiaCoin (SC)
- BitShares (BTS)
- DigiByte (DGB)

- Verge (XVG)
- Steem (STEEM)
- Pundi X (NPXS)
- Holo (HOT)
- Waves (WAVES)
- TrueUSD (TUSD)
- Metaverse (ETP)
- Golem (GNT)
- Iostoken (IOST)
- Augur (REP)
- Stratis (STRAT)
- Komodo (KMD)
- ChainLink (LINK)
- Electroneum (ETN)
- Status (SNT)
- Populous (PPT)
- Aurora (AOA)
- Wanchain (WAN)
- Ardor (ARDR)
- MaidSafeCoin (MAID)
- Ark (ARK)
- Ravencoin (RVN)
- GSENetwork (GSE)
- Mithril (MITH)
- Aion (AION)
- KuCoin Shares (KCS)
- aelf (ELF)
- Bankera (BNK):
- Digitex Futures Exchange (DGTX)
- NEXO (NEXO)

>> Veritaseum (VERI)

>> HyperCash (HC)

>> Reddcoin (RDD)

>> ...N)

>> ...)

>> ...vork (POLY)

>> ...MANA)

>> ...(C)

>> ...)

>> ...ET)

>> ...IA)

>> ...D)

>> ...C)

>> ...OM)

>> Nebulas (NAS)

>> TenX (PAY)

>> Dentacoin (DCN)

>> Kyber Network (KNC)

>> Bancor Network Token (BNT)

>> Power Ledger (POWR)

>> Zcoin (XZC)

>> Ino Coin (INO)

REMEMBER

Keep in mind that finding a consistent source for cryptocurrencies is pretty difficult, and the info on Crypto Briefing about the cryptocurrencies' market capitalization may be different from the info from other sources. You shouldn't consider what you find on any website a definitive interpretation of the markets, at least until all websites start using similar metrics for the cryptocurrency market. At the moment, they don't.

Cryptos ranking 101 to 200

This list, ranking cryptos from 101 to 200 at the time of writing on Crypto Briefing (https://cryptobriefing.com/), includes many cryptocurrencies that top investors are putting major bets on because they can buy them cheap, and these cryptos have the potential to overtake higher ranking cryptos in the future. (See the previous section for information on how to find additional details on these cryptos.)

>> NXT (NXT)

>> Theta Network (THETA)

>> SALT (SALT)

>> Dragonchain (DRGN)

>> Gas (GAS)

>> Syscoin (SYS)

>> Ambrosus (AMB)

>> Enigma (ENG)

>> Bytom (BTM)

>> Dai (DAI)

>> Genesis Vision (GVT)

>> Ether Zero (ETZ)

>> Civic (CVC)

>> Kin (KIN)

>> Elastos (ELA)

>> Nexus (NXS)

>> EmerCoin (EMC)

>> Dent (DENT)

- » Cindicator (CND)
- » MobileGo (MGO)
- » Cortex (CTXC)
- » GoChain (GO)
- » Nuls (NULS)
- » Storj (STORJ)
- » Eidoo (EDO)
- » Bitcoin Private (BTCP)
- » Sirin Labs Token (SRN)
- » Factom (FCT)
- » Enjin Coin (ENJ)
- » Neblio (NEBL)
- » Storm (STORM)
- » Gifto (GTO)
- » Substratum (SUB)
- » WaykiChain (WICC)
- » Nectar Token (NEC)
- » Matrix AI Network (MAN)
- » Groestlcoin (GRS)
- » Request Network (REQ)
- » RChain (RHOC)
- » Centrality (CENNZ)
- » SmartCash (SMART)
- » Bibox Token (BIX)
- » ODEM (ODEM)
- » Iconomi (ICN)
- » SingularityNET (AGI)
- » Docademic (MTC)
- » Hydro (HYDRO)
- » Noah Coin (NOAH)

- Mainframe (MFT)
- Quant (QNT)
- Hycon (HYC)
- Endor Protocol (EDR)
- Skycoin (SKY)
- iExec RLC (RLC)
- Byteball Bytes (GBYTE)
- Red Pulse Phoenix (PHX)
- Ethos (ETHOS)
- Vertcoin (VTC)
- Cryptaur (CPT)
- Scry.info (DDD)
- Time New Bank (TNB)
- Ignis (IGNIS)
- SmartMesh (SMT)
- IoTe (IOTX)
- Clams (CLAM)
- PayDay Coin (PDX)
- Infinity Economics (XIN)
- Gold Bits Coin (GBC)
- Streamr DATAcoin (DATA)
- Crypterium (CRPT)
- THEKEY (TKY)
- Pillar (PLR)
- Telcoin (TEL)
- FUSION (FSN)
- High Performance Blockchain (HPB)
- Po.et (POE)
- SONM (SNM)
- Santiment Network Token (SAN)

- Linkey (LKY)

- Bluzelle (BLZ)

- Libra Credit (LBA)

- Peercoin (PPC)

- Wagerr (WGR)

- CyberVeinToken (CVT)

- Aragon (ANT)

- NIX (NIX)

- Content Neutrality Network (CNN)

- Zipper Network (ZIP)

- ARBITRAGE (ARB)

- NavCoin (NAV)

- PumaPay (PMA)

- TokenPay (TPAY)

- CRYPTO20 (C20)

- Penta Network Token (PNT)

- Gnosis GNO (GNO)

- Raiden Network Token (RDN)

- Ubiq (UBQ)

- TomoChain (TOMO)

- Quantstamp (QSP)

- ProCurrency (PROC)

Cryptocurrency Information Websites

As cryptocurrencies become more mainstream and investors allocate a higher percentage of their portfolios to digital assets, you can expect traditional financial media to cover crypto-related topics more often. However, there is definitely no shortage of crypto-specific information websites that you can follow. Different websites focus their energy on different topics, such as breaking news, mining information, market information, and so on. In this section, I provide information resources for different aspects of the industry.

Cryptocurrency news

In this section, I list both crypto-specific websites as well as traditional news websites that also cover cryptocurrencies.

Crypto-specific news sites include the following:

» AMB Crypto: https://ambcrypto.com

» Bitcoinist: https://bitcoinist.com/

» Bitcoin Magazine: https://bitcoinmagazine.com/

» Blockonomi: https://blockonomi.com

» CCN (Crypto Coins News): www.ccn.com/

» CoinDesk: www.coindesk.com/

» CoinGape: https://coingape.com/

» CoinGeek: https://coingeek.com/

» CoinJournal: https://coinjournal.net

» Cointelegraph: https://cointelegraph.com/

» Coin Insider: www.coininsider.com/

» Crypto Briefing: https://cryptobriefing.com/

» Crypto Crimson: https://cryptocrimson.com

» Crypto Daily: https://cryptodaily.co.uk/

» Crypto Recorder: www.cryptorecorder.com/

» Crypto Vibes: www.cryptovibes.com/

» Cryptolithy: https://cryptolithy.com/

» Ethereum World News: https://ethereumworldnews.com/

» ETHNews: www.ethnews.com

» Hacked: https://hacked.com/

» NewsBTC: www.newsbtc.com/

» Ripple News: https://ripplenews.tech/

» Smartereum: https://smartereum.com

» The Daily HODL: https://dailyhodl.com/

Traditional news sites that offer crypto updates include the following:

>> Bloomberg: www.bloomberg.com

>> CNBC: www.cnbc.com/

>> Forbes: www.forbes.com/crypto-blockchain/#1c35cd8b2b6e

>> Market Watch: www.marketwatch.com/

>> Wall Street Journal: www.wsj.com

>> Yahoo! Finance: https://finance.yahoo.com/

If you're looking for news on a specific cryptocurrency, you can simply search its name on your favorite search engine and click on the "News" tab to get the latest coverage.

Cryptocurrency investment analysis

Many of the websites I mention in the previous section also provide investment analysis on the digital assets. Here are some that are more investment focused:

>> Cryptovest: https://cryptovest.com/

>> FXStreet: www.fxstreet.com/cryptocurrencies/news

>> Invest Diva: www.investdiva.com/investing-guide/category/cryptocurrencies/

>> Invest In Blockchain: www.investinblockchain.com/

>> Investing.com: www.investing.com/crypto/

>> Nasdaq: www.nasdaq.com/topic/cryptocurrency

Always make sure you understand your risk tolerance and investment goals before following investment strategies provided in such websites. Check out Chapter 3 for more on risk, Chapter 17 for more on short-term strategies, and Chapter 18 for more on long-term strategies.

In Invest Diva's Premium Investing Group, I provide investment strategies for cryptocurrencies, stocks, and forex and for diversifying your portfolio among these assets. You can join at https://learn.investdiva.com/join-group.

Crypto-related stock news

As I cover in Chapter 13, you can diversify your portfolio by investing indirectly in the blockchain and cryptocurrency markets through stocks with exposure to these industries. Many traditional financial news sources provide such information. Here's a list of some of the most dominant ones:

» Benzinga: https://pro.benzinga.com?afmc=2f

» Business Insider: www.businessinsider.com

» CNBC: www.cnbc.com/

» Financial Times: www.ft.com/

» Fortune: http://fortune.com

» New York Times: www.nytimes.com/section/technology

» Reuters: www.reuters.com/

» Wall Street Journal: www.wsj.com/

Cryptocurrency live market data

Many cryptocurrencies' news websites provide market data on a select page. However, some websites put most of their energy on providing live data. Here's a list of such websites:

» CoinCap: https://coincap.io/

» CoinCheckup: https://coincheckup.com/

» CoinCodex: https://coincodex.com/

» CoinGecko: www.coingecko.com/en

» Coinlib: https://coinlib.io/

» CoinLore: www.coinlore.com/

» CoinMarketCap: https://coinmarketcap.com/

» Coinratecap: www.coinratecap.com/

» CryptoCompare: www.cryptocompare.com/coins/list/USD/1

» Live Coin Watch: www.livecoinwatch.com/

» OnChainFX: https://onchainfx.com/

Comparison tools

Some websites are dedicated to delivering comparisons and alternative sources to resources you may already be familiar with. For example, if you're looking to find an alternative to a crypto data source like CoinMarketCap, you can simply search that on these services' sites to find the alternatives. Here's the list of the top comparison service providers:

>> AlternativeTo: https://alternativeto.net

>> finder: www.finder.com/cryptocurrency

>> Product Hunt: www.producthunt.com

Cryptocurrency Marketplaces and Wallets

All types of crypto enthusiasts can find an appropriate marketplace, from active traders to investors to those who simply want to buy a digital asset and hide it away under the mattress. The following sections list the places you can conduct these activities.

Crypto exchanges

As I explain in Chapter 6, exchanges are one of the main places where you can buy and sell cryptocurrencies. Here are some of the most popular ones as of the time of writing:

>> Binance: www.binance.com/?ref=18381915 (note that this is a referral link)

>> Bisq: https://bisq.network/

>> Bitfinex: www.bitfinex.com/

>> Bittrex: https://bittrex.com/

>> Coinbase: www.coinbase.com/join/59d39a7610351d00d40189f0 (note that this is a referral link)

>> Gemini: https://gemini.com/

>> Huobi Global: www.huobi.com/

>> Idex: https://idex.market/eth/aura

>> Kraken: www.kraken.com

- » KuCoin: www.kucoin.com/#/
- » NEXT.exchange: https://next.exchange/
- » Poloniex: https://poloniex.com/
- » Qurrex: https://qurrex.com/
- » Stellar Dex: www.stellar.org/developers/guides/concepts/exchange.html
- » Waves: https://wavesplatform.com/product/dex

REMEMBER

The preceding list includes different types of exchanges, and you should compare them based on security, fees, the number of cryptocurrencies they carry, and so much more. I dive into the methods to choose the best crypto exchanges for you in Chapter 6.

Brokers

Brokers are alternatives to exchanges and operate similarly to traditional stocks and forex brokers as I explain in Chapter 6. Here are some brokers that provide cryptocurrency trading services:

- » AVATrade: www.avatrade.com/?tag=87597&tag2=~profile_default (note that this is a referral link)
- » eToro: http://partners.etoro.com/A75956_TClick.aspx (note that this is a referral link)
- » Plus500: www.plus500.com/
- » Robinhood: http://share.robinhood.com/kianad1 (note that this is a referral link)
- » Voyager: www.investvoyager.com/?campaignId=H0guzEW4egR4AcSwgu Cgd1FnPGM&referralCode=hGCBM99&code=ZINGER (note that this is a referral link)

TIP

More brokers may start offering cryptocurrency trading services. You can track the best ones in your location here with my referral link: https://forestparkfx.com/?id=UU1UckhZSVN3OW1WNnNuNHIxaHlqUT09.

Other services

Besides trading and investing, many other services enable you to buy Bitcoin and other famous cryptocurrencies as I explain in Chapter 6. Here's a list (all these links are referral links):

- » CoinTracker: https://www.cointracker.io/i/eALc60xcyXpD
- » Coinmama: http://go.coinmama.com/visit/?bta=53881&nci=5360
- » LocalBitcoins: https://localbitcoins.com/?ch=w7ct
- » XCoins: https://xcoins.io/?r=62hcz9

Cryptocurrency wallets

Many of the exchanges I mention earlier in this chapter provide investors with an online wallet. However, as I explain in Chapter 7, saving your cryptocurrencies in more secure hardware wallets is best. Here are the most popular ones as of the time of writing (note that these are referral links):

- » Ledger Nano S: www.ledger.com/products/ledger-nano-s?r=2acaa6bf4b8d&tracker=MY_TRACKER
- » Trezor: https://shop.trezor.io?a=investdiva.com

Charting and Tax Resources

To analyze the price action of cryptocurrencies, you need a charting tool to conduct your Invest Diva Diamond Analysis (see Chapter 9) properly. But your job as an investor isn't done when you make or lose money. As cryptocurrencies become a recognized asset, you must make sure that you complete your residence responsibility by paying taxes. For that, you need to keep track of your trading activity.

TIP

Most crypto exchanges and brokers provide trading tools such as charts for technical analysis. However, their charting services may not enable you to use the advanced technical analysis techniques I showcase in Chapter 16. One of my favorite charting tools is TradingView (www.tradingview.com/).

In most countries, including the United States, you must pay capital gain taxes on your cryptocurrency activities. Here are some resources (via referral links) that help you with managing your activity for tax purposes (see Chapter 21 for an introduction to taxes and cryptocurrencies):

>> CoinTracker (www.cointracker.io/i/eALc60xcyXpD)

>> CoinTracking (https://cointracking.info?ref=I248132)

>> CryptoTrader.tax (http://cryptotrader.tax?fp_ref=behp6)

Appendix **B**

Resources for Personal Portfolio Management

Portfolio management is an art, and I strongly believe you're the best person to manage your own money. Even if you eventually decide to hire someone to manage your investment portfolio for you, getting a basic understanding of how the markets work is still wise so that you can supervise the way that person is handling your money. At the end of the day, no one cares about your money as much as you do!

In this appendix, I introduce supplementary resources to help you become the master of your money, whether you're investing it in cryptocurrencies, stocks, foreign exchange (forex), or a combination of them all.

Making Your Money Work for You MasterClass

Are you the type of person who works very hard to earn money? Or are you one of those who get their money to work for them to create even more money? Which type of person do you think ends up with more money? If you said the second type, you're correct.

Why do the rich keep on getting richer? The answer is that they've discovered the secret to getting their money to work for them and not the other way around. In my *3 Secrets to Making Your Money Work for You MasterClass*, I reveal the exact strategies I use for my own and my students' investment portfolios to generate wealth by making money work for us. You discover how to

>> Make more in 1 year getting your money to work for you than you could in 15 years working a nine-to-five job

>> Not have to stick to your screen and analyze the markets all the time

>> Start with a little initial investment

TIP

If you want to discover the three secrets to making your money work for you, go to www.InvestDiva.com and click on the "Get Started" button to receive the directions on how you can attend the free master class. Otherwise, you can simply go to https://learn.investdiva.com/free-webinar-3-secrets-to-making-your-money-work-for-you to join the next available broadcast.

Putting your money to work

My day job is being the CEO of Invest Diva. I love what I do, but that isn't where I make most of my money. In 2017, I made over six figures putting my daytime job's profit to work, without spending hours in front of the screen or selling my time in the process. How can that be possible?

Say you have the goal of generating $1 million in one year. You have a couple of options. The first method is to become a VP at a tech company with 15 years of experience and work your butt off. Even if you get to do this, most of your income at a top corporation generally comes from bonuses, which are a result of selling the stocks you get from the company. On the downside, time restrictions and penalty fees are involved in accessing 401(k) or employer's stock rewards. Worst of all, you may end up spending all your life in the office and missing out on doing things you love, like spending time with family or traveling the world.

The second method is to let your money work instead of you and generate a compound income without requiring you to hang out in front of your computer screen all the time.

Making money without chaining yourself to your computer

Time is your biggest asset in life. The thing I love the most about Invest Diva's investment strategy is that I don't have to be online analyzing the markets all the time. Personally I'd rather be sleeping or spending time with my daughter, Jasmine, instead. Plus, this kind of constant monitoring has its drawbacks:

>> It's not good for your health, eyes, or overall happiness in life.

>> Day trading the markets brings out the worst fear and greed in people, and those emotions may lead you to make poorly thought-out, snap investment decisions that hurt your portfolio.

>> You lose time you can be spending with your family and friends.

In the 3 *Secrets to Making Your Money Work for You MasterClass*, I walk you through the steps you can take to set a financial plan, create an investment strategy based on your unique financial situation and risk tolerance, and create a budgeting plan so that you can sit back, relax, and let your investment strategy do its job of making you money.

REMEMBER

You need to learn about this stuff only once. It's not rocket science, and every money manager that makes you feel intimidated by throwing out vocabulary you don't understand is trying to prevent you from discovering his or her secrets. As far as time management goes, I probably spent more time with a shady money manager ten years ago as he tried to sell me his products than I do managing my portfolio now.

Creating a strategy unique to you

Many investing gurus create one-size-fits-all trading signals, which can sometimes become one of the fastest ways of losing your money or preventing you from getting the most out of your investment. In fact, a study by Online Trading Academy in 2016 showed that 86 percent of managed funds underperform market average. Realize that each individual is different. You're different from the investment guru, and from everybody else in the guru's group for that matter. Your money mentality, your financial history, your current financial situation, your risk appetite, your risk tolerance, your financial goals, and your timeline for achieving those goals are all different. By understanding the fundamentals of financial planning and calculating your own risk tolerance, you can create an investment strategy that is just right for you and can give you a greater return than parking your money in a managed fund.

REMEMBER

The fund managers may have years of experience. They're probably incredibly good at managing their own money and have created a huge amount of wealth for themselves by setting up strategies that are unique to them. But what worked out for them may not work for you and may not help you generate true wealth. How many people have you heard of who've become millionaires by parking their money in a managed fund? I haven't heard of any. All those self-made millionaires like Warren Buffett managed their money themselves, and they weren't even geniuses.

Taking a Look at Textual Investment Resources

TIP

In this section, I list a number of supplemental books that offer you information about alternative markets and thus help you diversify your portfolio. Check your local bookstore, library, or favorite online book seller for these helpful titles.

Invest Diva's Guide to Making Money in Forex

The foreign exchange market, or forex, was my first investment love. With one single trade, I made the most money I had ever made in a given month in my life, and that was when I knew absolutely nothing about how the markets work. I obviously got lucky. But by getting more involved in the industry, I learned the methods any investor can use to stack the odds in their favor.

TIP

Keep in mind that the forex market is one of the riskiest markets you can get involved with. That's why educating yourself before jumping in is so important. (See Chapter 15 for an introduction to the forex market.) In my book *Invest Diva's Guide to Making Money in Forex* (McGraw-Hill Education), I walk beginners through the steps necessary to become successful forex traders. You can get the second edition at `https://education.investdiva.com/guide-to-making-money-in-forex`.

Stock Investing For Dummies

Stock investing is one of the most popular methods of investment, so established strategies exist that you can use for your own portfolio. Personally, I allocate at least 50 percent of my portfolio to stocks. (I talk about stocks with exposure to the cryptocurrency market in Chapter 13.)

In his book *Stock Investing For Dummies* (Wiley), Paul Mladjenovic lays out the process of selecting, investing, and taking profit from this market. He also points out what to stay away from, when to cut losses short, and what basics of risk management are necessary to be a successful stock investor. The strategies in this book are suitable for newbies and high-level investors alike.

You can find this book on Paul's website, Raving Capitalist, at `www.raving capitalist.com/home/stock-investing-for-dummies-5e/`.

Investment Psychology Explained

I talk a lot about psychological levels and market sentiment throughout the book you're reading right now. If you're interested in discovering more about what drives the markets in order to be able to overcome emotional and psychological impediments that distort decision making, I recommend that you check out *Investment Psychology Explained* by Martin J. Pring (Wiley). This book goes through the classic trading principles that may apply to the cryptocurrency market as well when the market becomes more saturated.

Ichimoku Secrets

My book *Ichimoku Secrets* (CreateSpace Independent Publishing Platform) is a fast and furious guide to using a technical indicator I introduce in Chapter 20, Ichimoku Kinko Hyo. I've aimed to make this complicated topic super easy. You can probably finish the book in a couple of hours and be ready to create investment strategies unique to your risk tolerance using a combination of Ichimoku and Fibonacci retracement levels.

You can get this book on Invest Diva's website at `https://learn.investdiva.com/ichimoku-secrets-trading-strategy-ebook`.

Index

Numerics

V

validators, 53
vanishing risk, 41–42, 110
VeChain cryptocurrency (VEN), 119, 122
Verge cryptocurrency (XVG), 119, 166
virtual private networks (VPNs), 154
VirWox exchange, 92
volatility
  avoiding with high market cap cryptos, 110
  volatility risk, 40
voting, blockchain technology and, 59
Voyager, 300
VPNs (virtual private networks), 154

W

Wall Street Journal, 297–298
wallet addresses, 93, 96–97, 105
wallets, 12, 95–107, 268
  brokers and, 89
  cold wallets, 96
  day trading and, 220
  hot wallets, 96
  overview, 95–97
  private key, 96
  public key, 96
  security for, 105–107
    adding security levels, 106
    backing up, 105
    encryption, 106
    multiple wallets, 105–106
    two-factor authentication, 106
    updating software, 106–107
    using strong passwords, 106
  security risk, 40

selecting, 102–105
  based on anonymity, 104–105
  based on crypto ownership, 103–104
  based on security, 102–103
  based on transaction fees, 104
types of, 98–102
  desktop, 100
  hardware, 101
  mobile, 99–100
  online, 99
  paper, 101–102
wallet addresses, 93, 96–97, 105
Waves cryptocurrency (WAVES), 161
Waves DEX exchange, 82, 300
web wallets, 99
whales, 41
white papers, 39, 129, 152–153, 161
WindowsWear, 152

X

XCoins, 86, 301
XEM (NEM cryptocurrency), 69, 119
XLM (Stellar Lumens cryptocurrency), 118, 123, 195
XMR (Monero cryptocurrency), 11, 119, 121
XMR Stak, 168
XRP. *See* Ripple cryptocurrency
XVG (Verge cryptocurrency), 119, 166

Y

Yahoo! Finance, 180, 193, 297

Z

Zcash cryptocurrency (ZEC), 121

About the Author

Kiana Danial is an award-winning, internationally recognized personal investing and wealth management expert. She's a highly sought-after professional speaker, author, and executive coach who delivers workshops and seminars to corporations, universities, and investment groups. She frequently appears as an expert on many TV and radio stations and has reported on the financial markets directly from the floor of the New York Stock Exchange and Nasdaq. Kiana has been featured in the *Wall Street Journal, TIME* magazine, *Forbes, TheStreet.com,* and many other publications as well as on CNN. She has won numerous awards, including Best Financial Education Provider at Shanghai Forex Expo in 2014, New York Business Women of Influence Honoree in 2016, and the Personal Investment Expert of the Year award from Wealth & Finance International in 2018.

Born and raised in Iran as a religious minority, she was awarded a scholarship from the Japanese government to study electrical engineering in Japan, where she obtained two degrees in that field and conducted research on quantum physics in classes taught in Japanese. Being the only woman and foreigner in her classes made her decide to dedicate her life to empowering minorities, especially women in male-dominated industries.

Dedication

To my sweet daughter, Jasmine, who was born right around the time I started writing this book and inspired me to finish it.

To my amazing husband, Matt, who supports me unconditionally.

Author's Acknowledgments

I'd like to thank numerous people for their help in making this book a reality. In particular, I would like to thank veteran *For Dummies* author Paul Mladjenovic, who selflessly handed me this project, trusted me with it, and sprinkled his support and kindness all over this book. I'd like to extend a special thank you to Michelle Hacker for shepherding this project to completion. Thank you to Georgette Beatty and Megan Knoll for your thorough edits, advice, and suggestions. Thank you to Kara Coppa for keeping the book accurate. Last but not least, thank you to Tracy Boggier and Sheree Bykofsky for all your help in pushing the project through and backing me to create a great guide.

Publisher's Acknowledgments

Senior Acquisitions Editor: Tracy Boggier

Project Manager: Michelle Hacker

Development Editor: Georgette Beatty

Copy Editor: Megan Knoll

Technical Editor: Kara Coppa, COO, EVP, and Co-Founder BLAKFX/Co-Founder Wickr and United Alert/Cyber-Security Expert

Production Editor: Mohammed Zafar Ali

Cover Photo: © Dario Lo Presti/Shutterstock

Leverage the power

Dummies is the global leader in the reference category and one of the most trusted and highly regarded brands in the world. No longer just focused on books, customers now have access to the dummies content they need in the format they want. Together we'll craft a solution that engages your customers, stands out from the competition, and helps you meet your goals.

Advertising & Sponsorships

Connect with an engaged audience on a powerful multimedia site, and position your message alongside expert how-to content. Dummies.com is a one-stop shop for free, online information and know-how curated by a team of experts.

- Targeted ads
- Video
- Email Marketing
- Microsites
- Sweepstakes sponsorship

20 MILLION PAGE VIEWS EVERY SINGLE MONTH

15 MILLION UNIQUE VISITORS PER MONTH

43% OF ALL VISITORS ACCESS THE SITE VIA THEIR MOBILE DEVICES

700,000 NEWSLETTER SUBSCRIPTIONS TO THE INBOXES OF

300,000 UNIQUE INDIVIDUALS EVERY WEEK

PERSONAL ENRICHMENT

Staying Sharp

9781119187790
USA $26.00
CAN $31.99
UK £19.99

Facebook

9781119179030
USA $21.99
CAN $25.99
UK £16.99

Guitar

9781119293354
USA $24.99
CAN $29.99
UK £17.99

Investing

9781119293347
USA $22.99
CAN $27.99
UK £16.99

Beekeeping

9781119310068
USA $22.99
CAN $27.99
UK £16.99

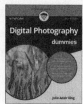

Digital Photography

9781119235606
USA $24.99
CAN $29.99
UK £17.99

Meditation

9781119251163
USA $24.99
CAN $29.99
UK £17.99

Pregnancy

9781119235491
USA $26.99
CAN $31.99
UK £19.99

Samsung Galaxy S 7

9781119279952
USA $24.99
CAN $29.99
UK £17.99

iPhone

9781119283133
USA $24.99
CAN $29.99
UK £17.99

Crocheting

9781119287117
USA $24.99
CAN $29.99
UK £16.99

Nutrition

9781119130246
USA $22.99
CAN $27.99
UK £16.99

PROFESSIONAL DEVELOPMENT

Windows 10

9781119311041
USA $24.99
CAN $29.99
UK £17.99

AutoCAD

9781119255796
USA $39.99
CAN $47.99
UK £27.99

Excel 2016

9781119293439
USA $26.99
CAN $31.99
UK £19.99

QuickBooks 2017

9781119281467
USA $26.99
CAN $31.99
UK £19.99

macOS Sierra

9781119280651
USA $29.99
CAN $35.99
UK £21.99

LinkedIn

9781119251132
USA $24.99
CAN $29.99
UK £17.99

Windows 10

9781119310563
USA $34.00
CAN $41.99
UK £24.99

SharePoint 2016

9781119181705
USA $29.99
CAN $35.99
UK £21.99

Fundamental Analysis

9781119263593
USA $26.99
CAN $31.99
UK £19.99

Networking

9781119257769
USA $29.99
CAN $35.99
UK £21.99

Office 2016

9781119293477
USA $26.99
CAN $31.99
UK £19.99

Office 365

9781119265313
USA $24.99
CAN $29.99
UK £17.99

Salesforce.com

9781119239314
USA $29.99
CAN $35.99
UK £21.99

Coding

9781119293323
USA $29.99
CAN $35.99
UK £21.99

dummies.com

dummies
A Wiley Brand

Learning Made Easy

ACADEMIC

9781119293576
USA $19.99
CAN $23.99
UK £15.99

9781119293637
USA $19.99
CAN $23.99
UK £15.99

9781119293491
USA $19.99
CAN $23.99
UK £15.99

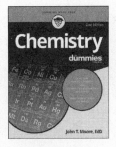

9781119293460
USA $19.99
CAN $23.99
UK £15.99

9781119293590
USA $19.99
CAN $23.99
UK £15.99

9781119215844
USA $26.99
CAN $31.99
UK £19.99

9781119293378
USA $22.99
CAN $27.99
UK £16.99

9781119293521
USA $19.99
CAN $23.99
UK £15.99

9781119239178
USA $18.99
CAN $22.99
UK £14.99

9781119263883
USA $26.99
CAN $31.99
UK £19.99

Available Everywhere Books Are Sold

Small books for big imaginations

9781119177173
USA $9.99
CAN $9.99
UK £8.99

9781119177272
USA $9.99
CAN $9.99
UK £8.99

9781119177241
USA $9.99
CAN $9.99
UK £8.99

9781119177210
USA $9.99
CAN $9.99
UK £8.99

9781119262657
USA $9.99
CAN $9.99
UK £6.99

9781119291336
USA $9.99
CAN $9.99
UK £6.99

9781119233527
USA $9.99
CAN $9.99
UK £6.99

9781119291220
USA $9.99
CAN $9.99
UK £6.99

9781119177302
USA $9.99
CAN $9.99
UK £8.99

Unleash Their Creativity

dummies.com

dummies
A Wiley Brand